CW01628546

Praise for *Remembered Fragme*

Compelling, informative and entertaining.

—**Pat Quigley**, biographer of Constance, Casimir and Stanislav Markievicz, *The Irish Times*

In marking his unique place within a territory where who-owns-what-space is often a highly contentious issue, the County Down born writer blends sharp observation, humour and affection to call up memories from the people, the music, the meeting places, the watering holes and the dance halls of growing up around the beautiful shores of Carlingford Lough in the second half of the last century.

—**Colum Sands**, folk musician and winner of the Living Tradition Award for services to Folk and Traditional Music

---

Stephen Shellard tells his story with care and attention to detail, without dwelling on negativity. I learnt a lot.

—**Pat Kirby**, author of *The Last Year* novel series

The title somewhat belies the content and execution as both are far from fragmented. The primarily chronological presentation of Shellard's life is narrated seamlessly while the quality of the writing is finely modulated, drawing the reader in and sustaining interest in the memoir throughout.

—**David Mark Williams**, poet and short fiction writer

An enjoyable account of growing up in Ireland in search of a path to adulthood. Erudite, touching and poetical, it also addresses societal issues such as that for outcasts in need of compassionate help. A different take on life in Northern Ireland as generally described in literature.

—Amazon review

Chatting with Stephen when we happened to meet in a pub, for some reason the topic of the Irish troubles arose, at which point I mentioned that I found the whole thing all very tricky to figure out. To which he replied 'Oh, I have just written a book which may help understanding'. Well yes; I think it does.

"It gives a feeling of how it was to grow up in the difficult times, from somebody clearly possessing a warm personality which enabled him to navigate the social boundaries and consequently describe several points of view empathetically. The account left me rather heartened about people's nature in general. Well, most people, anyway. I also enjoyed the tales of travels, amorous pursuits, punk and leftie politics, Thatcher's Britain, Berlin before the wall fell. These, together with the accounts of his family and lots of touching little details were both interesting and enjoyable as were the snippets of the author's clever lyrics & poems. Stephen's openness helps to blend all this into a fascinating story. It's a good read.

—**Ben Humphrys**, Amazon review

A valuable addition to the literature on the psychological issues thrown up by the Northern Irish 'troubles'."

—**Alan Hamilton**, Former Lecturer in the University of Ulster (1972-1989)

Remembered Fragments

A Memoir

Stephen Shellard

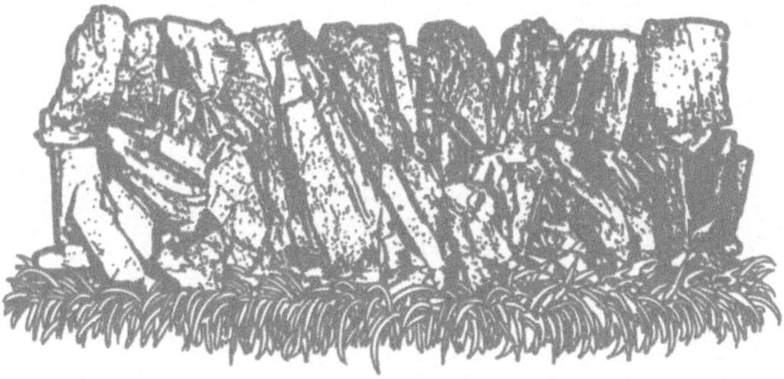

Carruchan Press

Nether Carruchan
Troqueer
Dumfries
DG2 8LY

This is a memoir grounded in the author's coming of age during the civil and political disintegration in Northern Ireland in the 1960s and early 1970s. It tells the story of his Anglo-Irish family with its roots in Dublin, Limerick and Bandon, Co. Cork, where his parents met, and married in 1945. Following the Second World War, they moved to Belfast and then to Newry, where the author was born in 1953. These relocations did not diminish enduring family affections and interests which crossed all the vexed geographical, political and religious divisions of Ireland.

The author is sharply critical of the failures of unionist politics to respond constructively to the changing world of the 1960s. From the perspective of his wider experience in the 1970s and 1980s, in Canada, in Reading, in Ballycastle, Co. Antrim, in West Berlin, the author reflects on the trauma of his homeland in the context of the national and international turmoil of that era. The narrative describes the various challenges which eventually led his entire family to move to southwest Scotland in the second half of the 1980s.

Remembered Fragments offers a perspective on the Northern Irish Troubles which reminds us that, amidst the violence which led up to the Good Friday Agreement, many people were unwilling to take a position on either side and were always seeking and hoping for a more agreeable way to live. It is a narrative defined by anecdote and a rich appreciation of human character. It is a political commentary which avoids rancour or invective and is a contribution to the literature and understanding of a period in Irish history which is still a painful memory for many but which the author recalls with a surprising degree of humour and affection.

Dedication

In memory of my mother and father and my brother Michael.

Contents

What
Are my foolish words when
Set against the last gasp
Of a wave over a stone

Or the intense disclosures
Of shadows
Dancing together?

Nothing. Yet it is this
Nothing that compels me
To wake in the nightsilence

And feel the need to speak
To you. This is a universe
Of voices. They make

Me want to be a voice
Telling my fragments in words
That bid your heart rejoice

At the spider lunging to the kill,
Every sharp unshareable pain,
Dust that gathers on the window-sill.

From Brendan Kennelly's poem *To You*

Introduction

These *Remembered Fragments* will not necessarily correspond with the recollections of others who were there. I will have got details wrong. At some points the narrative has been simplified; at others, I have used my imagination to fill in what I simply could not remember or otherwise make sense of. In a number of cases, details have been changed, including names of those involved, where I was unable to consult prior to publication or where I felt offence might be taken at the observations made. Much has been left out as I can't imagine it being of interest to anyone other than myself. Nevertheless, it has been my intention to represent accurately the spirit of what happened.

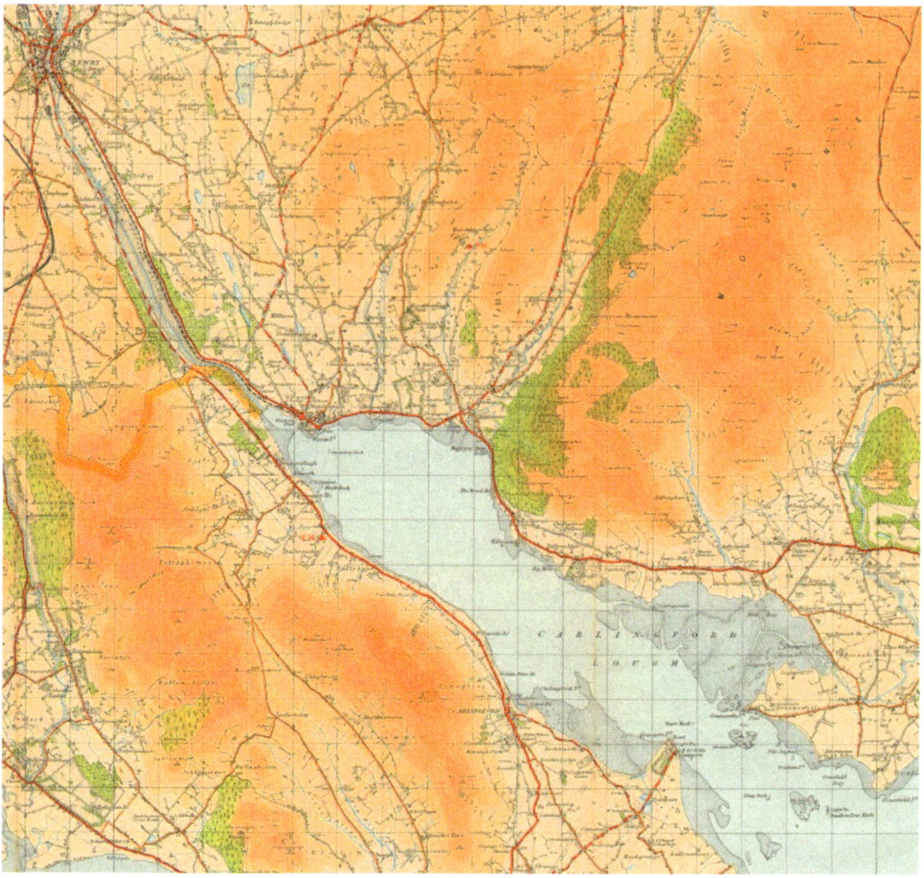

Newry and Mourne – Extract from Ordnance Survey one inch, sheet 11, Northern Ireland, published in 1955. Full map image available from Wikimedia.org.

1: A Different World

There's a wall, so there is, between us and them, there is
Throw the ball against the wall and back to me
Is there anyone can tell me that they didn't help in building it
Open up your eyes and tell me what you see

From *The Last House in Our Street*, on Colum Sands' album, *The March Ditch.*

One Long Holiday

My grandfather was fond of teasing me with the suggestion that my life was just one long holiday. This overlooked the fact that from the earliest days of my attendance, I didn't much enjoy school, but in the months of July and August his jest did have some substance. Early in July and before my teenage years, I would be invited by the Brownes to stay with them for a week in a little timbered holiday house in Cranfield at the northern tip of Carlingford Lough. Frank and Freda Browne were the parents of my friends, Nicholas and Philip. Later in the month I would be invited with them to stay in Sandycove, just south of Dublin, with their Aunty Ruby and Uncle Alan. Ruby was Frank's sister and her reception of her band of northern visitors was warm and welcoming.

My own father had grown up in Dalkey, just along the road from Sandycove, but it was in the company of Nicholas and Philip that I got to know the area well; the rocky shoreline that ran toward Dun Laoghaire harbour, where we could see the mail boat coming and going from Liverpool; the little beach at Sandycove where we would swim; the Martello Tower on Sandycove Point in which James Joyce had chosen to place the opening scene in *Ulysses*, though no one thought it worth informing us of this at the time. Just beyond the Tower, was the Forty Foot bathing place which, in those days, was for men only and where Nicholas and Philip's Uncle Alan went swimming each morning, winter and summer we were assured, before going to his job in the Bank of Ireland. Occasionally, cousins Geoffrey or Edward, older than ourselves, young sociable men in fact, would take us out sailing in Dublin Bay or we would explore Bullock Harbour where the oldest and more serious-minded of the three cousins, David, kept and treasured a little sailing dinghy. But once July was done it was my own family's turn to take a holiday.

My parents had met in Bandon, County Cork, where my mother was living at the time, together with her mother and her five younger brothers and sisters. My father had taken up a teaching post in Bandon Grammar. Following their marriage, they chose to move north of the border but they both retained an affection for the Republic of Ireland, and this largely determined our holiday destinations.

1: A DIFFERENT WORLD

My mother and father on their wedding day, 30th August, 1945.

In the late 1950s, when I was five or six years old, Da had purchased a second-hand four berth Sprite caravan, calculating presumably, that as the youngest and smallest I could be fitted in, with no great discomfort, in an improvised fifth bunk between my elder brothers, Peter and Michael.

After a great ritual of lists and packing we would set off across Ireland to some remote coastal outpost in the west: Mayo, Kerry, West Cork. On our outward journey, Michael had his harmonica with him and would entertain his fellow travellers with popular tunes of the day: *When Irish Eyes Are Smiling, The Mountains of Mourne, Galway Bay*. There were occasional games of I-spy. Sat in the back the three of us would be agog whether it was bog or tree-lined country roads, or the towns and villages we passed through where roadside hand pumps seemed a ubiquitous feature and we never needed to worry about running short of drinking water. Given the dearth of motor vehicles, the quality of these by-ways was remarkable, a motorist's paradise.

Our Austin A40 car was at the lower end of weight and power for the purpose of pulling our caravan, and so at speeds generally not much above thirty mph we made unspectacular progress across Ireland, there generally being at least one overnight stay, parking up in any convenient lay-by. The fact that the car was a little lightweight for the job did not discourage my father from seeking out the scenic routes even where this involved the negotiation of steep mountain passes, a strain on the engine on the way up and the brakes on the way down. Ma suffered the jeopardy of these exploits more than the three adventurers in the backseat who had unquestioning belief in their father's judgement on such matters.

Our main destination was invariably close to a deserted beach. There were no caravan sites in the West of Ireland at that time and we would simply find a sheltered place amongst sand dunes where we would set up our camp. Da would construct a rough table for us to eat our meals outside when the weather was fine. A little boxy tent was erected for the lavatory, a simple metal can on which rested something approximating a toilet seat. The can would be primed with a potion smelling richly of tar or creosote resulting in a memorable, not entirely unpleasant, odour. We would explore the beaches, picnic, and swim in the restless waters of the Atlantic Ocean.

At night, the caravan was warmed by the gas mantles which hissed gently and gave a pleasing light. Our principal evening diversion was for Ma or Da to read aloud to us. The chosen text, intended to suit all, could be a bit of a stretch for me. In the case of Dickens', *A Tale of Two Cities*, my abiding memory is of Madame Defarge knitting, for some dark purpose, which I never really understood. There were other books more pitched at my level, *The House at Pooh Corner*, Paul Gallico's *The Abandoned*, and *The Wind in the Willows*, a book rich in the enchantments of the modest lives of Mole and Ratty set against the comic vanities of Mister Toad in his Hall and the stern but reassuring figure of Badger, secure in the rustic comfort of his underground lair, at the very heart of the Wild Wood.

When we retired to bed there was further storytelling. Michael would entertain us with improvised tales of a character he had invented, Mrs Surprising, a kind of female superhero. Peter and I found her strangely diverting and we would eventually have to be silenced by Ma and Da, who slept in a made-up bed at the far end of the caravan, divided off from us by a wardrobe door which folded out across the passage.

Picking blackberries was one of the great holiday rituals. This was not a favourite activity for me, but I was required to play my part and to this day I find myself drawn to this late summer bounty. I have never quite understood why, in Seamus Heaney's poem, *Blackberry Picking*, the harvest of blackberries so invariably was left to go bad. I feel almost guilty when I read it, knowing the pleasure I have had from eating blackberry tarts and crumbles prepared by my mother.

Despite Da's preference for remote places, Ma's love was for the people, whether encountered in chance meetings or observed toiling in the patchwork of small rocky fields. In the West of Ireland at that time, in the late 1950s and early 1960s, there was little machinery and every farming task we witnessed in that impoverished landscape was still being done by hand. As in a Van Gogh painting, we would see figures cutting barley with sickles and forming the cut corn into stooks in the field before these were gathered in for threshing. I recall my mother remarking how, even in the hottest weather and whilst engaging in this strenuous work, the men, unfailingly modest in their behaviour, always kept their shirts on.

A common sight in the mornings was a donkey — the main beast of burden in that part of the world — pulling a cart loaded with grey galvanised steel milk churns, on the way to the creamery. People were welcoming and generous. Ma would quickly establish warm relations with the proprietors of the village shops where we purchased our groceries.

My first glimpse of Barley Cove in West Cork seemed almost visionary; our trek across Ireland nearly at an end, we looked across a lake in which swam a flotilla of swans, to a barrier of sandhills beyond which lay Barley Cove itself, and the vast blue of the Atlantic. We made our way across a causeway and found a place amongst the dunes for our caravan. A tidal channel wound its way from the lake to the sea and, at a couple of points, there was sufficient depth to swim. The water in these pools was warm, having been trapped by the back and forth of the tide and heated by the sun. From time to time, we would vary the experience and throw ourselves into the great waves that rolled in to break on the sands of the cove, the water cold, bracing.

Regattas were a feature of these Cork holidays, one such being at the little village of Crookhaven. A regatta was a great day out: stalls and side shows, races for sailing and rowing boats and for swimming. Michael was a strong swimmer and took part in one of the latter. I felt confident he would win. He proved unable to deliver my hoped-for triumph but this in no way dented my belief in his superior capabilities.

When at last, our fortnight was over and the time had come for us to set off for home, we packed up and took our leave with wistful goodbyes to our new friends. The return journey was again over a couple of days, though we always seemed to arrive home very late. Exhausted, I would savour the intense pleasure of falling asleep in my own bed.

Flags and Emblems

In those holidays in the Irish Republic, beyond the presence of picture postcards, I recall very little of the paraphernalia of tourism — trinkets which might be taken home to be put on a mantelpiece or given as a present — but on one occasion Michael did purchase a little triangular tricolour, its green, white and orange representing the flag of the Irish Republic. He was about twelve at the time. When he got home, he mounted this pennant on the handlebar of his bicycle and set off for the town centre, I am sure with some sense of pride in the impression he might make. He returned, not long after, in a state of distress. Somewhere near the junction of Sandy Street, Talbot Street and Windsor Hill a woman standing in her doorway had observed the colours of the flag and had felt it necessary to tell Michael that his pennant was unwelcome in that part of the town.

I do wonder, when I recall this, why my parents had not advised Michael against his display of this emblem of Irish republicanism. They had underestimated the symbolic potency of this shred of tourist ephemera. They of course had grown up in the Irish Republic, continued to have friends and family there and were happy to go there for family holidays. Whatever its failings, they had never experienced the Irish Republic as an unwelcoming place for Protestants and found it difficult to make sense of the hostility and distrust that was sometimes evident in those in the north towards their neighbour state.

There were other parts of Newry where the Union Flag would have been unwelcome and it should not be forgotten that between 1958 and 1961 there was an active IRA campaign. It was on a much smaller scale than what was to follow but, nevertheless, resulted in the murder of a number of RUC officers. Indeed, the first politically motivated killing that I can recall being spoken of by the adults around me was the death of RUC officer William Hunter in November 1961. He was fatally wounded in a gun battle with the IRA in South Armagh.

That IRA campaign was no doubt the reason it was felt necessary to have two armed policemen guarding the electricity transformer situated at the foot of Balmoral Park where we lived at the time. My main concern was not the possibility of a bomb at the transformer but that I would be arrested for cycling after dark without lights. As the nights drew in there would be the troubling decision as to whether the light had fallen to such a degree that I should dismount to pass by their forbidding gaze to complete the final stage of my journey home.

Cranfield

Cranfield, situated at the outer edge of Carlingford Lough, was to become a significant backdrop to my early years. It is, in simple terms, a holiday resort but with two distinct parts, the outer shore, overlooking the Irish Sea and the lighthouse shore, tucked just inside the Lough and looking across to Ballagan in the Irish Republic. I was to become familiar with both the outer and the lighthouse shores. Each had its own distinct social character and topography, separated by a rocky headland, Cranfield Point, at the northern tip of the Lough.

On the outer shore, a hundred feet or so above a sandy beach, a row of holiday cottages had been built, mostly timbered, though some in brick. This was the location where, when I was still at primary school, I was invited for a number of years to join Philip and Nicholas and their parents, Frank and Freda, to spend a week in one of those dwellings. Philip was a little older than me and Nicholas, a little younger. They fought quite a lot at that stage in their lives and I thought sometimes that I had been drafted in as a kind of buffer between the two fractious red-headed brothers, yet both were to become my friends.

We swam, played football on the beach, watched the gulls just off-shore plunge diving for fish and explored the rock pools at the southern end of the strand. At night there would be card and board games, or comics, the latter never encouraged in my own house, but which I read with interest and which doubtless informed my early ideas of social class, with stories ranging from *Dennis the Menace* and *Minnie the Minx* to *Alf Tupper, Tough of the Track*. Comics were also my unlikely introduction to the literature of classical antiquity. A good deal of what I know about Homer's *Iliad* came from a comic strip story about the Trojan wars, and the great clashes between Achilles and the Trojan hero, Hector. Though I was later to take Latin classes for a couple of years, my comic book introduction to Homer remains the greatest thrill of my classical education, the more formal side of which was shorn of any sense of narrative or history.

There was no television in the holiday house and so we were a captive audience for Frank's disarming commentary on the small events of the household. Much of this was gentle humour at the expense of Freda's finely developed sense of propriety. I thought a good deal of what informed Freda's decorous approach to life was her admiration for the royal family and, in particular, the Queen. The Queen was to live long enough to become a very dignified elderly lady but, in the late 1950s, she was young and beautiful and had a handsome husband with a distinguished war record. They were a dazzling couple, their growing family respectfully presented in a compliant media, quite unlike the aggressively intrusive paparazzi which lay waiting in their future, ready to overturn at least some of this idyll. The royal family set a standard to which Freda aspired. Much was made of good manners, 'courteous' behaviour and correct speech. Freda might perhaps attempt to council Philip or Nicholas in the finer points of their table manners but Frank, though broadly in support of her objectives, could not resist a little subversion of Freda's best intentions: "Thankfully dear, in the circles in which our boys will be moving, nobody'll notice that kind of thing."

Philip picked up his father's irreverent take on such matters and found he could make his own contribution to this bantering conversation. Freda took this in good part and stuck firmly to her programme, thus providing a fairly steady stream of prompts for Frank and Philip to have some fun. I think she enjoyed the straight role she played in this improvised family comedy.

Fionn mac Cumhail's Binoculars

Close to the southern end of the unsurfaced road running in front of the houses there was a coastguard station, a little white block of a building, looking out over the Irish Sea. Philip, Nicholas, and I were once invited to enter. What impressed me most at the time was a huge pair of binoculars, big as a church bible, big enough for the giant, Fionn mac Cumhail. The binoculars had been captured from a German ship during the Second World War. Nobody seemed able to bring anything into clear focus with them, a great disappointment to me, as I assumed their size to be a reliable indication of their superior power and potential to see into worlds beyond our own.

Yet our own world absorbed us. We explored the outer limits of the beach and beyond, the headland on the northern tip of Carlingford Lough, where memory has dissolved into a single discovery: a dead seal, a great slice of flesh cut from its flank by the propeller of a boat.

The weather cannot always have been perfect, but on one of these visits there was a week of pure blue skies where, on the first day, the three of us were in and out of the sea from an early hour in a state of blissful abandon, only to find, as the evening fell, that we were badly sunburned. The cooling breezes off the sea had hidden the painful reality of what was happening until it was too late. Nicholas and Philip, with their red hair and fair skin, suffered much more acutely than I did. Freda's remedy for our affliction was gentian violet, much of which was applied. This experience was distressing, and yet, though I was away from home, I felt myself safe and cared for, an honorary member of another family. The worst had passed in a day or two and we recovered, a little wiser as to the dangers of unfiltered sunshine.

Later in that week we went swimming at about ten o'clock at night, with the air still mild, the water balmy and the sea calm. When, eventually, we tired of this and started to feel the chill of nightfall, we climbed the steep ascent back to the house and warmed ourselves by the stove in the back kitchen.

The Sunday School Militia

I was never an enthusiast for school and Sunday School was no improvement, but at least it didn't last very long. My earliest experience of this unwanted religious annex to my education took place within St. Patrick's Church, which stood magnificently atop a hill, overlooking the town, surrounded by streets and rows of small one and two-storey houses. As I walked home alone following one such session, along Pound Street towards the Fullerton Road, a gang of small boys, about my own age, surrounded me demanding to know whether I was Protestant or Catholic. I imagine in retrospect that they were Catholic but the problem, in the circumstances, was that I really didn't know the answer to their question. Perhaps if I'd been listening with more attention to my Sunday School teacher, I would have been able to provide an answer, though whether that would have been to my advantage is anybody's guess.

My confession of ignorance on the subject was clearly not what the boys were hoping for. Unable to determine whether I was friend or foe there came from my inquisitors a kind of collective groan of exasperation. One lad fired off a catapult loaded with a rolled-up ball of paper, which struck me squarely in the forehead. Though I felt a snap, it was only a momentary pain; they dispersed, with much head shaking, leaving me to make my heathen way homeward unhindered.

What would they have done had I been able to answer? I don't imagine theological discussion was any part of their plan and yet, in broad daylight on a Sunday morning, I was probably not at risk of any great harm. On arrival home, I asked my parents what I should say in such circumstances, but the truth is, I was never again required to provide the answer to such an aggressive inquiry regarding my religious beliefs.

Whilst open and direct enquiries about one's religion were uncommon in Northern Ireland, where they did occur, there was undoubtedly a risk that they were hostile. In my teenage years, my brother Peter related to me a story about his school friend Billy, with whom he went to Queens University in Belfast. Billy was getting home late one night in 1968 or 1969 and was confronted by a gang of youths who demanded to know his religion. As it happens, Billy was not only the product of a mixed marriage but also a confirmed atheist: in the circumstances, and presumably on the basis of the area he was in at the time, he thought it best to say he was a Protestant. His answer did not convince these young zealots and so they said, "Well, you'll know the words of *The Sash*, then." This was a tight spot for Billy as his knowledge of *The Sash* didn't go far beyond the opening lines. Quick thinking as he was, he pointed out that a Catholic might well know the words of *The Sash*. This gave the lads who had accosted him pause for thought. "Well, how can you prove you're not a Catholic?" they asked. Says Billy: "If I were to say, 'Fuck the Pope', that would prove I wasn't a Catholic." This was immediately accepted as a sufficient test of the matter and Billy duly said the words and passed on his way.

Peter had his own personal story to add to this tale. This took place in 1972 when he was living and working in Belfast. By that point, the Provisional IRA campaign had become a dominant force in republicanism and loyalist terrorists, unable to find legitimate targets for their fury, began "reprisals" which took the form of random shooting of Catholics; to be confronted by a gang of young loyalists was an unnerving experience. Here is the story in Peter's own words: "Late at night, walking alone on the Donegal Road, I was stopped by a small group of youths and faced with the challenge to repeat the words of *The Sash*. I was at a loss: notwithstanding my heritage, I had no interest in the song, and I could only have repeated what I believed to be the first line: 'It is old but it is beautiful, and the colours they are fine.' I was aware of and, naturally, worried about my predicament. Fortunately, another youth came out of the shadows and, to my surprise and relief, vouched that he knew me, and I was 'alright' … I felt extremely grateful to this Protestant stranger and proceeded on my way."

Travelling North

My family took our caravan holiday in the six counties of Northern Ireland on only one occasion. We stopped off at a caravan site in Cushendall, and then settled, for a few days on an industrial-scale site just outside Portrush. I enjoyed the novel experience of the more commercialised holiday, the amusements and the candyfloss, the play park on the site, the toilet block and showers. We also visited the Giant's Causeway and the Carrick-a-Rede rope bridge. I swam in the outdoor pool at Portstewart, memorable to me for an earnest conversation I had with one of the pool attendants who seemed to regard me as a fellow adult, worthy of thoughtful attention. Da was restless and not really at his ease until we had left the caravan site and moved on to a spot by a stream in the Sperrin Mountains where we were to pass several days. I seemed able to find entertainment lighting campfires, skimming stones and building dams, though this early interest in engineering went unnoticed and unnurtured by my parents.

As Michael, Peter and I grew older and, more importantly, bigger, our caravan could no longer contain us, and the format of holidays started to evolve. We would book into fixed caravans, more generously appointed and more comfortable than our own. I continued to enjoy these holidays, swimming, fishing, rather unsuccessfully, off the rocks and experiencing, in Donegal, the most astonishing deserted beaches. But as the years passed, I could see Michael and Peter becoming unsettled, pushing against the old holiday rituals — the long walks seemed a particular trial for Peter — and I knew that the days of our family holidays were numbered.

A Mongrel in the Family

It was about my fourth Christmas that my family acquired a Lakeland Terrier pup, a pure-bred dog, whom we called Claus. Claus seemed a brave little fellow but before he was much more than a year old, he was run over whilst playing with his pal Bruce, the Alsatian from up the road. This was really a piece of bad luck, for the semi-detached house in which we were living at that time was situated in the upper end of Balmoral Park, a quiet road on the way to nowhere and with little traffic. Claus did rally following the accident, but as the severity of his injuries became clear, the decision was taken for the vet to end his life. Claus was to be the only pure-bred dog that we owned and thereafter we stuck to the mixed-breed economy route to dog ownership.

Our next dog was a smooth haired collie cross, who we called Easter, this being the time of year at which he joined the family. Easter was a great dog as I remember him, though a little ill-disciplined. On one occasion, when on holidays, he declined to get in the car for our return journey. The solution was simple enough. We drove off, slowly, at which point Easter charged after us, and having caught up, obligingly jumped in. Perhaps because of his nature and no doubt because he was an unneutered male, Easter was prone to wandering, and would disappear for several days at a time roaming the town in amorous adventure and causing the family a good deal of anguish until his return. He did not, however, come back from one of these expeditions, and with much heartache we gradually came to accept that he had met with some misadventure. Remarkably, this seemed to be confirmed by a story in the *Newry Reporter* telling of a dog, fitting Easter's description, who had suffered fatal injury after being struck by a train at Newry Station. The best thing that could be said for this was that it was a conclusion to his life with a distinction equal to his bold character.

Neither of these stories suggests that we were particularly responsible dog owners, but in those days, dogs were fairly generally turned out to fend for themselves with little thought being given to the problems this might cause.

A curious appendix to this commitment to the waifs and strays of the dog world occurred when I was about fourteen years old, following our move to a house on the Belfast Road. Ma sent me on an errand to Damolly village where her friend Mrs Copeland lived. Damolly was a short distance from our home and amounted to a single terrace of houses on a promontory overlooking the Clanrye river. Beyond the village and down the hill at the level of the river was a textile mill, the village clearly having been constructed to provide accommodation for the workers.

Having fulfilled my obligations with Mrs Copeland, walking back up through Damolly, I noticed a young man playing with a pup. I went over to admire it. I asked the young man what proved an unwise question: "Is it a mongrel?" In a moment he had me by the throat, pushed up against the wire fence overlooking the river. I was shocked. He was probably older than I was, certainly stronger. Quite what would have happened next, I am not sure, had not a woman, standing on her doorstep on the other side of the road, coolly observing the scene, intervened: "Just let him be." She could, I imagine, see that, whatever kind of fool I was, I had not intended to offend. On being released, I made my apologies as best I could and skulked off.

In my mind, to be a mongrel meant no deficit. Ma spoke warmly of "hybrid vigour," added to which there seemed to be general agreement in our family that mongrels were more inclined than pure-breds to be rich in character and intelligence even if a little wayward in their manners.

The author and Easter, interrupted by a door-to-door photographer, whilst enjoying some early reading material.

Our own family had something of a mongrel character, but then, is this not true of every family when the matter is examined? We could be loosely categorised as Anglo-Irish, my great-grandfather, Henry Shellard, having come to Dublin from Bristol. My great-grandmother's name, by contrast, was Kelly, an Irish name, though I formed the idea that she may have been Manx. This notion could have arisen because of my grandfather's fondness for the music hall song *Kelly from the Isle of Man* and the fact that, before he came to live with us, he had regularly taken holidays there. Following his move to live with us in Newry, his holidays were always taken in Dublin. He nurtured his attachment to the city and in particular to St Patrick's Cathedral where he had sung in the choir as a boy. My mother's family name was Foley, very much an Irish name, traceable to my mother's great-grandfather who had, it was said, converted to the Church of Ireland around the time of the famine. My maternal grandmother was Twigg, again an English name. One of my mother's younger sisters, Olive, perhaps unconsciously betraying a prejudice against the Catholic Foleys, I once heard say: "The Twiggs, of course, were always Protestant," as if ignoring the fact that, before Henry XIII fell out with the Pope, everyone in the kingdom including, presumably, the Twiggs, had been Catholic.

The Language Problem

Ma and Da chose to come to the North of Ireland because my father had no gift for languages and in the Irish Republic, in order to rise in his profession as a teacher, would have had to pass further exams in Irish, beyond the basic certificate that I assume he did possess. I never heard him utter a single word of Irish. He decided to take what must have seemed an easier route at the time and moved north to where the authorities cared nothing for the language. My mother had been a primary school teacher in the Republic of Ireland and assured me that she had taught through Irish but was scornful of her own abilities in the language and clear that she was far from being fluent. I don't recall her speaking any Irish apart from occasional words, such as geansaí and crios — jumper and belt. Still, when we were close to Irish-speaking areas in the West of Ireland, she encouraged Michael, Peter and I to try to pick up a little of the language. None of us appeared to have much aptitude for the task, yet we were all a little enamoured by the mystery of this other language so close to us and so much a part of the country's history; we listened attentively and, though we understood not a word, were as thrilled as if hearing the call of the bittern, to be in the presence of that rare thing, the cadences of native Irish speakers.

Border Town

Newry was a port and so had some claim to being the gateway to a wider world. This is not to suggest the town was a great cosmopolitan melting pot but ships loaded with coal, perhaps from Liverpool or Glasgow, regularly chugged their way through Carlingford Lough and when the tide permitted would enter the Clanrye estuary and steam up beyond Narrow Water Castle to find their way into the Newry Canal and from there to the Albert Basin on the eastern margin of the town. The heyday of this commerce was past, and the development of the Port of Warrenpoint gradually took over.

In two senses, Newry is unarguably a border town. Situated on the Belfast-Dublin Road, it is just five miles from the crossing into the Irish Republic which, in the 1960s, was definitely a hard border, with customs posts both north and south and the requirement to declare goods on which duty might have to be paid. With good access to both Belfast and Dublin, Newry is a fine location for anyone interested in the larger world these cities have to offer, whether in commerce, sports or the arts and, as a consequence of this situation, wasn't quite such a backwater as might have been expected for a place so economically down-at-heel.

Newry is also on the border between South Down and South Armagh. The Clanrye river, which runs through the town, demarcates the county boundary, the most striking element of this border being the town hall built on a bridge across the river. I won't pretend that, whilst growing up in Newry, I knew this red brick building to be of 'neoclassical design with Italianate detailing' but its prominent position straddling the river definitely gave it some style.

The Qually

Before Newry Grammar School evolved into a comprehensive school, rebranded Newry High, prize-giving and school theatrical productions were staged in the town hall. Indeed, it was whilst I was a pupil at the Prep School annex to the Grammar, that I was first pushed into the spotlight to play the part of a frog in some otherwise forgotten production. It was a role which I was to reprise, equally reluctantly, the following year. Ma had made the costume, and other parents had been similarly engaged. Probably there had been some push back from those, perhaps including Ma, with better things to do than sew theatrical outfits, and so my frog suit which, unfortunately, I had not outgrown, was reused in some further benighted animal drama in which I was obliged to reprise my croaking talents. Nicholas was a rabbit in these productions. I don't recall him hating his role quite as much as I hated mine, though he may have been similarly scarred. We never spoke about these indignities. Things got a little better a year or two later when I was offered the part of the Mad Hatter in a production of the Mad Hatter's Tea Party. I enjoyed that.

My enrolment in the Prep School was a consequence of my father being a teacher at the Grammar. It was there I met Philip and Nicholas, whose father also taught at Newry Grammar. The Prep School, however, was on its last legs, my final year there being the final year of this anachronistic little two-teacher school, with its ever-shrinking roll. I imagine that at one time it had been the choice for the children of the local gentry on their way to a private education, perhaps in England, certainly not in Newry, and indeed when I attended there was still some evidence of this.

There was also evidence, however, that the Prep School was the choice for parents who sought an education for their children not entirely focused on the eleven-plus. This exam was generally known as the Qualifying or, still more colloquially, as the "Qually." It was a big deal: success or failure determined one's future educational options. Michael had stumbled at this hurdle; Peter had passed. Certainly, the atmosphere in the Prep was very relaxed when I was there. Somehow I became aware that Windsor Hill Primary School, just across the Rathfriland Road from the Prep, was hot-housing pupils for the Qually, and so I was very relieved when I managed to pass and perfectly content when I took my place in the B class in my first year as a Grammar School pupil rather than in the A class, where I knew competition would have been a good deal tougher.

Newry Grammar Preparatory School, circa 1954. Back row, first on left, Michael Shellard. Front row, second from left, Peter Shellard.

Stony Ground

Whilst I was still in the primary stage of my education, my parents became friendly with Toby and Elizabeth Truell. The Truells had arrived in the area following their purchase of a small farm of about twenty acres situated on The Commons, to the north-east of the town. The land was stony and poor and, indeed, an enjoyable day out at the Truell's was burning whin — or gorse — in an effort to free up more pasture for their cattle. They had a tiny farmhouse and a few farm buildings where they also kept goats, pigs and hens.

The Truells were not from farming stock but had decided to take on the challenges of a farming life. They became included in the close-knit community of small farmers around them. Toby had a talent for reading government literature on the grant aid available to support his own enterprise but was generous in sharing this knowledge with his neighbours and doubtless in return he received guidance on some of the skills necessary to make a living from this marginal land.

Even as a primary school child, I understood Toby and Elizabeth Truell to be unusual. They were small farmers — yet with a lively interest in the arts and politics. They submitted paintings to local art exhibions. They appeared able to find friends right across the spectrum of social class and religious difference and still defy any such classification themselves. They were respectful of the religious beliefs of others but there was absolutely no evidence of religious observance or affiliation in their own case.

A story told to me with some relish by my brother Michael involved an attempted pastoral visit to the Truells by the vicar of St Patrick's, the church of which my own family were members. Toby was working in the farmyard at some noisy task and, unable to gain his attention, Reverend Furnace had approached him from behind. At the final moment, suddenly aware of a looming presence, Toby swung round and doubled up his presumed assailant with a punch in the midriff. I am sure that once the scale of the threat posed by the Reverend Furnace had been properly assessed he would have been offered the usual Truell hospitality before being sent on his way.

Toby did not seem like an obviously aggressive or angry person but when, many years later, following his death, I reminded Elizabeth of the story, she was delighted, and suggested that his reaction had been the consequence of

The Truell family, farmers, milliners, artists, free spirits.

his military training; Michael's enjoyment of the story, however, was derived, I am quite sure, from his sense that a mere glimpse of an approaching cleric had been the trigger.

After a few years farming on the Commons, Toby decided to open a shop on Trevor Hill in Newry, the Hat Box. He saw an unlikely gap in the market and an opportunity to supplement what, I can only imagine, was a subsistence income from the farm. He had no experience in millinery, but his business plan was solid enough for him to finance the venture and to include buying trips to Paris and Milan. He learnt the trade as he went, much like he had done with farming. He employed a neighbour from Ballyholland, Bernie, who was to work full-time in the shop, and who proved adept at selling the hats he had selected on his overseas buying trips.

When I reflect on this business venture, at that moment in the history of Northern Ireland, in a town like Newry, it seems crazily optimistic. We needed more of that spirit — but in 1967 the Truells, who could clearly see what was coming, emigrated, taking their talents and their young family to New Zealand.

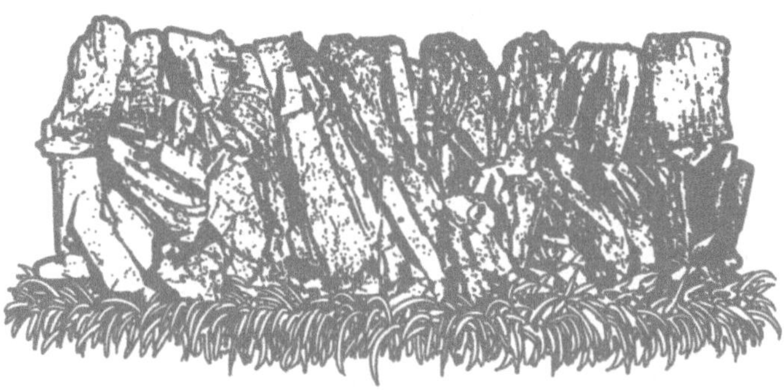

2: Never! Never! Never!

The Sash My Father Wore — updated

It was old but it was beautiful and its colours they were fine
It was worn at Derry, Augherim, Enniskillen and the Boyne.
My father wore it as a youth in the bygone days of yore,
And on the 12th I loved to wear the sash my father wore.

I was taught the Orange Order stood for independent minds
But I fear it's long been colonised by the bigoted and blind.
My father marched with families to fill a sunlit field,
Now they march where they're not wanted to meet with truncheon and with shield.

All That Guff: Updating songs from the Orange and the Green traditions for the modern era.

Paddy

To my mother, my father was "Fred". To his Dublin relations, he was affectionately known as "Freddie". However, all teachers in Newry High School had nicknames and my father's was "Paddy," for the simple reason, as far as I could discern, that he had a southern Irish accent. In England, the name "Paddy" is frequently used as a convenient way to refer to any passing Irishman. Northern Irish Protestants are probably more resistant to this labelling than are the Irish in general, and there was an implicit note of disrespect in the use of this nickname for my father, but then disrespect is really the reason for all such teacher nicknames. I did not think my father singled-out any more than "Moosey", or "Ma Hen", or "Popey Joe", the latter being a Presbyterian Minister and teacher of religious studies. The fact of my father's accent was entirely lost on me until one day, when about fifteen years old, I had occasion to speak with him on the phone. I was suddenly struck by his distinguished southern Irish cadences emerging from the receiver. Michael, Peter and I, in our turn, were nicknamed "Paddy" and this moniker was consistently applied whilst we remained in school.

I had no problem with being called "Paddy". Coincidentally, I had been christened "Stephen Patrick" and, though the name "Paddy" would not typically have been used within earshot of my parents, Ma picked up what was happening and at one point asked me would I prefer being called "Patrick" within the family. I liked having both an informal and a formal name, so I opted for the status quo. One of my small disappointments in life was that, after a single term at university, nearly all of my erstwhile school friends seemed to be overcome by paralysis as to how I should be named now that I was no longer a lowly schoolboy. To my disappointment, they chose the safe option of calling me Stephen.

For Peter, Michael and I, being taught maths by my father was not always a comfortable experience. His methods had an originality, even eccentricity, which could raise some amusement at his expense. On one occasion I recall him bringing his bicycle into the classroom to illustrate some point of geometry. In the current era of education improvising in this way might be considered commendable, but to appreciate the impact of his unusual teaching aid, it should also be said that he was the only teacher in Newry High School of that era ever to come to work on a bicycle. That bicycle, in itself, had achieved the status of a comic icon, with its high saddle, adjusted to fit his six-foot-two-inch frame and handlebars of a design no longer available in any shop. It didn't seem to cross his mind that such things might be considered odd.

My father taught games as well as maths. Boys' hockey was his chief responsibility and he had himself played for Leinster schools as a boy. Quite a small number of schools provided candidates for this honour so the achievement should not be overstated, but he also played quite a good game of tennis. In general, his philosophy was to encourage all games, and to promote team play rather than great individualism. Freddie Martin, who went on to play hockey for Ireland, reports that my father was always agitating for him to pass the ball. Freddie didn't really need to pass the ball and could easily weave past his opponents with style. On the First XI, assisted by another talented player, Noel Mears, Freddie had the status of a George Best, with teenage girls gathering on the touchline to watch him play.

Few teachers go through their career without upsetting at least some of their pupils but, within my hearing, my father has always been spoken of by former pupils with some affection and frequently with tributes to the quality of his teaching. I know that Peter and Michael found the public nature of my father's idiosyncrasies difficult. Likewise, I would not call my father a social asset in my teenage years and yet, whatever he did seemed to wash over me without being a serious burden. Philip and Nicholas's father, a geography teacher at Newry High School, nickname, "Charlie", after the cartoon character Charlie Brown — though I never felt inclined to call him that myself — had an entirely different style, genial and humorous, and I might have wished for my father to be more like him. As I grew older, however, I came to better appreciate my father's unselfconscious quirks and to realise that he had a good sense of humour, though not the quick wit and relaxed manner to use it in his teaching.

Occasionally I come across debate as to whether it is a good idea for teenagers to be enrolled in a school where one of their parents is a teacher. There is no doubt that our father did present the three of us with challenges. He did not seek to draw attention to himself and was careful not to cause offence, but he could not resist a simple and practical solution to a problem, however absurd it might appear to others. He would have had our whole house fitted with fluorescent tubes — cheaper to run, better light to read by — if Ma had not put her foot down. He was deferential to Ma on such matters and, where formality was expected, happy to conform. But where formality was not required, or the rules not clearly defined, he went his own way.

At the conclusion of our summer holiday in 1960 my father did something strikingly unexpected which I think unnerved him as much as it did the rest of the family, though which also seemed evidence of a certain talent for dealing with a crisis. That year, we travelled to the Blacksod Peninsula on the extreme west of County Sligo. The holiday was memorable for a number of things. There was a family living in a tiny, thatched cottage, quite close to where we situated our caravan. Electricity had only just arrived in Blacksod with this particular cottage rejoicing, for the first time in its existence, in electric light. I became friendly with the two lads from the cottage and was invited into the front room. The family were still cooking all their food over an open turf fire (which my mother assured me would never be allowed to go out, winter or summer). Both of those boys addressed me in Irish, though when I quite obviously could not understand, they switched easily to English. Perhaps it was this family which offered us a donkey to take home with us for what seemed liked the very reasonable price of five shillings. It was a thrilling idea, but we were clearly not serious customers.

On this particular holiday my father had borrowed an 8mm cine camera. Some memorable images came home with us, for example, a sequence in which Peter attempted to get on a donkey and, instead, tumbled off on the other side. This being captured on film was a source of special pleasure to the whole family in years to come, excepting of course, Peter.

The gateway to the Blacksod peninsula was a small town, Belmullet. Belmullet was well provided with a range of shops and a filling station. Almost every store in the town was also licensed to sell alcohol to its customers, the tradition for many in that part of the world being to complete their visit to the town for provisions with a stop at the bar for a pint of Guinness. This sale and consumption of alcohol was conducted in the darker recesses of the premises and so customers, such as my parents, who had no interest in this offer, could simply make their purchases and exit. Even as a seven-year-old I understood that the effects of alcohol were not always benign, but the atmosphere in these shops seemed relaxed and friendly, and the smell of porter, agreeable.

On our final day we rose early for breakfast and completed our packing. It was probably mid-morning as we drove onto the forecourt of the petrol station just east of Belmullet. Our attention was soon drawn to the worrying spectacle of two men fighting one another amidst the pumps and parked cars. Apparently, one of the two had pulled in to refuel in a state of complete inebriation. He had been doing some early morning shopping and having filled his own tank at the bar, now wished to do the same with his car. The other individual involved in this altercation was the proprietor of the filling station who knew the drunk man and, concerned for his safety and that of others on the highway, had thought it best to remove the keys from his customer's vehicle. This expression of good citizenship had, however, not been well received by the owner of the keys. The potential of an 8mm cine camera to bear witness to the resulting brawl got the better of my father and before any of us could say, "It'll be the ruination of a fine day", he was on the forecourt filming.

My father, never an inconspicuous presence, was instantly the main focus of attention for the drunk man who clearly understood this development not to be in his favour; in a moment he was lunging for the camera. The three of us boys, lined up on the back seat, being unused to seeing our father treated with anything other than deference, were immediately in a state of high emotion, myself leading the chorus. My mother remained outwardly calm in the face of this drama, though must, no doubt, have been in some anxiety herself, with the entire family apparently in jeopardy.

The extraordinary thing was that my father emerged from this fiasco with both himself and the camera intact. This miraculous escape was, I imagine, due to his ability to make a peace which was not just in his own interest but also in the interest of the other warring parties. An agreement was struck that, once it had been developed, the offending section of film would be destroyed. Quite what happened to the confiscated keys I cannot say, but relative harmony was established on the forecourt such that we were able to fill our own tank with petrol. Without so much as a "good riddance" from the local citizenry, we headed for home.

My father did not crow about his achievement in brokering this deal and I am sure understood perfectly well that, in his duties as a husband and parent, he had taken a seriously wrong turn. Still, once I had calmed down, these events did little to dent my seven-year-old's belief in my father's invincibility. The incident naturally became a part of the family legend, albeit not a part that I felt able, at the time, to share with my pals. The film was duly processed and the agreed section removed and destroyed, though not before we had all gathered, on a single memorable occasion, to run it through the projector and reassure ourselves that it really had happened.

Rocklands

My paternal grandfather had been part of my life for as long as I could remember. He would visit regularly from his home in Dublin driving up to see us in an immaculately clean and tidy Morris 1000 motor car. Then, in 1964, when he was over eighty years old, he retired from his partnership in the Land Agency firm of Townshend and Dickinson, where he had spent most of his working life, and came to live with us in Newry. I was about eleven years old at the time. Quite how he had come to be the senior partner in the business is something of a mystery. The firm had been founded by Charles Townshend. Indeed, ten years before my grandfather was born, Townshend took on George Bernard Shaw as a junior ledger clerk in his estate agency, on a salary of £18 per annum. Shaw resigned on 29 February 1876, by which time he was head cashier on an annual salary of £84. By the time my grandfather was taken on by the business, I imagine in a somewhat similar role to the one in which GBS had started out, the business had acquired a further partner, Charles Dickinson but presumably these founders grew old and passed on and unlike George Bernard Shaw, my grandfather did not leave the business to become the most famous playwright and wit of his age, but remained in post and eventually, I feel sure, by hard work rather than sharp practice, ascended to the position of senior partner. My grandfather never made anything of the association of Townshend and Dickinson with George Bernard Shaw and indeed, so far as I could tell, had no interest in Shaw's career as a critic and playwright or in his socialist ideas.

One piece of good fortune which came my grandfather's way as he rose in his employment was a house in Dalkey, Alberta Lodge. This had been on the books of the firm for many years with no traceable owner and, eventually, it came into his possession. The situation of the house, close to a railway line, may not have been ideal, but it became the fondly remembered home in which my father and his younger brother Dell were to grow up.

It was in anticipation of my grandfather's relocation to Newry that we moved from our semi-detached house in Balmoral Park to Rocklands on the Belfast Road. The new house offered an additional bedroom for my grandfather and came with some acres of ground attached. The house was purchased from a pair of ageing spinsters, the Misses Leadley. Their father had built Rocklands, so it was not a house of any great antiquity though to my eye it was old fashioned in its style with a small scullery and kitchen and a range cooker in what became our dining room. The house, modest in scale, had a very favoured setting, with views across the river to the south. The Misses Leadley were austere in their ways and devoutly attached to some form of evangelical Christianity. Evidence of this was clear from the placard nailed to a tree which stood just inside the wall that ran along the front of the property and which proclaimed the words of Jesus as recorded in the Gospel according to St. Mark, Chapter 2, verse 17: "I came not to call the righteous, but sinners to repentance." An admirable sentiment I thought. My parents would never have put up such a placard but saw no reason to remove it and it remained in place until wind and weather did their inevitable work.

By contrast with the house, the garden at Rocklands had been set out according to an elaborate plan, but under the care of the Misses Leadley it was running wild and in need of modification to make it manageable by anything other than a team of gardeners. Both of my parents had an interest in the garden, but it became my grandfather's purpose in life to keep it all in good order. This he seemed to manage, for the most part, with the aid of a petrol lawn mower and some shears. To my mother's delight there was a hen run and a rickety hen house and she immediately installed hens though these seemed inevitably to come with an entourage of rats. From somewhere we had acquired a small-bore shotgun, a "garden gun" my father called it. He had no inclination himself to make use of it, but I was not discouraged from having a go at the rats and also the rabbits which were taking a generous share of the produce from my father's beloved vegetable patch. Whilst the gun seemed fairly effective in dealing with rats the power of this weapon was so feeble that it was necessary to stalk the rabbits in order to deliver a lethal shot and, even then, I always had to finish the poor creature off with a blow to the head. I didn't much like doing that but on the other hand I wasn't ready to become a vegetarian and so thought this hunting a challenge I should be prepared to take on. After things started to turn bad in Northern Ireland my father dutifully handed our garden gun in to the police, lest it fall into more irresponsible hands.

Rocklands also had a couple of fields, one stony, the other adjoining the Clanrye and liable to flood when the river was up. Some attempt was made to rent out these assets though I can't imagine they would have brought in much income. One of my jobs was to try and control the thistles with a sickle but where the ground was clear of thistles there were reeds or whin, and very little grazing. There was also some woodland with a few mature trees and a little stream running down to the Clanrye. With the hire of a digger an unpromising rectangle of ground surrounded by high thorn hedges was levelled and turned into a serviceable tennis court. Old fishing nets were obtained from Kilkeel and put up to stop the balls running into the hedge. Rocklands seemed quite a grand house to me at the time, a step up in the world of some kind. Its purchase was, I am sure, made possible by my grandfather's savings.

My grandfather's unionism had a very Dublin stamp to it, and he did not have much time for the politics he encountered in the North of Ireland. He had an antipathy to the Orange Order and an impulse to make fun of anything that came out of Ian Paisley's mouth. Despite these irritations I think my grandfather's final decade in retirement was a very contented one. He made an essential contribution to maintaining the garden, he went for a daily walk, played bridge once a week with his regular partner, Mrs Kelly, went to church on Sunday, and complained a good deal about the inferior quality of the church choir. His objections to the choir were focused on someone he chose to discourteously title, "Teymo Codwallaher." Teymo sang lustily in a grating and tuneless tenor. My grandfather's judgement of his musical talent was unkind but not entirely unjust. Teymo had been my Sunday school teacher, an earnest Christian who had worked in Fisher's timber yard, an experience from which he drew much of his moral commentary. It was, it seemed, a place of rampant immorality, mostly taking the form of bad language. I don't recall Teymo having any great scriptural learning to share with his charges. His principal purpose was to warn us against the rough habits of speech and excessive drinking that he had observed in his fellow employees at Fisher's.

Perhaps my grandfather would have been more forgiving of Teymo's musical misdemeanours had he known more of this mission.

In later years I would occasionally visit Fisher's yard, usually to scavenge timber from the off-cuts bay. These scraps were available at very reasonable prices. In these visits I don't recall any of the questionable behaviour against which Teymo had warned us. Neither can I recall making anything memorable from those off-cuts. I could blame lack of tools or parental encouragement but Peter, inspired by the great snowfall and freeze of 1963, constructed a very serviceable toboggan using timber, quite probably from the same source. Painted red and equipped with metal runners this creation was taken a short trek across fields and through hedges, from Balmoral Park to Monk's Hill, where there was a lengthy incline, satisfyingly steep, at the foot of which was an extended and uninterrupted run-off. Through that long winter, under clear blue skies in the freezing cold, local boys would gather at the summit and, at a run, launch themselves onto a variety of contraptions to exhilarate in the descent powered by nothing more than the pull of gravity.

The Cathedral Quartet — T.V. Shellard, left. The Cathedral was St. Patrick's and the Quartet were, on one occasion at least, in the pioneering days of such broadcasts, invited to Belfast to sing on the wireless.

In all of his activities, my grandfather remained vigorous and clear minded until his ninety-third year when he succumbed, in short order, to pneumonia.

Yet despite the contentment of these final years, he retained an overriding nostalgia for the Dublin of his youth. He was fond of retracing journeys through the city's byways, invariably, it seemed, involving passage along Wine Tavern Street and past Christ Church Cathedral. This latter detail is odd, for his real loyalty was to St Patrick's Cathedral, where he had attended the choir school and, before his voice broke, been a leading chorister. From this musical beginning he had developed a refined appreciation of church music and church organs. In every other department of life than church music he was obstinately middlebrow in his tastes; Bing Crosby, Val Doonican, film musicals, television comedies, such as *Steptoe and Son*, *Dad's Army*, and I am afraid, *Till Death us Do Part*, and *The Black and White Minstrel Show*. The latter two are not favoured with repeats on the BBC owing to racist content that, when they were originally broadcast, passed unremarked. As a young adult my grandfather had enjoyed some success as a tenor, being engaged, for example, to sing at Masonic functions. He was a member of a couple of male voice quartets but whatever their repertoire his own preferences were more music hall than classical.

His Dublin nostalgia was notable for its focus on his early years and indeed it would have been easy to conclude that nothing much of great interest had happened to him in the long life he had lived beyond the age of twenty. What he had done before that was, he believed, worthy of fairly insistent repetition, to the point that Michael, Peter and I became weary of details which, for more occasional listeners, were a fascination. He had served as an ordinary seaman on a merchant sailing ship, the Loch Venachar and on three occasions had made the return trip from the Port of London by Cape Horn to Sidney, Australia. We were left in no doubt that the rounding of Cape Horn was a very great test of character. In the course of these three voyages, he had, as he liked to remind us, endured much hardship, survived on a staple of "hard tack biscuits," and had caught an albatross on a fishing line and subsequently had it mounted in a glass case. The Loch Venachar was eventually sunk, somewhat unglamorously, whilst at anchor off Thames Haven. The ship went down with the loss of one man when the SS Cato, the crew of which were drunk, ploughed into it with devastating effect. Also lost, by the way, was that albatross in a glass case. Clearly none of the sailors on the Loch Venachar had paid any heed to Coleridge's *Rime of the Ancient Mariner* and all the misfortune that ensued from the killing of an albatross.

2: NEVER! NEVER! NEVER!

'God save thee, ancient Mariner!
From the fiends, that plague thee thus!—
Why look'st thou so?'—With my cross-bow
I shot the ALBATROSS.

Having been in the merchant navy he naturally had a tattoo. It was on his forearm generally covered up by shirt sleeves. Occasionally, in hot weather perhaps, those sleeves would be rolled up and this memento of his time at sea made visible. My abiding impression is of an indistinct image, perhaps featuring an anchor and floral intertwining; had I ever been tempted to get a tattoo myself I would always be reminded by this glimpse that they do not age well.

At one point my grandfather featured in a two-page spread in the *Newry Reporter* under the heading "Old Thomas Looks Back." There will be no prizes for guessing the content of this item. I certainly did not feel the need to read it.

My grandfather had a repertoire of anecdotes from the Dublin of his youth, notable amongst which was a story of a man, Endymion, who was to be seen walking the streets of the city carrying under his arm a bundle of swords. In my grandfather's telling of this story there was always a group of small boys on Endymion's tail and eventually a point would come when these urchin hangers-on would become intolerable to the sword carrying Endymion and he would suddenly swivel round to confront them with a fiercely delivered single word riposte: "Heh!" I imagine that this was received with great delight by his tormentors. Years later I was to discover that Endymion's presence on the streets of Dublin early in the twentieth century was well documented, no doubt assisted by the fact that he appears in Joyce's *Ulysses*. His real name was Cashel Boyle O'Connor Fitzmaurice Tisdall Farrell, and he came originally from Dundalk before making his name as a Dublin character.

My grandfather had little interest in literature, I am sure disapproved of Joyce's *Ulysses* and probably never knew of Endymion's appearance in its pages or stopped to ponder the fact that Joyce, who was younger than him by only a few months had, in his youth, criss-crossed the same city streets and, coincidentally, shared his talent for singing. They could so easily have met, though given my grandfather's lack of interest in the arts and his conservative and unionist view of the world, it is hard to imagine that they could ever have become friends. An additional complication in imagining such an encounter is the fact that my grandfather was teetotal and so would never have set foot in any of the Dublin hostelries which were such a feature of Joyce's life and work. On the other hand, there is some evidence that my grandfather did have a lively appreciation of Dublin's vernacular culture, as exampled by his story of a judge having to enquire as to the meaning of the word "mot" in the testimony of a witness in a court case. "Mot? What's that he's saying? Mot?" The council for the defence comes to the aid of the judge. "Ah, a mot, m'lud, is a lady friend."

And then there was the pup we acquired soon after our arrival in Rocklands. He came to us via a friend of my mother and had been picked up from a farm in Castle Bellingham which, hitherto, I knew only as a hamlet we would pass through enroute to Dublin. He was part springer spaniel and part keeshond, the latter being a breed of which none of us had ever heard. The mix however had produced a striking patchwork of brown, white and black with spaniel ears and a handsome plume of a tail.

The new arrival showed early signs of character and intelligence and my grandfather immediately christened him "Jem". At the time, I misunderstood the significance of this and thought our new arrival was being called "Gem," as in "precious stone". I thought this saccharine and undignified. Only later did I realise that "Jem" is the Dublin vernacular for any person encountered whose name one does not actually know, and rather suited this mongrel addition to our family.

Why was my grandfather teetotal? He was not an evangelist for temperance in general. He felt no need to wrestle with the question of why Christ had thought it fit to turn water into wine at the wedding in Cana. One family theory is that, because he was regularly invited to sing at Masonic functions around the city, it was easier for him to say he did not drink than to manage his intake on an ad-hoc basis. It is just possible that, like me, he did not find the experience and after-effects of intoxication pleasant.

Literature may not have been important to him, but he did enjoy C.S Forester's *Hornblower* novels and occasional crime fiction. In his later life, when he came to live with us in Newry, it was the television which entirely occupied his attention in the long winter evenings and it did not go unremarked that his given names, Thomas Vincent, abbreviated neatly to TV

Shellard and fitted him well for this. Ma and Da both watched little television, whereas every night, apart from Wednesday when he went to Newry Bridge Club, my grandfather sat down after his high tea to enjoy an evening in front of the box. There were of course only two channels so there was little to fight over as regards what we might watch, but when *Top of the Pops* came around on a Thursday night this did result in some tensions between Michael, Peter and I, and my grandfather.

Whilst Ma and Da may have shared some of my grandfather's reservations about *Top of the Pops*, they also appeared to believe that our right to this half hour of television, once a week, should be protected. For the duration of *Top of the Pops* my grandfather would withdraw behind his copy of the *Belfast Newsletter*, at that time a broadsheet. He would turn the pages noisily and occasionally, when provoked by some particularly cacophonous offering, lower the page he was reading to ask: "Is that the tune the old cow died on?"

It would have been ridiculous to expect someone born in 1881 to welcome the musical developments of the 1960s with an open mind, though probably it was long hair and outlandish clothes which were the principal obstacle to such an appreciation. Indeed, I am conscious that the picture I am drawing of my grandfather might suggest he was a tolerated rather than a valued part of our household and that would not be a fair summary.

My grandfather was a complete contrast to my father, dapper in his dress, his tailor-made suits from Brown Thomas in Dublin's Grafton Street. My father gave sartorial matters only the minimal required consideration and had a much more serious and thoughtful turn of mind than his father; yet there was no evidence of conflict between them.

My grandfather may have been too ready to poke fun at his three grandsons, but he was generous, particularly where Christmas and birthdays were concerned. He spoke warmly of Mrs Kelly, his bridge partner, and his other friends at the club. Most important of all, he was very fond of my mother and always enjoyed cordial relations with her; and then of course there was his role as an unpaid gardener which helped keep us all in slightly more style than we might otherwise have managed.

Dell

This recollection of my father's family would be incomplete without mentioning his younger brother Sydney, or Dell, as he was known. Dell went on a holiday in Tramore, in County Waterford, in July 1943, from which he never returned. He had cycled down from Dublin with a group of friends. Amongst other things, he was there to celebrate his twenty-fifth birthday, which fell on the twenty-eighth of that month. On the morning of the twenty-ninth his friends noticed that he was not in his room, but it was not until the first of August that his body was found at the foot of cliffs, close to where he had been staying.

The *Waterford News*, dated 6th August, records the verdict of the coroner, that the spinal cord of "the deceased" was severed and that all his injuries were consistent with a fall from the cliff. There was no evidence of excess drink or anything that might implicate another person in his death. Nobody had witnessed the tragedy, and the precise circumstances of his fall were unclear. The same paper also notes that Dell was "employed in his father's estate office" and also includes the sad testimony of friends who say he was "a very popular man," that he could be "moody," and that he "was very healthy physically and mentally and was mainly interested in music." The *Dungarvan Observer* of 7th August 1943 adds further detail. Mr Shellard was "red haired and over six feet tall and was a well-known saxophone player... a member of Phil Murtagh's band … and also played with a Dublin band in Tramore Hotel last year."

Amongst various family photographs of Dell there is one of him as a member of an accordion, drum and saxophone quartet. Dell is one of the two saxophonists. Very little was ever said in the family about his musical influences, but I find it hard not to invest his memory with a sense that he was part of the emerging jazz scene in Dublin which, according to Liz Evers in her online essay, *A Short History of Irish Jazz*, "By the mid-1940s … had become a popular Irish youth subculture."

In contrast to this, there is also a photo of Dell in the uniform of the Irish Marine Service. He was evidently playing his part as a citizen in the "The Emergency," as the Irish government referred to the period of the Second World War. I do not recall my grandfather or my father ever saying very much, if anything, about Dell. What I knew of his story, when I was younger, mostly

Dell Shellard, second from right.

Dell in the uniform of the Irish Marine Service.

came via my mother and she made it clear that the few days during which Dell was missing was an agonising trauma for the whole family, and the confirmation of his death, devastating.

I recently came across an online history of the Killiney Estate in Co. Dublin. That is not a subject of any great interest to me, but the estate archive included a copy of a letter from Townshend and Dickinson, who were employed to manage affairs on behalf of the owner, a Mrs Talbot, resident at the time in Hampshire, England. That letter is dated 29th March 1943 and is signed, in fountain pen, by my grandfather. It is a single typed page containing some dry business details including discussion of the possible need for the "ejectment" of a tenant who is in financial difficulties and has fallen behind with his rent. Then, a little incongruously, the final paragraphs of the letter turn to the subject of "the very mild winter" and reference is made to the daffodils and crocus being in bloom and the garden seeds doing well. "I hope we will not have any late frost to spoil the good work," comments my grandfather before concluding that the mild weather has been very helpful in "coping with the fuel problem." During the war, coal imports from across the water had come to a halt and it was necessary to bring turf to Dublin from the west of Ireland by canal on specially constructed barges. It is a curious thought that my Uncle Dell was working in the Townshend and Dickinson premises as that letter was being prepared and that, just a few months later, he would go missing, having fallen to his death from a cliff top in Co. Waterford. It is hard not to imagine that one of the reasons my father got on harmoniously with my grandfather, despite their differences of character, was the shared experience of this tragedy.

The Count, the Countess and the Governess

These distinctions of character can be better understood by examining the insubstantial scatter of information that I have about my grandmother. She died when I was less than one year old. Michael spoke warmly of her, Peter had fewer memories and I had none at all. I have seen photographs of her in her older age, in particular, a colour enlargement, arm in arm with my grandfather, which would appear to support the family narrative that they were devoted to one another. And yet the evidence also suggests that the quirks of my father's character, his seriousness and thoughtful turn of mind came from my grandmother.

Kathleen Shellard, née Pemberton.

Apart from photographs, there is a further image of her which has followed me, perhaps even haunted me a little, since my earliest years. It is a portrait of her, aged about twenty, in a long dark dress with a white lace collar and wearing a showy dark hat, feathered I imagine, though it is difficult to say, given the dark background of the painting. The artist is Count Casimir Markievicz and, in its original full-length form, in 1905, it was hung for a time in the Royal Hibernian Academy. Early in the century, before she met my grandfather, my grandmother was employed by Count and Countess Markievicz as tutor to Stanislas, the Count's son from a previous marriage.

At the time my grandmother was in the Count and Countess's employment, they were living in Dublin and deeply involved in promoting the visual and literary arts. It seems that the Count took a liking to my grandmother and that she agreed that he might paint her, though had to insist that this could only happen if she were fully clothed. The clothes she does wear in the painting are not her own, but from the wardrobe of the Countess. And yes, that is Countess Markievicz, who features in Yeats's poem *In Memory of Eva Gore-Booth and Con Markievicz:*

> *The light of evening, Lissadell,*
> *Great windows open to the south,*
> *Two girls in silk kimonos, both*
> *Beautiful, one a gazelle.*

Lissadell was the country house in County Sligo where Countess Markievicz had grown up. In later years she was to gain, depending on your point of view, notoriety, or celebrity, as a prominent participant in the 1916 Easter Rising. Following the Rising, the Countess was sentenced to death for the part she had played. Her sentence was commuted to life imprisonment, and she was released in 1917 as part of an amnesty granted by the British Government. In the general election of 1918, she became the first woman to win a place in the British House of Commons. In line with the abstentionist policy of Sinn Fein, she never took her seat.

> *But a raving autumn shears*
> *Blossom from the summer's wreath;*
> *The older is condemned to death,*
> *Pardoned, drags out lonely years*
> *Conspiring among the ignorant.*

The "lonely years," which Yeats alleges, may in part explain why, later in his life, her stepson Stasko would, from time to time, knock the door of my grandparents' home in hope of a little money to pay his bills.

Casimir Markiewicz had, by 1913, returned to live in Poland and Stasko too was to leave Ireland in 1915, his destination a Markiewicz family estate in Ukraine. However, he was conscripted into the Russian Navy, and posted to

Archangel. Sometime during that posting, he met and married a Russian girl. But then, in 1919, Archangel was captured by the Bolsheviks, and he was imprisoned for several years. He was never to be reunited with his wife. By 1927 his step-mother was dead. He returned to Ireland in the 1930s and became a loyal defender of her reputation but was to fall on hard times. At the beginning of the war he had a room, for a while, in Sorrento Terrace in Dalkey, a rather fine address, but he was short of funds. My grandparents were also living in Dalkey during World War Two, a little over a mile from Stasko's lodging. It is probably in that era that Stasko paid a visit to his erstwhile governess in the hope that she might help him out. I'd guess that he was not sent away empty handed but that my grandfather will have harrumphed at it all.

The painting eventually came into the possession of my grandmother and was, for many years, given the unionist affiliations of her family, an unloved and somewhat ridiculed encumbrance. The picture was rolled up and left to gather dust in an attic. It is even suggested that Dell planned at one point to make a curragh from the canvas, a curragh being a type of boat which used to be common in the west of Ireland, made by stretching skins — or canvas in this case — over a wooden frame, and covering it with tar. Somehow the painting was rescued from this fate, so despite ambivalence towards its provenance, some sense that it was an artefact of historical significance must still have lingered.

It was my mother who eventually decided the picture should be taken from its hiding place and put on display. As we weren't living in a mansion house it was deemed necessary to commit the crime of cutting the painting and removing the bottom so that it might find a place at the top of the stairs in our semi-detached home in Balmoral Park, Newry.

In the intervening years and flittings, the cut section was left behind in the attic of some previous home though my father preserved a little rectangle of canvas, carefully tucked into the stretchers on which is just discernible, the signature of Count Markievicz.

The surviving fraction of the picture now hangs in the stairwell of the house where I live in Dumfries in south-west Scotland.

Grand-père

I have accounted for my paternal grandparents, but it may seem odd that my maternal grandparents have so far made no appearance in this story. Part of the reason for this is the simple fact that my maternal grandmother died in 1950, three years before I was born. As I grew older a picture of her gradually emerged from my mother's occasional comments and reflections on her character and also from little black and white contact prints in dusty photo albums which showed her as a benign presence in a rambling country house outside Bandon in County Cork. That was Overton, which was to become my mother's home in her late teenage years when the family moved there sometime around 1934, together with her younger siblings: Bill, Brian, Olive, Rose and Myrtle. Malcolm, the eldest in the family had by that time left home in pursuit of his studies.

We once visited Overton on one of our caravan holidays in County Cork but it was by that time unoccupied and ruinous; yet this only seemed to add to the allure of the house which occupied a rather sun-drenched place in my mother's recollections of the period in which she had been resident despite the fact that, even then, the house was in a poor state of repair. Overton had enough ground to keep four cows, a pony, a donkey, hens, and then of course there was the dog and three cats. My Aunty Myrtle recalls milking the cows at the weekends and churning butter from the cream. Potatoes and other vegetables were grown in an old walled garden. A boy and an old pensioner, often drunk, helped out with the garden and there were maids, to assist my grandmother in the house. According to my Aunty Myrtle, the maids were paid "a pittance," but she also took care to add, "we loved them, and they us."

The house was big enough to accommodate visiting cousins and friends in school holidays. Overton was a place of great sociability, cycling, tennis, swimming in the river. It was where my mother was living when she first met my father. There were some hints in my mother's recollection that her young brothers, Brian and Bill, were restless and less easily pleased with life at Overton and my Aunty Olive was later to recall that they couldn't get away fast enough to join the British forces once the war broke out. But where in all this activity was my grandfather?

2: NEVER! NEVER! NEVER!

This was a question which I had never thought to ask, but then one day, out of the blue, an answer was provided. It was August 1965, and we were off to spend a fortnight in a static caravan at Toormore, Co. Cork when my mother announced that we would be breaking our journey to visit her father, my grandfather. She explained that he had, just prior to the Overton era, begun a second family and that I had an Uncle Noel and Aunty Joan, previously unknown to me. Their mother, my grandfather's second wife, was no longer living.

Perhaps some clues had been laid in the years before these facts were made clear to me, but if so, I have no recollection of them. With this revelation, a curtain was drawn aside to reveal details of a family history that was not just unexpected, but scandalous. My Uncle Noel was born in 1934 and Joan three years later in 1937. My grandfather had moved out of the Foley family home to live with his new partner, Grace. They were unable to marry until my grandmother's death in 1950, but then formalised their relationship, and were together as husband and wife until Grace's death in 1954, aged just forty years old. My mother and all of my aunts and uncles had been estranged from my grandfather during this period.

It was my father who persuaded my mother that she should make some attempt to reconcile with her father before it was too late and she did indeed maintain connections with him until his death, though I never formed the impression she had forgiven him for what he had done. To understand the challenges that my grandfather's departure from his first family presented for her and for the rest of the family, it is necessary not just to appreciate that the breakdown of my grandfather's marriage took place in a very socially conservative era, but also to know that he had been a clergyman in the Church of Ireland. It is not hard to imagine that the family he chose to leave will have found his behaviour not only bewildering but humiliating and shameful. And then there was the extended family to be considered, though they, in important ways, came to the rescue.

My grandfather was himself from a large family. At the time of his separation from my grandmother, his own father, also a clergyman, and his mother, were still alive. In addition, he had four living brothers and three sisters. His eldest brother, Thomas William Winspeare Foley, in fact a half-brother whose mother had died in giving birth to her only son, had lost his life at Ginchy, in the Battle of the Somme, September 1916. He had been a lieutenant in the third battalion of the Leinster Regiment. Another brother had died in 1894, in the year of his birth.

And then there is my grandmother's family. She had three brothers living at the time of her separation from my grandfather. A fourth brother, Richard, had died in the 1918 flu pandemic, aged just twenty-nine years. There were also two sisters, Lucy and Muriel, Loo and Moo, as they were generally called.

Encouragement was given to my grandfather, I imagine from a consortium of these numerous relatives, to go to Canada with Grace, but he chose instead to make a new home in County Carlow. He could no longer be a minister in the Church of Ireland, but he had other skills and was able to earn a living by making furniture. The same consortium that had unsuccessfully attempted

My maternal grandparents on their wedding day, Limerick, April 13th, 1914, just three months before the outbreak of the First World War.

to export the family embarrassment were, between them, sufficiently prosperous to provide for my grandmother and her growing family. The principal source of this prosperity was my great-uncle Ernest, who had established a business importing bananas from the Canary Islands. Indeed, when my mother left school, she was offered the extraordinary opportunity to travel to the Canary Islands on a banana boat. For a year, she stayed with Uncle Ernest and his family and learnt Spanish, mostly, it would seem, from the maids employed in the household. She assured us Spanish was an easy language, though the only real evidence of her ability to speak it, that I can recall, was her attempt to teach Michael, Peter and I a well-known Mexican-Spanish song, *La Cucaracha*. At the time of this lesson, we were walking through sand-dunes to a beach near Dundrum in Co. Down. It was the first summer holiday of which I have any memory. Sadly, not much of that Spanish lesson has remained with me beyond the title of the song, *La Cucaracha* — the cockroach.

I cannot gloss over another story of my mother's, that Uncle Ernest, whilst living in the Canaries, had played golf with Franco. Franco was banished to the Islands in 1934 following a downturn in his fortunes in Spain. Whilst in exile in the Canaries he, nevertheless, retained a position as military commander in the Islands' administration, and so was a force to be reckoned with. This golfing story is made all the more remarkable by the fact that Uncle Ernest had lost his left leg in the First World War and so had the unusual golf handicap of an artificial limb when that apocryphal game of golf took place. As was my mother's way, she didn't have much interest in the outcome of the game, merely the fact that it had taken place.

She also told a story of how, not long after the First World War had ended, Uncle Ernest had taken a girlfriend to the cinema. It was only when he emerged onto the steps on the way out that it was noticed that his left shoe was pointing in the wrong direction. Evidently, he bore the loss of his leg with good humour.

I have no recollection of ever meeting my great-uncle Ernest and would not wish to paint him as a Franco supporter on the basis of this tenuous golfing connection. My mother never said anything to suggest that Uncle Ernest was anything other than a supporter of democracy, but he was a businessman, and I would be surprised if he had much sympathy for the communists and anarchists who were amongst Franco's opponents in the Spanish Civil War that was to come.

My mother made clear her reservations regarding my grandfather's character, but she did not try to turn me against him. On that visit to his home in Co. Carlow, deep in the countryside, I remember a vegetable patch near the house and a couple of bee hives. Noel, my uncle, had married and was in partnership with my grandfather in the furniture making business. He and his wife Elsie were also resident in the house. Noel's younger sister, Joan, had by that time, left home, and was living in England, though she was later to move to Moira in Co. Down, where I remember visiting her with my mother on a couple of occasions.

Noel took Michael, Peter and I out for a walk in the surrounding countryside. I imagine we were being kept out of the way whilst my mother made some kind of peace with the father she had not seen for nearly thirty years. Noel had a twelve-bore shotgun with him and was keen to show us that he could use it. Climbing over a gate, he spotted a crow on the far side of a field and, with remarkable fluency, raised the butt of the gun to his shoulder, took aim, and brought down his quarry. Even at the time, I could not see the point of killing a crow and would have been happier with a rabbit for the pot, but I was impressed by the manner in which the deed was done.

I was only to meet my grandfather that once and don't have a strong memory of the encounter, but it must have happened. He took an interest in me, surprising perhaps given that he had so many grandchildren most of whom he never met. He wrote me a few letters and my mother did not discourage this. I think he had hopes that I might go to Trinity College in Dublin and from there establish a more active connection with him, but nothing like that ever happened.

I don't remember much from his letters, other than talk about the game of chess which, he must have known, I played a little. He also shared with me his interest in the French language and sent me a couple of textbooks, *L'Art du Conjuger* and *A Précis of French Grammar*. I still have them, though they have contributed little to my continuing struggle to acquire a passable knowledge of the language.

Whatever questionable thing my grandfather had done, I was interested in his story. Scandal, when you are not actually at the centre of it, is endlessly fascinating. Even in Northern Ireland in the 1960s it was clear that the status of marriage and the family was changing. Mostly these changes were happening in other parts of the United Kingdom but one could not fail to be aware of them and, consequently, I understood what had transpired from a shifting perspective in which the break-up of families, however unwelcome, was increasingly an accepted part of life.

Some of my Foley aunts and uncles did not wish to have any connection with my grandfather. My Aunty Olive was an exception to this, and she sustained a correspondence with him in his final years. I have copies of some of the letters he sent her. Apart from touching on domestic themes, his letters contain evidence of theological concerns and, consistent with the letters he wrote to me, an abiding interest in French literature. In one letter he speaks of Voltaire's *Candide* and remarks on how, as with Rousseau, ideas came to him early in the morning, but unlike Rousseau, he did not have a secretary to write these ideas down for him. Chance would be a fine thing.

In their later years, Olive and Myrtle and Rose would occasionally come to visit me at my home in Dumfries. There was always talk of politics and Olive enjoyed trying to persuade me that my socialist ideas were a youthful error. Myrtle was much more on my side of the argument, but Olive was set in her conservative point of view. She relaxed by doing the *Daily Telegraph* crossword and was an early fan of Boris Johnston's columns in that paper at a time when I already had a strong impression that he was an untrustworthy clown. She was not impressed, however, by the scholarly pretensions in my grandfather's correspondence.

Olive had spent much of her adult life with her English husband, Bert, in Kenya but, in 1981 when my grandfather died, at the age of 93, she was living in Leicester and was the only member of his original family to attend his funeral. She told me about this years later saying that the church was "packed" for the event. I must have hinted this was evidence that he was well regarded in the community where he had lived. That may indeed have been the case; however, Olive was not prepared to allow this accolade. She was dismissive: "Ah, the Irish love a funeral."

At one point in my grandfather's correspondence with Olive, he detailed his progress on a little writing table he was making for her. Following Olive's death in 2009, that table came into my possession. Though I would be proud to have made it myself, it is not fine furniture, but is precisely made and serviceable and I am pleased to have it.

Annus Mirabilis

In his poem, *Annus Mirabilis*, Philip Larkin identified 1963, as a point of significance where his own sexual experience was concerned, wryly observing that was also the year in which Penguin Books defeated attempts to block their publication of D. H. Lawerence's novel, *Lady Chatterley's Lover*. Larkin also celebrates 1963 as the year in which the Beatles' first LP was released, though he himself was more interested in jazz.

I was just ten years old in 1963, and certainly knew nothing of the "Chatterley ban". Where sex was concerned, I was in the process of trying to discover what all the fuss was about, with absolutely no help from my teachers, and some rather unhelpful help from my parents who, I suppose at some critical indication of my development — I know not what — drew my attention to a book called something like *Love and Marriage*, which they conveniently located so that I might consult it at whatever moment I felt appropriate. I am sure I was given a few more clues as to what this book might concern, but not many. The generalities of this approach to sex education did have merit in letting me explore the matter at my own pace. The problem was, however, that even if I had had the patience to read my way through the chapters on courtship and love and the sanctity of the marital state, etc. etc., (which I did not) the description of the sex act was offered up in highly technical language and well buried within the wider messaging. On the whole, the explanations offered by my school friends were more useful, however implausible they seemed at the time.

By the time I got to secondary school, another source of authoritative, if somewhat crudely expressed knowledge, about the facts of life became available to me. Many of my new school friends were the sons of local farmers and the farm was an environment where the mysteries of procreation could not be concealed and where inferences were easily drawn between what was observed in cattle and sheep and the more obvious aspects of human anatomy. It may be that something of *Love and Marriage* had rubbed off on me, for I was instinctively uneasy with the business-like terms in which such matters were sometimes discussed.

On one occasion — I was about thirteen — my friend Charlie and I were pondering the mysteries of the female form, and like many teenage boys with a deficit of knowledge in such matters, we thought to acquire a pornographic magazine. Charlie had the money and made it clear that he was happy to pay the price if I were prepared to make the purchase. The prospect of going into a newsagent and making a request for a top-shelf magazine filled me with dread, but the deal was too tempting, and I agreed.

At that time, there was a newsagent, Eamonn Fitzpatrick, situated just off Trevor Hill, at the beginning of North Street, an area of the old town that was shortly afterwards to be completely demolished. With my heart beating hard in my chest, I stepped up to the counter, identified a magazine and made it clear that I wished to purchase it. Eamonn Fitzpatrick himself was serving. He sized me up. Many of my classmates sported sideburns, straight out of the 1950s, a clear demonstration of their manly credentials. I on the other hand would have to wait another few years before shaving became anything like a necessity. "You're a little young for that sort of thing," he said. I suppose it was not the first time Eamonn Fitzpatrick had encountered a young lad, hardly out of short trousers, making such a request. I was ready, however: "It's for my big brother." This, remarkably, seemed to do the job and I hurried off with Charlie to see what was between the covers.

The magazine in question would have been classified, even then, as soft porn. The girls' breasts, the curves of their figures were all very frankly shown, but there was never any sign of pubic hair, still less genitalia. Pornography of course is a very vexed matter: young girls, young women, exploited, objectified, possibly abused, for the rather sordid interest that men take in their bodies. Yet the pictures in this magazine seemed to offer something of an improvement on much of the information that had hitherto come my way informally on matters of sexuality, much of which was couched in a misogynistic miasma of slur and insinuation.

The notes that accompanied the magazine pictures — clearly written by the male editors to titillate and suggest the unqualified sexual availability of these young women — also gave some idea of their backgrounds. My recollection is that they were inclined to be factory workers, shop girls, typists, seduced by the seedy world of soft porn with the hope of some extra cash or escape from tedium into the world of glamour modelling. No doubt they had been selected for their appearance, flattered and groomed, and were risking their future reputation and peace of mind: yet, for a thirteen-year-old boy, viewing these young women unclothed, so apparently willing to display themselves in this way, was a thrilling transgression.

The Beatles' First LP

1963 was clearly not an annus mirabilis for me, as far as sex was concerned. I did eventually read *Lady Chatterley's Lover* in 1974 by which time all of its original notoriety had dissipated. But what of the Beatles' first LP? That was another matter entirely.

In 1963, even ten-year-olds in primary schools, were not just aware of the Beatles, but absolutely transfixed by them. All the girls I knew had a favourite Beatle and there would be lively arguments about who was the most attractive. Paul, I think for the more innocent, and the sharp edges of John for the more mature and worldly, though George and Ringo also had their supporters.

I now know most of the songs on the first LP, *Please Please Me* but it was the second album, *With the Beatles*, also released in 1963, which made me a fan. I credit my eldest brother Michael with bringing this into our house and thereafter bringing home every album that the Beatles released, through to *Sgt. Pepper's Lonely Hearts Club Band.* The singles were of course brilliant pop, but the albums offered more, with clever lyrics and, as I came to realise when I started to learn the guitar, they were more musically complex than Bob Dylan. I just couldn't play them.

The Beatles, having emerged from the Cavern in Liverpool, opened up a space in their wake for other bands, most notably the more edgy Rolling Stones. Much of the energy of this new cultural wave was centred on London, but no part of the United Kingdom was untouched by it, even Northern Ireland, and indeed, in 1965 something very exciting happened: Van Morrison and his band Them, made their first appearance on *Top of the Pops*, with a cover version of a traditional blues song, *Baby Please Don't Go.*

I was only twelve years old at the time, and knew nothing of the blues, but I was riveted by this performance. Some of this fascination naturally reflected the complete novelty of a band from Northern Ireland, or indeed any part of Ireland, being on *Top of the Pops*. But Van's performance was intense and uncompromising: unforgettable. Any teenager in Ireland who was able to tune in to that particular edition of *Top of the Pops* must surely have felt thrilled by the energy of the performance.

Baby Please Don't Go wasn't really a pop song, and how it had found its way to number ten in the charts is a puzzle. I saw Van in July 1973 at the Rainbow Theatre in London, by which time he had started to adopt a kind of awkward parody of rock performance and was evolving into the more dour, portly, pork-pie-hat-wearing public persona of his later career. In 1965, however, he was a youthful force of nature, not particularly stylish in his dress, but handsome, his face sensitive and, at that time, having all the benefits of a full head of hair. His performance was completely focused, no theatrical affectation, his voice, a diamond.

The B-side of *Baby Please Don't Go* was a song, penned by Van himself, which has become a pop standard: *Gloria.* I can't help wondering why this was not the A-side, for it seems such an obviously brilliant song. Them did produce more successful singles, but Van obviously had his eye on something more serious, and in March 1967 moved to New York to record his first solo album, *Blowin' Your Mind!* The track released from *Blowin' Your Mind!* as a single, was the song, *Brown Eyed Girl.* The BBC banned it because it contained reference to adolescent sexual activity and so, as a single, it was not particularly successful at the time of its release but has, over the years, acquired a reputation as a classic pop song. Van himself apparently does not think highly of it: "It's not one of my best. I mean I've got about 300 songs that I think are better." Whatever its ranking, it's a vivid evocation of what it must have been like to become a teenager during the cultural earthquake of the early 1960s. The fact that, for all its Americana, the song was clearly written against the backdrop of East Belfast, added to its impact on any sentient young person growing up in Northern Ireland.

1967 was also the year that a song was released by a young man from Ballymena, David McWilliams: *The Days of Pearly Spencer.* The theme of the song was difficult to pin down, but the lyric was full of images of urban decay and the desolation of Pearly Spencer. The production, which introduced a swirling orchestration and voice distortion, was very original for 1967.

At the time Pearly Spencer was released, McWilliams was being hyped as an "Irish Bob Dylan," a proposition that I found very hard to resist. Why not an Irish Bob Dylan? There were difficulties for him, however; the BBC declined to play the record because of Phil Solomon's involvement with the recording. Solomon was associated with the illegal "pirate" broadcaster, Radio Caroline. The song failed to chart in the United Kingdom. It was a hit, however, in many countries across Europe.

McWilliams was clearly a talented songwriter, but he did not build on the success of Pearly Spencer and the uniqueness of the song made it difficult for him to find his place beyond the realms of the folk world from which he briefly emerged. It was a striking piece of work, all the more so in that it originated from a young man who had grown up in Ballymena, a town at the very centre of Ian Paisley's support in the years to come.

The cultural wave that was sweeping through the United Kingdom as a whole, signalled the beginning of the end of unquestioning deference, of the automatic respect which had hitherto characterised the relations of the young with the old, those of ordinary people with the upper classes, of the powerless with those in authority. The establishment in every institution, political, religious, educational, felt threatened and characterised much of what was happening as immoral and dissolute: but their underlying concern was, surely, loss of control. Most threatened of all in the Northern Irish context, was unionism, for if young people from both sides of the divided community were starting to develop a shared culture, then the old unionist hegemony could not last.

The Only Book That Matters

Van Morrison and David McWilliams were never going to lead political change; they were harbingers of it. It was at about this time that the Civil Rights movement started to make waves in Northern Ireland. Their objective was not a united Ireland but rather changes to the institutions of government and administration in the Six Counties which would establish Catholic citizens as equal partners rather than perpetual underdogs. The rise of the Civil Rights movement was the prompt for Reverend Ian Paisley to move centre stage, to speak directly to the insecurities of the working-class loyalist community, and to activate ancient fears of "Popery". In language blending the character of rural Ulster and the Old Testament, he used his rhetorical force to resist the change being sought by the Civil Rights movement. His call for loyalists to "harass" the three-day Civil Rights march from Belfast to Derry was clearly instrumental in the attacks on the marchers as they passed peacefully through Burntollet on the 4th of January 1969. There were other politicians engaged in exactly the same project of disruption, but Ian Paisley was the name on everyone's lips and his trenchant resistance to change was a hallmark of his presence in the coming years, until, in 2005, he surprised everyone and endorsed the power sharing agreement by claiming the position of First Minister for himself with Martin McGuinness sitting alongside him as deputy. Over the preceding troubled years, it was Ian Paisley's mission to raise up the old demons of Protestantism, and to embed them in a deeply conservative loyalist culture. Into the vacuum created by the failure of the Civil Rights movement stepped the Provisional IRA, turning a hopeful moment into an abiding tragedy for all parts of the community.

In general, the Protestant middle classes of that era did not have much time for Dr Paisley and yet, at quite an early age, I felt I understood something of his appeal, the directness of his speech, the certainty of his message. I have heard many stories over the years of how he always treated his Catholic constituents with great fairness and would work in support of their interests as well as those of his Protestant constituents. I have seen instances captured on film of his interpersonal behaviour, when not addressing a crowd and how he could be humorous and personable. But most of all I have heard the late Martin McGuinness, former commander of the Derry Brigade of the IRA, talk about the way in which Ian Paisley had become his friend, had invited him into his home and made him feel welcomed: all of this speaks of a decency that was, somewhere, at the core of the man, and which was, I am sure, well known to his family, his political associates, his congregation.

Had he remained within the world of church and religion, known only as a firebrand preacher, a great deal less harm would have been done. He might be remembered now as charismatic, turbulent, out of touch with the changing world; capturing the attention of the media at such moments as his 1977 Save Ulster from Sodomy campaign, which resisted the decriminalisation of homosexual acts, the breakthrough legislation already having been passed in England ten years previously; or when, in the 1970s, he protested against the showing of such films as Monty Python's *Life of Brian* and *The Exorcist*; or in the early 1980s when his supporters demonstrated against the opening of sex shops in Belfast, using the — we must assume unintentionally amusing — slogan "Bump your horn for decency."

The politics of Northern Ireland had a tribal character from its inception. This exactly fitted with Ian Paisley's brand of unionism. Over the course of his political career, he contributed no big ideas which might make Northern Ireland work better for its minority population. His entire policy position was a defence of the status quo with the injustices and discontents endured by the minority "priced in." He made no attempt to criticise the record of previous unionist governments, reserving his hostilities for those more moderate than himself who saw that reform was a necessity if Northern Ireland was to prosper. The opposition to change, which he so successfully placed in the minds of the loyalist population, was then solidified by the equally tribal campaign of the Provisional IRA.

I saw him once in the 1970s at the height of his notoriety. We were both waiting to be called for a flight from Heathrow Airport to Aldergrove, Belfast's main airport. He must have been returning from that week's Parliamentary session. Nothing about his demeanour would have given away the fact that he was a politician. There were no newspapers scattered about him; no sheaves of documents to be studied. He was reading the only book that really mattered to him: his Bible.

Ill-Fitting Clothes

Unionism, it seemed to me, was like a suit of ill-fitting clothes that many Protestant people saw no other option than to wear. This unionist suit masked the vitality, diversity and decency of Protestant people. I knew that the institutions of Northern Ireland had been shaped in the interests of the loyalist population, but I thought the individual Protestants my family knew and that I knew, seemed not to be part of this corruption.

In saying this I think first of Mrs Ferris, who came to help out in the house as my mother became ill with multiple sclerosis. Mrs Ferris's family were members of the Orange Order and looked forward to the parades and the gathering which took place each 12th of July. Her husband and her father had both been members of the B-Specials, a reserve police force, disbanded on the recommendation of the Hunt report in 1970. These affiliations were alien to my own family and yet all of the Ferris and Copeland family, (Mrs Ferris being a Copeland before marriage) were valued friends to my mother. Mrs Ferris was beloved and respected by all of our family. She showed particular empathy to my eldest brother Michael, whose life from his late teenage years was tormented by intermittent and disabling mental health problems.

Undeniably, I did encounter occasional openly expressed sectarian tropes; people who would casually let it be known they thought Catholics were lazy, dirty, untrustworthy. Yet, in my experience, such comment was very far from commonplace. People got on with their neighbours, whatever their beliefs. But the message of sectarianism could be expressed in more subtle terms.

I was a member of the First Newry scout troop. As far as I was aware, the scouts had no rule against the membership of Catholics, yet there were none in the Newry troop. Indeed, it was my understanding that there was a Catholic scout troop in Newry, but they did not, as I understood the matter, identify themselves with the movement created by Baden Powell. Certainly, we had no association with them, and they never marched to the Cenotaph on Remembrance Sunday to commemorate the fallen of the two World Wars, as did the First Newry troop.

I had good friends in the scouts and my association with them was a happy diversion in a small town where there was not a great deal else to do. I enjoyed scout camps. We got on well with our scout leaders, and as we grew older felt ourselves to be treated by them as equals. One occasion, though, stands out in my mind as an instance of undue scouter influence. I was thirteen or fourteen at the time, and we were all summoned to assemble in the upper floor of the scout premises, situated in the little lane which connected Sandy Street to the back gate of Newry High School. One of the scoutmasters took the lead in what was said, and all of the others remained silent. Reference was made to the Catholic, St. John Bosco's sports club, which I understood to be located in the Upper Canal Street area of the town. Some members of the First Newry troop had been observed attending the club. I imagine this was boys who lived close to St. John Bosco's, and were already acquainted with other members, who found that their attendance was not unwelcome.

We were not told that attendance at St. John Bosco's was wrong, rather that our parents would not wish this to be happening. There was probably truth in this, but I was disquieted, pretty certain that my parents would not have discouraged me from such an association. In any case I did not think it the proper place for our scoutmasters to intervene. Yet I didn't feel sufficiently confident of this to speak up at the time.

I raised the matter with my parents, and got the expected answer: of course, if I wished to attend, that would be fine. Whatever they thought, my parents did not speak ill of the scoutmaster who had raised the matter. They were grateful to all of the volunteer scout leaders for what they did and understood that it was not necessarily productive to object to every small instance of behaviour which was so deeply embedded in the ways of the community and in the character of some individuals.

A favourite story of my mother's, gleaned, I believe, from a door-to-door salesman with whom she had made some common cause, concerned sectarianism in the Harland and Wolff shipyard in Belfast. According to this story, the workforce was largely Protestant but did include some Catholics. They were organised into work groups without any consideration for religious composition. These groups in turn were attached to distinct locations within the yard. An esprit de corps would develop within the groups.

From time to time, however, concerns would arise amongst the Protestant workers that the Catholics were gaining undue influence with the management, or otherwise securing unfair advantage. Plans would be hatched to deliver some kind of warning, punishment even. In my mother's telling of the story, this involved being thrown in the docks. Such plans would spread and develop without hindrance throughout the Protestant workforce, and yet no action was ever taken, for within each sub-group or team the instinct was to exclude their own Catholic members from any of the planned outrages.

This story has, to me, the ring of a parable, rather than being a description of real events. Nevertheless, in many contexts in Newry, there was association between Catholics and Protestants, and, as far as I was aware, much of it, perhaps most of it, was friendly and harmonious.

Small Talk — the Inner Shore

My holidays on the outer shore at Cranfield with the Browne family would have been in the very early sixties, in parallel with some of those early caravan holidays. As Philip and Nicholas and I grew into our teenage years the lighthouse shore at Cranfield came increasingly to occupy our attention. In contrast with the front shore, it was a more socially mixed and a busier holiday community, with people coming and going throughout the summer. For teenagers seeking some excitement, the lighthouse shore at Cranfield was, in the high season of July and August, a place to hang out and, a number of times, I went camping there with friends. It was on one such occasion, in the summer of 1969, that I had an early experience of intimacy with a girl; intimacy, I should say, of a fairly innocent kind. I had just turned sixteen.

I was mingling with a crowd of young people, some known to me, and some not. Adrian, a boy in my school year, from Rathfriland, and distinctly more practised than myself in such matters, had brokered an agreement in which the guys and the girls present were all paired off. The girl I was with, Andrea, was a little older than myself. We set off in our pairs, scattering in search of some private place.

This was uncharted territory for me, but I felt that it was probably my responsibility to take the lead, and so, unsure of where exactly I was going, we found our way to the beach and set off westwards. I was painfully conscious of my inability to think of even the smallest thing to say as we walked, hand in hand, in the direction of the setting sun. We rounded a corner at the inner end of the beach and were heading towards the ferry crossing point at Greencastle. We might well have ended up there had we not, by some negotiation, which may have involved words, brought an end to this long march, and found a place to lie down together.

The physical closeness which ensued was a welcome release from my sense of conversational inadequacy and the circumstances of our encounter, an obvious invitation to embrace and to kiss. My desire to explore the mysteries of her body were not rebuffed. Eventually, it seemed time to return, before the search parties crashed in on our intimate adventure. We set off back along the strand. Not a word was spoken that I recall, and we parted, never again to meet, perhaps an inevitable conclusion, but one which I came increasingly to regret in the weeks that followed. There was, however, no way back. What bothered me most at the time was not the inept nature of my caresses, but rather, my inability to engage Andrea in a conversation which might have put us both at ease. Even though she was older than me, I felt strongly, the failure was mine. I did not know how to make small talk. It was not the first time I had floundered in such circumstances, and it would not be the last.

I am sure our walk along the strand at Cranfield will not have gone down as a high point in Andrea's early experience of boys. Still, what we shared that summer evening is evidence that, in the late 1960s, just beneath the surface of the puritanical society in which we were growing up, young people were exploring the complicated territory of sexual encounter as best they could, just as they have always done. Plus ça change, plus c'est la même chose.

The Beautiful Game

My early teenage years had been marked by an unrequited romantic interest in Julia. However, she was already resolutely committed to a good friend of mine, Brian, someone capable of growing sideburns, though he did, no doubt, have other fine qualities that I could not match. Once I had come to terms with this reality, and despite her commitment elsewhere, in the coming years, Julia became a good friend. She shared some of my literary and artistic pretensions, and did not glaze over when, for example, I tried to explain what had captured my attention in Richard Harris's performance as a professional rugby league player in the film, *This Sporting Live*. She was happy to mull over with me the BBC's Wednesday Plays, one of the cultural events of the TV week in the late 1960s. The opportunities to discuss such matters, and doubtless other more prosaic details of our daily lives, came in school during free periods in Room 1 when we were supposed to be studying for our A-levels, and Brian was helpfully tied up by some other class commitment.

There were occasional phone calls, where, I am not sure on what pretext, I would ring Julia from home. Our family only acquired a telephone when my grandfather retired and moved from Dublin to live with us in about 1964. Newry and district numbers had just four digits at that time. Home telephone ownership was far from ubiquitous; we were at the cutting edge of the domestic rollout, though the technology was spreading rapidly. My end of this telecommunication event involved closing myself into the cupboard under the stairs, the cramped and austere space allocated to our imposing green apparatus with its curly cord and circular dial. For all its claustrophobia, this under-stairs cubby-hole offered a pleasing privacy that, no doubt, added a sense of intimacy to our calls which I, at least, savoured.

In my middle teenage years, I did have a girlfriend, Emma, but it was a short-lived affair. She was a year below me in school but, though I liked her and was grateful for her interest in me, I never really settled into the relationship and my involvement, consequently, was half-hearted. Unsurprisingly, we drifted apart.

Part of the problem, perhaps, was that the fate of those in Newry High School who were "going steady" seemed to be to spend their breaks and lunch hours standing in the school yard, lined up along the red brick wall of the old High School building, in — what seemed to me — an enchantment of mutual admiration. I really couldn't visualise myself in this amorous company and was mystified as to how this practice could be sustained over months, if not years. But there was, so far as I was concerned, a further problem with the wall of love: lunch hour was for football.

It was the chance of a game before school which got me there early most days, and the opportunity for a further game at the end of the day which kept me late most evenings; but that was clearly not enough, and I was unready to sacrifice my lunchtime to anything other than football. Football — soccer that is — occupied a unique position in the culture of Newry and District for it was not an official game in any of the schools, whether Catholic, where Gaelic football and hurling were played, or state schools, such as Newry High School, where the official sports were rugby and hockey. I'd played both of these in my first year and opted for hockey, which I enjoyed; but my first love was "the beautiful game".

My passion for the game was a common one amongst my friends and so we sought opportunities for a more organised expression of this shared interest. This we found in the Carnbane League, a phenomenon of voluntary organisation worthy of an OBE, though I suspect that those who might have been offered the award, would have felt it necessary to decline it and the accompanying trip to the palace.

My friends and I entered teams in the appropriate age groups in the Carnbane League over several seasons. The sides that I played in were conspicuous only by their lack of success. The team names in general were like those I see listed today: Camlough Rovers; Rossowen Celtic; Millburn United. On one occasion I persuaded my friends to enter a team under the name of River Plate, which I knew to be one of the top Argentinian teams. I knew nothing about them, but I was very taken with the ring of the name. It must have been a knockout competition, for I remember playing only one game as River Plate in which we were well thrashed, 6-1. In this particular match, however, somewhat to my own astonishment and late in the "second moiety", as the man from the *Newry Reporter* would surely have recorded the moment — had he been present

— I shimmied past a couple of players and slotted the ball into the corner of the net for our only goal. I watched the *Newry Reporter* very closely that week on the day it came out, to see if the panel who awarded "goal of the week" had heard of the glories of my own effort. Apparently, no one had seen fit to pass on the good news.

The fact that football has such a strong cross-community profile in Northern Ireland made it all the more mystifying to me that the national soccer team was, and continues to be, divided, a Northern Irish team and a team for the Irish Republic. This does not mirror the situation in other sports such as rugby and hockey, where a single team represents the island of Ireland. In my teenage years, this was a matter of distress to me. In the late 1960s and early 1970s, George Best was indisputably the greatest player in the world. Newry's own Pat Jennings was a goalkeeper — the *Newry Reporter* would have called him a "custodian" — in the very top rank. It seemed obvious to me that if we could just add John Giles of Leeds United and the Republic of Ireland, we would have a midfielder of world class who could stitch the whole team together. With these three very great players and the best of the rest, there was no doubt in my mind that — to paraphrase Marlon Brando in *On the Waterfront* — "we coulda been contenders." I don't just mean that we could have got to the final stages of the World Cup; this was a once in a thousand-year opportunity for a small nation to go all the way, squandered, as far as I could see, on the altar of an archaic squabble.

Apartheid

In my early teenage years, I played quite a lot of badminton in the Sandy Street Presbyterian Church youth club and drank coffee in the Copper Grill on the corner of Sandy Street and Trevor Hill, just across from Newry's Court House. On a Saturday afternoon I might hope to meet up with friends in Foster's Coffee Bar, Foster's being quite a grand department store on Hill Street. It was school friends I was meeting in these places. The religious segregation of our education had determined the friendships we developed. I would glimpse the uniforms of other schools about the streets of the town: the green of the Sacred Heart, the blue of Our Lady's and of St Colman's College, the black of the Christian Brothers. I only properly knew the location of one of these schools. St. Colman's College was clearly visible from where I lived on the Belfast Road. It lay across green fields on the other side of the Clanrye River, a handsome redbrick building with fine playing fields where I could see the lads playing Gaelic football and hurling. I was never to discover where my Catholic age cohort disappeared to when they were out of uniform. This religious apartheid was, I imagined, preferred by both the unionist establishment and the Catholic Church.

Newry High School was a little exceptional in, to some degree, breaking ranks with this status quo. In the early years of my education, both primary and secondary, all my classmates were from a Protestant background. However, somewhere in the latter part of the 1960s, Headmaster, Joe Clements, or "the Boss" as we called him, had started to welcome pupils from Catholic schools who wanted to repeat O-levels or A-levels. There was a certain amount of resistance to this from some Protestant quarters and, on one occasion, a pupil protest was directed against this Catholic intake. It was an unseemly event orchestrated, I believe, by some disgruntled parents, who did not accept the idea that Newry High School was open to all comers. The Boss, an unlikely champion of integration, stood firm.

I had met a few Catholic people of my own age before, and was friendly, for example, with the O'Hare family, who ran a shop across the road from us on the Belfast Road. All the family who were still living at home, worked in the shop from time to time. They were all clever, obvious university material. Teresa, who was about my own age, was studying for a range of A-levels which intersected with my own, chemistry, physics and mathematics, and so we were not short of things to chat about; but such encounters were not that common. Suddenly, I had Catholic friends. I remember in particular Irene, a sweet-natured girl, and Bronagh, clever, but something of a rebel, who did not go out of her way to be popular. I liked them both and corresponded with Irene when I left for university though this communication did not last. Bronagh, I admired for other reasons. When I reflect on her character, I can imagine that in the future which awaited, she might have embraced the spiky values of punk rock or become an outspoken feminist. Sadly, I lost touch with her completely so cannot say whether she fulfilled this promise.

Then there were the boys; Feargal Sweeney in my A-level maths class, and Hugh Dowd, whom I encountered on the concrete tennis court where we played our lunch break games of football. Hugh was an exceptionally talented player. I have a vivid memory of him rolling the ball back and forth beneath his right foot, a ruck of opponents vainly trying to take it from him as he calmly looked up to find a well-positioned member of his own team to whom he might deliver a perfectly weighted pass. Hugh went on to have a professional career, playing for Northern Ireland on several occasions. Apart from this distinction, he never quite broke through into the top-flight of football, and I have always supposed this may have had something to do with his reputation, even when at school, for being a bit of a party person.

I cannot pass this reflection on Catholic pupils who attended Newry High without mentioning Leo White. I didn't really know Leo that well. He was not taking any of my subjects, but he was the kind of a person who you felt you knew well, even from a distance. He was a tall, slim, gangling figure, with unruly red hair. He was lively and sociable and, as far as I could judge, well-liked by everyone. His father was in the Royal Ulster Constabulary and, I suppose, at least part of the reason Leo had enrolled in Newry High School was that being the son of an RUC man in an exclusively Catholic secondary school, would have been tough. In 1971, Leo's father was ambushed in Jonesborough in South Armagh and was shot eleven times by two gunmen. Miraculously he recovered and went on to work in the Crown Prosecution Service in Newry for another decade but remained a target of interest to the IRA. In 1982 in the company of his wife, he was again ambushed, and this time did not survive. The moving story of Leo's father and their family's life when they were based at Crossmaglen in South Armagh is told in a book written by Leo's younger brother Shane, titled *Before the Bandits*.

Songs from a Beach

On two occasions when I was camping in Cranfield, as the evening closed in, I wandered out with friends to the eastern end of the beach. There we lit a driftwood fire. The first of these fires was in the summer of 1970, the second in 1971. With whatever scraps of food, or maybe even alcohol we could gather, we sat around the flames and whiled away what remained of the day. As the sparks rose, teenagers staying at the caravan site joined us. I had a guitar with me and, with a little encouragement, played through my slim repertoire of songs.

It was my eldest brother, Michael, who had introduced me to the four chords necessary to play the Dylan song, *Love Minus Zero*. From that beginning and, after some false starts, I built up a set of songs and enough confidence to play for a few friends. My guitar playing wasn't up to much, but I could sing in tune and gradually I dared to think my performance had become a welcome part of small, informal gatherings. I wasn't really the kind of singer who could compete with much background chatter. *The Wild Rover* was definitely not part of my set. However, if conversation faltered, and a more reflective humour settled on the company, someone would, as likely, ask me to play.

Of all the songs I was playing at that time, Leonard Cohen's *Story of Isaac* was an unexpected favourite. It came off Cohen's album, *Songs from a Room*. Cohen was at that time a fairly obscure figure and I knew the album only because my elder brother Peter, who was at Queens University in Belfast, had brought a copy home with him. I learnt a number of songs from the collection. In another context these songs would have been considered "boring" or "too melancholy," but when introduced by a fireside in the fading light of a July evening they really did seem to capture the attention of my small audience in a manner that could have deceived me into thinking I had a future in the music business.

Songs from a Room was not the only piece of intriguing media which Peter brought home with him, and I'd have to admit some fascination with a copy of *Oz* I discovered in some secret place in the bedroom we shared when he was in residence. *Oz* was a magazine of international disrepute, a mouthpiece of the emerging 1960s counterculture. I caught a glimpse of a vivid pop-art inspired montage of images and text, which on closer inspection I could see was built around a central image of a very lovely and very naked girl. This was definitely not content for sharing with the family. I hastily replaced it and kept quiet about my discovery.

The songs of Leonard Cohen presented their own challenges to the conventions of the day but that, of course, was part of their appeal to my friends, though the fact that they were couched in poetic language and occasionally imagery familiar to us from the Bible, imbued them with an additional mystique. The appeal of the *Story of Isaac* surprised me, but then, perhaps I really hadn't understood, when I first learnt the song, how contemporary its message was, this story of a man preparing to sacrifice his son on the altar of his belief and then realising at the eleventh hour that it did not have to happen.

When I went camping at Cranfield in July 1970 the group included my friend Charlie and his girlfriend Jean. They were sharing a tent. They were pitched fairly close to the tent I was sharing with some other lads. What I had not anticipated in this arrangement was that I could, without much difficulty, hear Charlie and Jean in the next tent. I did not find this a congenial experience. It was close enough to be pretty clear that they weren't having sex: it was equally clear, however, that they were having fun. Some of the details of this were being transmitted across the short space and the two layers of canvas which separated us. Apart from what seemed an unavoidable disturbance of my sleep, there was an additional complication to my response: I rather fancied Jean, which would have constrained me from passing some sardonic comment, had that been my style. I tossed and turned my way through the night. Charlie and Jean probably slept more than I did. The following morning, I was not in a great humour, but did not feel able to explain myself, and knew that I couldn't really stand another night of this torment. I decided to head for home. I had a bicycle with me and so my sudden departure was made easy, though I suppose it must have caused some head-scratching.

On the 20-mile journey home, I decided to stop off to see my friend Christopher. Because he lived in Warrenpoint, he was not normally someone I had much to do with outside of school hours. He was, besides, a somewhat different character from my other friends: quieter, more serious, more studious. We had become firm friends in our first-year science class where we had prospered as a team carrying out the required practical tasks. His father was a Presbyterian Minister. Christopher, as far as I knew, did not dissent from his father's beliefs. Nevertheless, though we never discussed matters of religion — by that stage I was well on my way to giving up any religious beliefs — I knew that he could think for himself and that he certainly didn't have any sermonising tendencies. Whatever was the case, we seemed to get along well. We shared sporting interests, football in particular, though unlike me, he was a rugby player. He was humorous and interested in the world in general, an important friend. Yet, there was an unspoken understanding between us that some of the usual topics of conversation between adolescent boys should be treated with circumspection. I had no problem with this and so, without offering a full explanation of why I had turned up so unexpectedly, I accepted the offer of lunch with his family, settled myself down, and headed for home in the afternoon.

Astral Weeks

I had to wait until 1971 for my first encounter with Van Morrison's *Astral Weeks*. In the summer of that year, my pal Victor and I set off to hitch-hike around the Republic of Ireland. Newry was very unsettled as we started our trip, but over the border everything was calm. On our second night we stayed in a youth hostel in the Wicklow Mountains where we got talking to a couple of girls from Dublin. They invited us to visit them, which we did, and it was one of these girls who introduced us to *Astral Weeks*. It was quite unlike anything I had listened to previously and it took a little time for me to appreciate the significance of this jazz-inflected poetic and musical wonder. The references to Belfast and Dublin drew me in, but the mysterious qualities of the vocal performance, musical arrangements and lyrics, kept me listening. Van Morrison has produced many fine albums since, but nothing really compares to this either in style or quality. I suspect Van himself doesn't really know where it came from. He's a bit of a shaman really.

After Dublin we stayed a night at a youth hostel in Kinsale where a young man from Belfast read his own compelling poem in which he had personified his hometown in a character called Belferiel, who wheeled a "handcart of hatred" through the streets of the city. I don't always get poetry, but I liked his performance and regret that I cannot remember more of his verse.

The following day we visited my Uncle Brian and Aunty Joan, and my cousins in Cork City, and then moved on to Limerick, my mother's birthplace. Uncharacteristically, I got into a fight there, of all things, coming out of a poetry reading. I quickly made peace with the guy who I had so unwisely pushed, but not before he had put a hole just above my lip which required stitches inside and out. At the local hospital, an Asian doctor, not something I expected at all in that part of Ireland, performed a very tidy job at no cost.

On leaving Limerick, we moved north. Just outside Galway, in very hot weather, Victor attempted to drain the last drops from a bottle of Guinness and got stung on the inside of his lip by a wasp which had got to the dregs ahead of him. This was an agony for him, but with some help from passing locals, we were provided with ointment which soothed the pain. After a long wait outside Galway, we hitched a lift into the centre of Ireland. We knocked on a door asking for suggestions as to where we might stay overnight. The couple that answered were helpful, though strangely reluctant to enquire into the causes of our sorry state. We were directed to a shed a mile or two along the road where we passed the night before embarking on the final stage of our journey across the border and home. It's hard not to assume that the couple we had approached judged the two rather beat-up and wild-looking characters who had turned up on their doorstep as, "on the run," from something or other, about which it was safer not to know.

Not long after our return to Newry, I saw plumes of smoke rising above the town as shops were burning. One of these was a draper's in Hill Street. The son of the owner was in my class at school. Two young men had broken in and set the premises alight. In the version of the story I have heard, it is not at all clear that they belonged to any terrorist organisation. They became trapped between the fire and the display window with its security grill. The two lads either burned to death or were asphyxiated by the fumes from the fire they had set.

I was given an account of this event later by Bronagh who lived in the town and had been an eyewitness to the tragedy. She described how a crowd of people had gathered. They could clearly see what was happening and were horrified that the two young men were trapped. Members of the crowd pleaded with the British soldiers who were attending to shoot off the locks which were preventing the young men from escaping. Bronagh told me that the soldiers ignored these requests.

I believed what Bronagh was telling me. She was no apologist for any kind of terrorism. I understood that, from the soldiers' point of view, letting off a weapon in such circumstances carried a few risks, the most obvious being ricochet and injury to onlookers. Indeed, raising a loaded weapon and pointing in the general direction of the young lads might also have provoked a difficult response in the crowd: yet these seem lame excuses for callous inaction. I cannot help wondering why some smart British Army officer did not manage the situation and at least show willing to help the boys escape to safety. Not to do so in the face of this human tragedy was a moral failure and, there is no escaping it, a public relations disaster.

Another Saturday Night

As my teenage years progressed, Saturday night became a growing challenge and often seemed empty. I recall passing time during winter evenings with my pals from the Venture Scouts. We would gather around the stove in the scout hall, a location where I brought my guitar, and I might occasionally be invited to sing a song or two. It was a scene redolent, I thought, of *Bob Dylan's Dream* and I did learn a few verses of that song at the time. However congenial this gathering around the coal-burning stove may have been, the element of female company was absent; but where were the alternatives?

I had some awareness of dances in the Henry Thomson's Memorial Orange Hall on Downshire Road, but that wasn't a location in which I was drawn to spend my leisure time. In truth, the reason I was aware of these Orange Hall dances probably owed much to the fact that, on a Saturday night in January 1961, a nineteen-year-old girl, Pearl Gamble, had been murdered following her attendance at a dance in that very venue. Robert McGladdery, who was found guilty of this crime, had also been at the dance. I was just eight years old when this happened and, in my own home, the details of this wrongdoing were not spoken of when I was present. Newry, though, is a small town, and this brutal murder was intimately embedded in the even smaller community of Newry Protestants. By whatever means, overheard snatches of conversation, whispers, newspaper headlines, the dark and disturbing details seeped into my eight-year-old consciousness; the discovery of the body in Upper Damolly, not far from where we lived at the time, the blood-stained clothing found in a septic tank, the fact that Robert McGladdery was a distant cousin of his victim; and then the trial. "McGladdery," as he was called in any of this talk, pled "Not guilty." The jury, having been presented with the evidence, took a different view of the matter and he was sentenced to hang.

For me, as I grew older, this crime and these details took on a more concrete aspect. Robert McGladdery had grown up in Damolly Village and his story was not forgotten. Tales of his eccentric behaviour continued to be told, how he would strip to the waist to wash under the flow of water from a pump in the village, perhaps more evidence of deprivation than deviance. In that same single row of terraced houses where McGladdery had grown up lived my mother's friend, Mrs Copeland. Mrs Copeland had taken it upon herself to communicate with McGladdery whilst he was awaiting execution in Belfast's

Crumlin Road Prison. I believe it will have taken some courage for her to do this, but she was clearly motivated by her strong Christian faith. On the eve of his execution, McGladdery wrote a letter to her in which, at that eleventh hour, he confessed to the crime he had committed and also accepted Jesus as his Saviour. I recall this document being soberly discussed and wonder now whether it is just my imagination that I was, on one occasion, permitted to view it. The day following the date on that letter, 20th December 1961, Robert McGladdery was the last person to be judicially executed on the island of Ireland.

Apart from the Orange Hall dances, I would occasionally hear talk of barn dances. I understood these events to be a stamping ground of the local young farmers. I imagined a strong country music influence on the proceedings though, at that point in my life, this was not really a recommendation. In my mind's eye there would be bales of straw scattered about, an accordion playing, or perhaps, music from the top twenty rounded off by a slow dance with a favourite partner, to the hypnotic baritone of Jim Reeves singing *Distant Drums*: but this vision was not put to the test as no invitations ever came my way.

There was a hall in Warrenpoint, located close to the Harbour Quay, where each week a disco took place. I understood that this gathering would be more working-class in character than I was used to and, probably, exclusively Catholic. I did not expect to know anybody if I went, and yet, I decided to give it a try. I told none of my friends. Quite what I told my parents I am not sure. I travelled by bus to Warrenpoint, and found my way to Harbour Quay, and bought my ticket. My memories of the experience are vague. The place was packed with young men and women, a little older than me, as best I could tell. There was music and dancing. There must have been alcohol, though I don't remember taking any. I wasn't yet eighteen, a fact no doubt blindingly obvious to all others attending. I struggled to engage. My deficiencies in small talk were no doubt part of the problem, but clearly, I stood out as an oddity. Nobody attempted to speak to me, though nobody was hostile or unpleasant. There may have been suspicions, as if a teenage Ian Paisley Junior had broken free of the bonds of his father's church and, on his journey to better understand the deeper truths of the divided country he was growing up in, had landed up in the dance hall of Warrenpoint's Harbour Quay. By midnight, I was back on the street, and hitch-hiking my way homeward. The bleakness

I associate with this particular outing mostly arises from the uncertainties of that wait by the roadside in the early hours. Had I lived in Warrenpoint I might well have returned for another crack. It is obvious that I lacked the talent for finding my way into a new social scene, but I feel sure somebody would have taken pity on me eventually and come to my aid.

Wine of the Country

Ma and Da were not by any means tee-total but they had no interest in alcohol as a social lubricant. My father never went to the pub. They never attended parties where drinks were served, yet they did not attempt to lecture Michael, Peter and I on the evils of drink and seemed to understand that to do so would probably be counterproductive. Indeed, for a period, from hedgerow fruit they picked, they very diligently made a variety of country wines, fermenting them in demijohns. The most successful I remember was elderberry, but there was also blackberry and elderflower, and sloe. The possibilities were endless. They would serve up modest amounts of these potions with our Sunday lunch. As an eight-year-old, I was entitled to about half a glass. To be truthful, the vintage I most enjoyed in those early tastings was one which had failed to ferment properly and was more or less sweetened fruit juice. In my teenage years, my palate became a little more sophisticated and I had a go at making crab-apple wine which I imagined might deliver something interesting. The result was initially encouraging, a beautiful clear golden liquid, which was definitely alcoholic, but there was a very disappointing musty aftertaste.

It was in July 1971 that I was, at last, legally able to take a drink in licensed premises. I had, like many of my friends, made earlier attempts to pass myself off as eighteen years old, but my youthful appearance generally gave the game away. Having gained a driving licence the previous year, I could back up my claim of adult status and, on my eighteenth birthday, as I started into my final year of schooling, things started to look up a little in my teenage social life. The prospect of greater freedom was on the horizon.

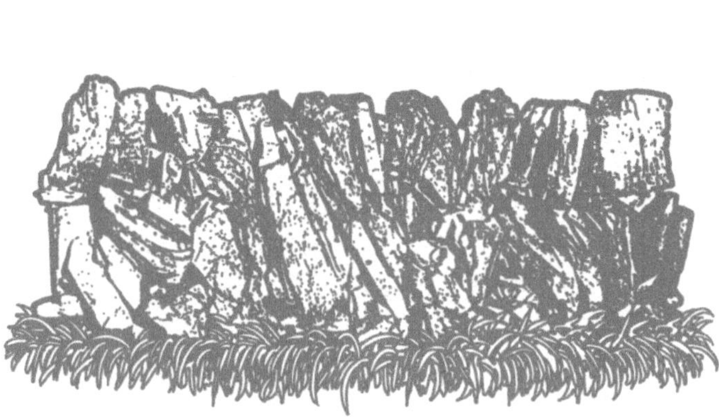

3: Promised Lands

Kevin Barry — updated

In Mountjoy Jail one Monday morning, high upon the gallows tree
Kevin Barry gave his young life for the cause of liberty
Just a lad of eighteen summers yet there's no one can deny
As he walked to death that morning he proudly held his head on high.

Just before he faced the hangman, in his dreary prison cell
British soldiers tortured Barry just because he would not tell
The names of his brave comrades and other things they wished to know
"Turn informer or we'll kill you!" Kevin Barry answered "No!"

But British soldiers battled Hitler and for that we should be glad
While DeValera walked the side lines, thousands starved in Leningrad
Every army has its villains, its mad dogs that break the chain
And every army has its heroes, its sacrifice and pain.

Another martyr for old Ireland? There's too much talk of martyrs now
Let the families mourn their loved ones, let the rebels take their bow
But lads like Barry are no cowards if they say "Let's burn the past,"
Let the flames light up the nighttime and show us Ireland free at last.

All That Guff: Updating songs from the Orange and the Green traditions for the modern era.

The Best Laid Plans

In June 1972 I was to take my A-level examinations in Physics, Chemistry and Mathematics. I had, however, decided to forsake the sciences and had applied for a place at Reading University to study Sociology. I knew nothing about Reading, or Sociology for that matter, but the subject was a fashionable choice for the time, and not one I have ever seriously regretted. With my parents' encouragement, I planned to defer my university career to take advantage of an offer from my mother's brother Bill and his Canadian wife Mary. They agreed that I might spend a year with them and their young family in Canada, my assumption being that I would return the following year to take up my university place. The Canadian hospitality on offer to me was also extended to my friend Christopher, though in his case he was only interested in staying for the summer months. He too was to fly to Canada at the conclusion of the school year,

If I was to find work in Canada for a year it seemed I would have to emigrate, in order to get the necessary visa. In applying for this, I was frank about my intention to go for a limited period, and this proved not to be the kind of commitment the Canadian immigration authority was seeking. They turned me down flat. I accepted the offer of a 3-month holiday visa as compensation, but this was to be a limitation on my ability to earn whilst I was in Canada.

Christopher fared better as my Uncle Bill, who had a good position in the Toronto Public Library service, had been able to arrange a summer job for him, filling in for staff on leave over the holiday period. For Christopher, the work visa came with the job. Library rules determined that Uncle Bill could not do the same favour for a member of his own family and so I was left in limbo. When the time came, Christopher flew out early to start his job whilst my departure was deferred by a couple of weeks.

The State We Were In

On the 30th of January of that year, thirteen unarmed civilians were shot dead at a rally in Derry's Bogside, organised by the Northern Ireland Civil Rights Association to protest at internment without trial, a policy crudely directed at Catholics suspected of having some connection, whether historic or current, to the IRA. 1972 was to be the deadliest year in the entire history of the

Troubles. Four hundred and ninety-seven people were killed as a consequence of politically motivated violence, over half of them civilians.

Despite this, all the young people I knew were getting on with their lives regardless. There certainly was a spectrum of risk, those most acutely in danger being the British Army, the Royal Ulster Constabulary, the Ulster Defence Regiment, and those actively engaged in terrorist activity. Politicians also spoke their mind at some considerable risk. For those at the low-risk end of the spectrum, where I would have placed myself, there was always the possible misfortune of being caught in some crossfire or of just being in the wrong place at the wrong time, but in general these hazards seemed roughly equivalent to the dangers of crossing a road and I did not lie awake at night worrying about them.

For many years Newry had been a town in decline. Unemployment was a problem which long predated the Troubles. In later years I hitch-hiked a good deal. I remember once being given a lift by an economist. I told him where I was from. "Ah!" he responded immediately, "Highest unemployment in the United Kingdom." Partition had split the hinterland of the port of Newry, and the Unionist government showed little interest in this Catholic town. Newry was a place of limited opportunity and significant deprivation.

There was another side to Newry, however, for every small town, even when times are hard, has its middle class; its doctors and dentists, its solicitors, its teachers, its small businesses, such as the butcher and the baker. In Newry this group of people, many of them Catholic, enjoyed a modestly comfortable lifestyle, notwithstanding the sporadic savagery in the background, which disfigured all our lives. The more prosperous of this middle class had, over the years, relocated to nearby Warrenpoint and Rostrevor, their homes and gardens strung out along the inner shore of Carlingford Lough. Much of this middle class was well-integrated from a religious point of view.

My family would not have identified or socialised with the more prosperous end of this middle class. My father, at that time, preferred to relax in his vegetable garden or to explore the ancient monuments to be found in the area, but he was to find friends across the religious divide in the Newry Choral Society and following his retirement, when my parents moved to Warrenpoint, in the Cloughmore Male Voice Choir, which he and Michael both joined. My mother and my grandfather, both members of the Newry Bridge Club, played each week with their Catholic bridge partners. Golf also was a game which seemed blind to religious differences. Philip and Nicholas's mum and dad were prominent members of the Warrenpoint Golf Club and thoroughly integrated into the wider social scene which spread from it. There was a sailing club at Killowen, out beyond Rostrevor, which was also a place where, so far as I could see, the religion of the members simply did not figure as a matter of significance.

As we grew older, Philip, Nicholas and I, and a fair sprinkling of my other friends, fitted easily into the social scene in which the sons and daughters of this middle class played an important part.

The Seven Steps and the Ballyedmond Hotel

When, eventually, the great day of my eighteenth birthday arrived in July 1971, new venues opened up for me: mostly these were in Warrenpoint and Rostrevor, though I do remember Philip and I going to the Sheepbridge Inn, a few miles north of Newry, where there was a very attractive, lustrous haired barmaid, Eithne, who we hoped might favour us with her attention; I don't recall much of that coming our way. The venues which were to become most significant for me were the Ballyedmond Hotel (firebombed in 1979) and the lounge bar of the Seven Steps hotel, (firebombed in 1983).

The Ballyedmond Hotel was situated east of Rostrevor, close to the northern edge of Carlingford Lough at the foot of Slieve Fadda. In a previous July, I had, with a group of friends, climbed to the summit of Slieve Fadda and in a little hollow, pitched a tent for the night. Had the wind or the rain been bothered to show up with any force, we would have had to hang on tight to our tent and our possessions: but luck, more than any considered reading of the weather forecast, was on our side. We slept well and awoke to a perfect, still and cloudless morning with a view of the lough and the Carlingford and Cooley Mountains across the water in County Louth.

The Ballyedmond had, at one time, been a mansion. I knew it only as a hotel and the location for discos on a Friday night at which time its distinguishing features were masked by the lights, the loud music, the throng of people talking, drinking, dancing. I don't think I ever visited the Ballyedmond during daylight hours.

3: PROMISED LANDS

With encouragement from my parents, who recognised driving as a very useful competence, I had passed my test before my eighteenth birthday. At least some of my peers had similar good fortune in having access to driving lessons and a family car in which to hone their skills. There was an element of competition in passing and gaining a full licence without evident strain. The occasion of the test itself was a difficult secret to keep. To fail, felt like a public humiliation. Success, at the first attempt was a passport to an immediately enhanced sense of status which, in my own case, came with a certain amount of showy driving and risk taking when there was anyone looking who might perhaps have been impressed. I doubt now that anyone was very much impressed, and I look back with some embarrassment at the extent to which I pushed the limits of the highway code.

I wasn't alone in exhibiting this kind of March hare madness. I remember one lad, Willie, who was on the first eleven hockey team. He had grown up on a farm, which invariably meant driving experience from the earliest possible age, albeit short distances on country roads between field and yard. On one occasion we were playing an away game and Willie had somehow persuaded the staff member supervising the team that, instead of travelling on the bus, he would find his way to the venue independently in his recently acquired second, or, possibly, third-hand Morris Oxford. Early in the journey, occupants of the bus seated in the rear spotted that Willie was following immediately behind. A lively channel of gestured and, no doubt, provocative communication was opened with him. All of this went unnoticed by the master in charge who sat at the front of the bus. Willie for his part could not resist playing the showman and started weaving about on the road. He was suddenly obliged to apply his brakes and the car spun out of control, turning completely around. I was one of the lucky ones who witnessed this thrilling vehicular pirouette. By good luck Willie managed to avoid oncoming traffic and keep out of the ditch. Coolly correcting his trajectory, he proceeded without further incident to our destination by which time he seemed to have recovered his customary ebullient manner. In the subsequent analysis of this stunt, Willy let us know that his car was a recovery from a serious accident. The chassis was skewed, resulting in the need for particularly careful handling. It was in effect un-MOT-able, and, quite certainly, uninsurable. This incident very much bolstered my idea that the world of farming was a law unto itself.

My father, who was well shielded from my own boy racer tendencies, was pleased to have provided me with what he believed would be an advantage in life. In his way, he was generous in lending me the family car for my own use but he had a clear set of rules governing how this privilege was to be awarded, and going to the disco at Ballyedmond on a Friday night was certainly not high on his list of priorities. Mostly I was reliant on the transport of others to attend these events; however, I don't recall ever being left behind for want of space in someone's car.

No one that I knew ever went early to the Ballyedmond disco. The Seven Steps, right on the seafront in Warrenpoint, conveniently split the journey from Newry and was an obvious gathering point, well established as the first stage of the Friday evening action. The Seven Steps Hotel had an imposing facade overlooking the Lough. The lounge bar was a contrast with the external grandeur of the premises, modern, and comfortable, with a warm yellow touch of Scandinavia in its style.

There were a number of people who made a charismatic contribution to these Friday night outings, above all, Declan. Declan worked in Dublin as a sales assistant in a shoe shop, I imagine, a rather classy one. His family owned a shoe shop in Newry, Cahill Brothers, and in later years this would become his business. In the interim he had a flat in Dublin where, it was generally assumed, after his working day was done, he would spend much of his time in the city's wine bars, pubs and discos. He was in his early twenties, longish black hair and a full beard, always immaculately groomed, as befitting his line of work. He certainly took a drink but was never drunk. He was charming and garrulous, always a centre of attention, and yet in my experience, able to take notice of more marginal figures in the throng of people around him, to adjust his register when it was appropriate, good humoured but instantly serious if the situation required. Declan was accompanied by his friend Brendan, also working in Dublin as a male model; tall, dark-haired, with a moustache and, like Declan, very well turned out. I mention these two because it seemed extraordinary to me that, every week, they saw fit to return from the metropolis to play a central part in the Friday night social proceedings of this more parochial location. There was a larger cast of players contributing to the gaiety of the gathering, not all of whom I could name, even at the time.

The crowd I became a part of was religiously mixed, a good many the sons and daughters of the local middle classes, but class wasn't really the defining feature of this scene. In my recollection there were more Catholics than Protestants but no one cared which tribe you had come out of or whether you were republican or unionist. A liberal approach to such matters seemed to be implicit in the determination to forget, at least for a short time, the army and police checkpoints, the bombings, the shootings, the hopeless political deadlock and the fact that paramilitary violence was digging in for the long haul.

I was drawn to this social scene despite not having developed any of the necessary qualities to prosper in it, but I turned up every week full of hope and it was in the Seven Steps in July 1972 that I had an encounter, the fallout from which was to add an unexpected complication to my first year at university.

The Lighthouse Cafe

This story begins at the Lighthouse Cafe in Cranfield. I had gone there with a friend. It was busy. I knew none of the others present but my attention was drawn, by my companion, to a girl called Patricia.

There was a game of pool being played. Whether she was a participant in this — at that time — rather male preserve, I do not remember, but when I think back, that seems entirely possible. She was definitely the centre of attention, fielding questions and engaging in conversation coming from different quarters of the room. A voice called out from over by the jukebox, "What do you want me to put on next?" There was a pause, whilst this question was considered by the group before Patricia offered her suggestion: "*Breaking up is Hard to Do.*" It didn't seem the coolest choice to me but when it came on, I could hear her singing what I thought was a perfect duet with David Cassidy. Her unselfconscious performance was pleasing. She, however, was not looking my way and that cameo appearance in the Lighthouse Cafe would have been forgotten had I not encountered her, less than a week later in the Seven Steps

When I arrived in the Seven Steps that Friday night, just under a week from when I had first seen her, Patricia was sitting amidst a crowd of people, some of whom I knew. I found a seat close by and was sufficiently intrigued to listen in on the conversation. She evidently had opinions of her own and I thought was showing some determination to hold others to account for theirs. I was impressed. Before long I saw an opportunity to say something and launched into a summary of my thoughts on J. D. Salinger's book, *The Catcher in the Rye.*

It is a novel written in the teenage voice of Holden Caulfield, in which he offers up a critique of the world and the people around him, who he regards in large part as "phoney," lacking in authenticity. My own teenage years, I would even admit, my adult life, were influenced, for better or worse, by this book.

What I had to say was, I am sure, an unexpected contribution to the conversation. Perhaps on some previous occasion I had heard the words "James Joyce" uttered in the Seven Steps, but literature was not the usual fuel to make Friday nights burn brightly. Patricia, however, was listening. We moved closer and before long I knew that, for that evening at least, I had her attention.

She was in the Seven Steps under false pretences. Her parents thought she was visiting friends. No, she hadn't lied to them, just hadn't told them the full story of what was planned. Her family owned a holiday house further along from where I had stayed with the Brownes. Her father was a medical consultant. They were from Holywood on the south-side of Belfast Lough, not far east of the city.

The party moved in due course to the disco at the Ballyedmond, where loud music made talk impossible. We danced together; the last thing I remember of that night was being with her in the back of a car which was taking her home. There was no overexcited snogging, but we were close, reclining together, my back propped against the angle of the door and the rear seat, my arms wrapped about her, her right hand with the curve of her fingers lightly caressing my neck. It seemed at that moment that something significant was happening, but there was a catch. I explained to Patricia that I was scheduled in the coming days to fly to Toronto where I would stay for the rest of the summer and then, if my A-Level results came out right, I would be going to university in England. She gave me her address and we parted.

Canada

It was a six-hour flight to Toronto with a stop in Montreal to refuel. As Uncle Bill and family were on a week's holiday, I experienced the disorientation of arriving at a busy international airport with no one to meet me. A long slow descent had given me a headache. My reception by the Canadian authorities was less than friendly, and they were clearly suspicious of my assurance that I would not be staying long, but eventually I emerged from this unwelcoming interrogation to take a taxi to 117 Glencairn Avenue, where Christopher was already in residence and had been left in charge whilst the family were away.

As it swung out of the airport, the taxi merged into dense traffic. Highway 401, onto which we filtered, was busy; through the city it expanded to four carriageways, two interlinked highways on both sides of a central barrier, each with three lanes of traffic. Newry was a town where people would not infrequently draw up their vehicles in parallel in the middle of the main street and wind down their windows for a conversation, with very little sense that this might lead to a traffic jam or detain anyone unduly, though occasionally it did. Highway 401 was another world, of constant movement, vehicles swinging between lanes and carriageways and slip roads. My sense of smell seemed in some way affected by my flight. I felt a long way from home. I was met at the door by Christopher, as if I had just turned up at his front door in Warrenpoint. He seemed to have settled well and to be enjoying his work at the library.

A few days later the family, Bill, Mary and my three cousins, returned from their excursion. Mary, who was Canadian, was warm and easy-going. Bill, whom I did not know at all, was amusing and enjoyed quizzing Christopher and I, perhaps even unsettling us a little. He very much identified as Canadian, and had little sentimental feeling, that I could discern, for "the old country."

The house at 117 Glencairn Avenue was detached and comfortably accommodated us all. It was set amongst other similar timber-clad houses. There were wire screens fitted on all the exterior doors, so that the house could be left open in hot weather without the danger of insect infestation. The neighbourhood was spacious with tree-lined streets, long and straight, meshed into the grid pattern layout of the city. The garden was modest yet large enough to provide a space for outdoor social gatherings.

The Girl at the Lido

To begin with I had quite a lot of time on my hands. Christopher was at work during the day. It was then that I made the first move in my correspondence with Patricia and wondered what I might get in return. What did I say in that letter to someone I hardly knew at all? I honestly cannot remember but to each letter that I wrote came a reply which responded encouragingly to my meanderings and so I wrote again.

The one scrap that survives from that exchange of letters is a five-line verse which I think captures a little of my impression of Patricia when we met and also my sense of uncertainty as regards the future viability of our friendship.

You in light blue jeans came singing, full of summer air,
But soon, when leaves come tumbling,
When I look round, will you be there?
Across the miles between our eyes
Can words on crumpled paper keep us tied?

Patricia had her own story to tell, not all of it what I might have hoped for. I learnt that, shortly after my departure for Canada, she had formed a friendship, I imagine more than a friendship, with a chap from the Newry scene, Joe. I knew Joe a little, quiet and handsome. I liked him. This jolt of reality gave my thoughts about Patricia a much-needed perspective. Still, I continued to write.

In the early days in Canada, I did odd jobs around the house and garden, I explored the area, I listened to Toronto's CHUM radio, a popular music channel. There was less banal chat and more music than on Radio 1. Bill Withers' *Lean on Me* was riding high in the Canadian charts and I became a little addicted to its simple rhythm and chord progression and its equally simple endorsement of friendship.

The weather was hot, sometimes, owing to high humidity, uncomfortably so. I found my way to the local lido, a beautiful pool with plenty of space surrounding it for people to sunbathe. The open-air swimming pool on the seafront in Warrenpoint was a rather sordid experience by comparison. On one occasion I noticed a girl, about my own age, lying close to where I was sitting. She was slim and tanned and, unlike many others there at the poolside, was on her own. I was close enough to notice a few golden hairs on her inner thigh, escaping from beneath the edge of her bikini bottom, close enough for me to speak to her, perhaps even to say how great it was to have a pool like this on such a day; but no words came. She lay there, a shimmering Canadian girl and I, a pale-skinned Irish youth, such male vigour as I may have possessed, eclipsed by the tanned athleticism of the presiding lifeguards. Before long she rose gracefully, glided towards the edge of the pool, and was gone.

Talk

My uncle was a convert to Christian Science, which was Mary's religion and that of her family. They did not attempt to evangelise, but we did accept an invitation to attend Sunday service on one occasion. In their home, talk of politics was welcome at the dinner table and there was interest in Northern Ireland, but the Cold War was at its height, and so the merits of communism versus capitalism and the question of nuclear arms were more to the fore in our discussions. Mostly though, I remember Mary's cooking, the generous helpings she served, and the astonishment expressed by my relatives as regards the amount of food I could put away. Even at the time I was aware that there was some element of comfort eating in this impressive consumption, but as I never put on weight, I was a source of wonderment rather than concern.

The lifestyle was relaxed, sociable. I had other relatives, second cousins of my mother, living not far away. My English Foley cousin, Jane, was passing through Toronto and I had the pleasure of getting to know her a little. Members of Mary's family, with their more established Canadian identity were also an interesting part of the network in which we moved. The climate was continental, very hot in summer and, we were informed, fiercely cold in winter with lots of snow. Mary and my cousins loved skiing. Bill, however, though he had sporting talents in other areas, could not stay upright on skis. He was resigned to skiing holidays in which he had to find other ways to pass the time. I developed a taste for burgers. The only fast food I had previously encountered was fish and chips and even that, not very often.

My cousins were two boys, Brian and Peter, and their younger sister, Alison, aged nine, spirited and, it seemed to me, with an energetically challenging approach to her parents, who remained steadfastly patient and tolerant. Peter, aged twelve, was a keen ice hockey player, and Brian, aged fourteen, was quieter and more serious than the other two. We were included in all of the family activities and taken on a trip to Niagara Falls which straddles the border between Canada and the USA; it could have been all the rivers of Ireland gathered up and cascaded into a single chasm.

Like many families in a similar income bracket, Mary and Bill owned property up-country, where they might retreat at weekends. They had plans to build on their patch. Canada was vast. There was, it seemed, plenty of space for everyone. On one weekend we stayed with members of Mary's family in a beautiful location out on a wide-open prairie, with mountains in the distance. There was a swimming pool by the house and we lounged about in the summer heat.

Ice hockey was a passion for the whole family. In September of that year, the Canadian national ice hockey team was engaged in an eight-game series with the Soviet Union, with the first match taking place in Montreal on the 2nd of September. Christopher and I were encouraged to watch the live broadcast. We took our places in the relaxed and comfortable furnishings of the basement, where there was a television. I became aware that Bill was having some difficulties with our interest in, but emotional detachment from the game, neutrals, as we might have thought ourselves. Why were our passions not stirred in favour of Canada? For Canadians, this was not just an ice hockey game. It was a contest between two systems of governance: a failing autocracy, in the shape of the Soviet Union and an open and prosperous democracy, the promised land of Canada. This game was the Cold War on ice and not taking sides didn't appear to be an option, so far as Bill was concerned.

A Gunman on the Forecourt

Eventually, with the help of Mary and Bill, I did manage to find work; for a while I delivered newspapers and then, a step up, I became an ice cream salesman.

Dickie Dee was, to be honest, very much a company at the bottom of the ice cream world. When I reported to the depot, I was provided with a tricycle fitted with a cool box in which the day's stock was stored. There was little guidance as regards the best place to set up my stall, but over the few weeks that I was with Dickie Dee, I selected my pitch more by personal interest in its location and less by its sales potential. Conversations with customers and passersby were plentiful and I spent my days talking to oddball characters, dropouts and people selling cannabis around the corner from me. I was showing more talent as a social worker — or an undercover policeman — than an entrepreneur and yet still able to make enough, before my stock all melted, to keep a little pocket money for myself.

One night, after some weeks of this, I was returning quite late from the depot, crossing the forecourt of a garage, when I spotted someone being robbed at gunpoint. The thought of intervention never crossed my mind. I ran in the opposite direction to find my way to the next underground station, and then home. It was the first and only time I have seen a handgun brandished with such obviously threatening intent.

The author during his short stint as an ice-cream salesman on the streets of Toronto.

City Lights

Gradually Christopher and I discovered more of interest in the city for ourselves. I think, for us both, Yorkville's Riverboat Coffee House was the highlight. It was a tiny venue, long and narrow, but it seemed able to attract artists of a high order. Joni Mitchell, Neil Young and Simon and Garfunkel had all played there at some time. We were lucky enough to see Tim Hardin, whose reputation I knew from songs such as *How Can We Hang on to a Dream*. He was a slightly tetchy figure, happy to chastise his audience if they were not paying proper attention. Other performers at the Riverboat were new to me. John Prine was humorous, more at ease with performance than Tim Hardin, strongly influenced by early Dylan talking blues, Harry Chapin, a master of elaborate and idiosyncratic story songs.

At an outdoor venue on a much larger scale, and close to the waterfront of Lake Ontario, we saw Jose Feliciano, soulful, a virtuoso Spanish guitar player whom I knew from his cover of the Doors', *Light My Fire*. In Newry, I would have to admit, my most significant brush with celebrity hitherto was queuing up for Val Doonican's autograph when he came to open a store on the Merchants Quay. Even at the time I knew that Doonican was not really for me, but still, I could not resist the pull of celebrity and joined the queue, patiently waiting my turn for a few moments in his presence.

Towards the end of our stay Christopher and I hitch-hiked to the province of Quebec. My O-level French elicited only blank incomprehension from the Québécois that we encountered. Christopher was better on that front. Montreal was a difficult city to get a fix on in the short time we were there, but Quebec City, more European than North American in its architecture, located on a promontory high above the St. Lawrence River, was breathtaking.

Mistaken Identity

Following my sojourn in Canada there seemed no opportunity of seeing Patricia between the time of my arrival back in Newry and my departure for Reading University. I wonder now, was I unconsciously avoiding a meeting, not really confident that, in person, I could hold her attention, as I seemed to be doing in the safe place of our correspondence. I did not, however, sit at home moping about this matter and not long after my return, Philip and I went on a short trip over the border. On the way back we were pulled over at a British Army checkpoint. This was a common experience in that part of the world during the Troubles and I thought little of it other than to adopt my usual manner in the circumstances: studied politeness and cooperation. I was proudly sporting an ex-US Army jacket which I had picked up cheap in a store in Toronto. In retrospect it seems a crass purchase, given the militarised state of Northern Ireland.

On that particular day however, some permutation of my dress and behaviour seemed only to annoy the soldiers. We gave our names and addresses and showed our driving licences. We were both put into a stress position, leaning forward, hands outstretched against some convenient support, whilst we waited for our vehicle to be searched. That did not usually happen. Soldiers were positioned around us, their rifles at the ready, trained on the surrounding terrain, wary of attack. I heard one of the soldiers mutter, "Fucking US Army." Philip waiting nearby made the mistake of betraying a flicker of a smile: this kind of treatment was not what he was accustomed to. His expression of amusement did not go down at all well, and he was sharply advised against any further indication that his situation was anything but serious. Eventually we were permitted to move on, though I recall no let-up in the hostile attitude the soldiers were taking. No one wished us well as we went about our business.

I had heard plenty of reports of people being treated much more harshly, indeed being given a beating by the army. Our names and addresses would normally have been a reassurance to the personnel at a British Army, Ulster Defence Regiment or Royal Ulster Constabulary checkpoint. Had my address been Derrybeg Park in Newry, or any other estate where republican allegiance was strong, or the IRA in some degree of control, I knew that things could have been a lot worse. Any lack of cooperation, or hint of hostility would have been risky.

Had this particular patrol recently lost a comrade to the IRA? Or were they weary from dealing with the hostile environment of South Armagh? Whatever was the case, I was convinced that such a failure of discipline and civility was liable to have the perverse consequence of driving young men towards the IRA.

One of the things which Philip felt to be ironic about our experience was that his parents had some social connection with the commanding officers in the area. This was entirely informal; their home was situated adjacent to the army barracks in Newry. I was present on at least one occasion when officers from the barracks were in the house for drinks. Mr Browne had been born and grown up in the Irish Republic but had served in the British Army during the war.

Entertaining soldiers in this way may seem like a small gesture, but it certainly did carry risks. The barracks itself occasionally came under mortar attack from across the Clanrye River and Nicholas told me, in one such incident, he had taken refuge under the bed as he had little faith in the IRA's ability to hit their target.

I decided in my earnest way that a report of the experience that Philip and I had been through should be submitted to the commanding officers of the barracks. I wrote up a fairly detailed description of what had occurred, no doubt stressing the obvious points about making enemies rather than friends. Mr Browne listened to me politely but I could see had no enthusiasm for the idea that he might be an intermediary. Perhaps his sympathies lay with the soldiers to the extent that he judged their lapse an exceptional one, rather than quotidian behaviour. I am sure had we returned home bruised and bleeding, he would have taken a different view.

A Night Sailing

Not long after this, I set off to take up my place at Reading University. I caught an overnight boat from Belfast to Liverpool. Then, poorly slept, I travelled on by train to the strange and brightly lit subterranean world of Birmingham New Street station, where I made the connection for the final leg of my journey. I carried my few possessions and clothes in a rucksack, my guitar in its loose cover, an awkward accessory. It was a sunlit afternoon as I walked onto Whiteknights campus, a grassland park with mature trees and, scattered here and there, student residences and academic buildings. Grey squirrels scampered across the path I took to my new residence, Childs Hall.

My brother Peter had gone to Queen's University Belfast in 1967, just at that point in the 1960s when, responding to events elsewhere, liberal change in Northern Ireland had seemed possible, but that moment had passed, and by 1971, the country was spinning out of control, turning in upon itself. Peter's advice had been clear: leave Northern Ireland and go either to Dublin or to a university across the water. That is exactly what I, and many of my friends, were to do.

My choice of Reading University had been based on the perusal of the prospectus and little serious additional thought. If there was a single image that persuaded me it was the right place to go, it was of a study bedroom in a hall of residence, with a picture on the wall of a dramatic mountain landscape across which, in large letters, was the word "Canada". Though study was never to become my defining characteristic, I could see myself at work in this monkish setting; the modest space, with its austere furnishing, evoked a sense of freedom.

Being further from home than most other new students, I had been given preferential access to a hall of residence. Friends I made later in the year were in lodgings at the outset and recalled a less well-integrated experience of their first few weeks. Childs Hall accommodated only male students. It offered full board. I quickly became part of a social clique, made up largely of the people I had been sitting with on my first night at evening meal.

My new friends were mostly from "up north," apparently a superior part of the country, its chief distinction being "friendliness." "Strangers talk to you on the bus; in the south they just ignore you." Paul came from Manchester and was a little older than the rest of us, a joker, the most likely to derail a serious turn in the conversation. John was bluff and humorous, like Paul, an Agriculture student, though his extracurricular interests had an unexpectedly avant-garde character, exemplified by a passion for the music of Captain Beefheart and Frank Zappa. "Home rule for Yorkshire!" he would occasionally interject into any politically slanted conversation. Eddie was also from Yorkshire, quieter, liked by all of us, but separation from his girlfriend and his hometown of Doncaster did not suit him. Phil was cheerful but always ready to be serious. He was from the Midlands, studying Modern Languages. Mike was the only southerner in the group, from Cambridge, definitely the most studious of us, German was his subject. From the outset it was clear he was destined for the greatest academic success but he showed no signs of wishing to distance himself from the banter that characterised much of our conversation: despite the north-south divide and other differences of personality, we all got on well. Religious belief or affiliation was of no interest. There was no one fishing about below the surface to work out whether you had been to a school with a saint in its name or listening to see whether you said "aitch" rather than "haitch."

During my first term at Reading, I continued to write to Patricia. This was neither a daily nor even a weekly event. I took my time to compose letters commenting on the unfolding drama of my life at university. What I looked for in Patricia's response was mostly affirmation, a sense that she was enjoying what I had to say, some suggestion that her own interests lay in the same territory as my own. In the current era of email, letter post is mostly a disappointment: scraps of glossy paper fit only for the bin. In the autumn term of 1972, the arrival of her letters in my residence pigeonhole was a significant event and a stimulus to start composing a reply which might keep this exchange alive.

At some point Patricia sent me a book, *Bitter Lemons of Cyprus*, by Lawrence Durrell. In some way I understood it to be a response to my vaunting of *The Catcher in the Rye*. *Bitter Lemons* was a book I supposed she loved. I started reading it but seemed almost immediately to get stuck. Worse still, I couldn't identify quite what the obstacle was. This did not seem a good omen. I muddled my way through this embarrassment, but whatever may have been exchanged on the subject, Patricia did not seem unduly concerned by this failure to rise to the literary challenge with which she had presented me. Still, I was uneasy.

The Other Side of the Lake

My new Reading friends, John and Mike, at that time already had girlfriends, who would visit regularly, staying over at the weekends. Girls were not being sneaked in by back entrances or climbing up knotted sheets to enter via bedroom windows. They came in through the front door. It was always interesting to see them appearing at the breakfast table on a Saturday morning.

The other lads in my group of friends did not seem conspicuously adept at chatting to girls at discos or at other likely venues such as the Students' Union. I could see that Paul, given the chance, showed some talent for endearing himself to girls and managed to obtain an invitation to one of the kitchens in Bridges Hall, a girls' residence on the other side of Whiteknights Lake. Hangers-on did not seem unwelcome and I tagged along. This particular kitchen in Bridges Hall had become a busy meeting place and an invitation there opened up opportunities to talk to anyone who happened to be on the guest list. It was in that same kitchen that I first met my good friend Alan, sporting an ex-army great coat, not unlike one I had myself. Alan was a student of French, but something did not suit him about the undergraduate life and he eventually dropped out and went to live in France. There, without the need of a university education, he became a fluent speaker and eventually made his career in translation.

Before long I had developed a friendship with a girl whose room was almost opposite the door of the kitchen, Denise. She was from Southampton. She would invite me in for coffee, to chat or to listen to music. She had a stereo and a record collection, assets I could not match. I don't recall us ever going out together.

I began to visit more frequently, though when the clock struck eleven, I was turned out, and made my way back to my room in Childs Hall. Denise made it clear to me that she already had a boyfriend, Howard, who was studying for a PhD in another university. She was visiting him at weekends.

She was a Psychology student, took her studies seriously and was resistant to the disco and drinking culture that could be found elsewhere on the campus. Nevertheless, our talk developed a pleasing intimacy. She seemed flattered by my attention and a little amused by the person I was, though that, perhaps, was not the precise response for which I might have hoped. Where music was concerned, she introduced me to Roy Harper and Al Stewart, two very English poets of folk music. I in turn introduced her to Van Morrison's *Astral Weeks*.

Bums

When my brother Peter visited me in Reading later in the year, he pronounced my new male friends, "bums," a judgement, I imagine, based upon some laddish behaviour that he had witnessed. I thought this assessment unfair. Beneath the banter I found them all serious and considerate of the needs of those around them. Paul and John were definitely on the more laddish end of the spectrum. "I'd give her one!" was their go-to phrase in offering an assessment of an attractive girl who came into view. I was a little squeamish in the face of this blunt talk, yet I would have to accept there was not much evidence that what was going on in my head was really any different than theirs. None of us were in the vanguard of the feminist revolution.

So far as meeting members of the opposite sex was concerned, we seemed a pretty hapless lot, though of course John, Eddie and Mike, being spoken for, had less interest in such diversion. We tried various venues, Union discos, pubs in the town, occasional students' house parties. On a couple of occasions, a group of us made our way to a disco at a teacher training college a short distance from the university campus hoping to impress some of the girls there with our undergraduate status, but my recollection is of a somewhat dismal experience during which we failed to make any impression whatsoever.

Still, this group of friends and my friendship with Denise sustained me through that first term. I played a lot of table football, shared musical interests and watched *Monty Python's Flying Circus* once a week, the only television which seemed to be of any real interest at the time.

It occurred to me that Howard might perhaps have been troubled by the cosy connection which was developing between Denise and myself. Somehow our intimacy developed such that we would lie on her bed, chatting to one another. It was hardly surprising that this resulted in the exchange of some caresses and, pleasingly, led on occasion — if I may borrow a phrase from a Judie Sill song — to the "sweet communion of a kiss."

I had become fond of Denise, and she, I think, of me. I cannot deny that I had some thoughts of our liaison taking a more serious turn. One evening we were standing together in her room, facing one another, my arms about her waist, and her hands linked around my neck. We were kissing. I slid my hands under her jumper and unhooked her bra. "What are you doing?" she said. Of course, she knew what I was doing, but I also understood then that this was the line she was not prepared to cross. Regardless of her dalliance with me, her commitment was to Howard and whilst this reality caused me some sleeplessness and for a time, I harboured hopes that she would come to her senses and ditch him, I gradually came to accept that was never going to happen.

A Rolls Royce in Piccadilly

Early in December Patricia wrote to say she would be travelling to London on a school trip and that there was a chance that we might be able to meet, just for a short time. The logistics of such a meeting seemed pretty tricky to me. John took pity on me and offered to ferry me up on the back of his Triumph motorcycle. Somewhere off Piccadilly Circus we made our rendezvous, John, me, Patricia and three of her school friends who had been set loose for a period of free time, charged, for safety, to remain together. Patricia and her friends emerged from the neon and bustle of the London street in a state of excitement, obviously delighting in their temporary escape from the attention of their teachers; clearly, her meeting with me did not form any part of what she and her friends had shared with these guardians, but that clandestine element was no doubt part of the adventure.

We settled on a cafe, not a classy place, but cosy enough in its way. I found a table and Patricia sat across from me, with her friends nearby. John absented himself to the other side of the room. For Patricia and I this arrangement had the unintended consequence of making our encounter feel like a spectator event. Being a few years senior to Patricia and her friends, I felt myself under some pressure to make the conversational running, but I struggled. It wasn't that I couldn't talk; I talked too much, trying and failing to say something smart or knowledgeable.

The hour passed, for me, mercifully quickly. Patricia and her friends had to be back at the hotel at the time appointed by their teachers. We spilled out onto Piccadilly Circus with the intention of hailing a taxi. It seemed almost instantly that a Rolls Royce pulled over, the window lowered and the driver smoothly offered to take us to our destination — without charge. I was under no illusion that it was my presence which had conjured this Puck-like chauffeur from the traffic on Piccadilly. It was clearly Patricia and her friends who were the stardust which had brought him our way. Despite the bizarre, indeed risky character of his offer, we piled in. The negotiations which followed, did not go entirely smoothly. The girls explained where their hotel was situated. I heard our benefactor say, with a kind of patient exasperation: "Jesus wept." He was perhaps getting a little more than he had bargained for.

We reached a street adjacent to the girls' hotel and they hurried off, anxious to make their deadline. John and I were then ferried on to where his motorcycle awaited. Our mysterious benefactor glided off, one hoped, to perform further good deeds. John and I set off along the M4, west, to Reading, his parting comment before we went our own ways for the night: "I'd give her one."

The Crown Hotel

Whatever reservations I had about events in Northern Ireland, I loved going home for the vacation, meeting up with old friends, swapping stories about our new lives, visiting old haunts. However, the significance of my Piccadilly shambles with Patricia was difficult to ignore and I did not attempt to meet with her over that Christmas break.

I, like many of my friends, had a great fondness for the Crown Hotel, in the Square in Warrenpoint. It became an important meeting place when the student diaspora was home over Christmas and New Year. There was a picture hung on the wall there, a water colour, by R MacDonald Ross. It was of a Newry Street scene depicting Merchant's Quay where it intersected with Canal Street and Sugar Island. MacDonald Ross was the grandfather of my brother Peter's girlfriend, Deirdre. His paintings, usually in oils, were mostly of scenes in the Mourne Mountains, so this particular one was definitely an outlier, but I liked it very much. In 1983, the Crown was blown up by the IRA. I assume the painting was lost. A supermarket building stands there now. No restoration could have been possible. It is a piece of the heritage of Warrenpoint that is gone forever.

Sometimes we would go on to Fearon's in Rostrevor. Henry Kavanagh, the proprietor, was on one side of the long bar serving his customers. On the other side was a passageway with enough space for bar stools and some standing customers with a little room through the back for overspill. It was small, dark, and intimate, Henry presiding over it all with easy charm, appearing to enjoy the youthful nature of his clients, perhaps drawing on their energy to recharge that hint of eternal youthfulness in his own character.

McCullough

On visits home there would be serendipitous encounters, with friends of my parents and others who knew me a little and had some small interest in how I was getting on in the world, which might be expressed in the form of Yeats's "polite meaningless words." One such was Mr McCullough, or "McCullough", as Michael, Peter and I preferred to call him. McCullough had sourced all of our family's second-hand cars, had reliably kept them serviced over the years, and sold us the fuel for them at five shillings a gallon. His manner, so far as I was concerned, was taciturn, but my father was absolutely loyal to him. This loyalty may in part have had something to do with a tragedy which had befallen the McCullough family, for their eldest son, Ian, when playing hockey for Newry Grammar School First Eleven, in a match in Belfast, had been struck on the chest by the ball and had collapsed on the pitch and died. My father was refereeing the game.

I was less than ten years old when this tragedy occurred but remember my father's return from Belfast as a moment of great sombreness, though I was not at the time, informed of what had happened. Later in my life, my father described to me something of the return journey with the rest of the team, how they supported one another, and how when back in Newry he had contacted Mr Greenlees, the headmaster, to tell him what had happened, and to discuss the matter of informing the family. I think my father may perhaps have hoped Mr Greenlees would accompany him on a visit to the family home, but no; my father was to go and see the family alone and tell them what had happened to their son. However difficult this task was, carrying it out had, I suspect, an important part to play in the significant place the McCullough family played in our world.

It was, I think, my brother Michael, who conceived the idea that, even after we had all left school, McCullough's opening gambit, in any encounter, was to ask the question: "Still at school, young Shellard?" The pronunciation of our family name, in this enquiry, would more accurately be rendered as "Shallard".

The mischievous quality of this question appealed to us, as if McCullough had understood that none of the Shellard boys were headed in a direction that could be easily grasped, such as teacher, doctor, accountant, or whatever, and were instead on some odyssey, possibly involving education, to destination unknown, even to ourselves. In my own case, formulating a concise explanation as to why I was taking a degree in Sociology, what the purpose of that was and where it might lead, was daunting, a challenge unsuited to the forecourt of a petrol station. In such circumstances it was generally best to move the conversation quickly on to the price of oil or the likelihood of seeing any blue sky in the coming week.

A Political Imbroglio

Following my return from the Christmas vacation, I found that the slight sense of homesickness which had tainted my first term, was gone. Eddie, however, had stayed in Doncaster — Donny — to marry his hairdresser girlfriend. Ay up, Eddie.

My circle of friends started to expand gradually beyond the limits of the serendipitous group I had become part of on my first evening. Danny was from Leeds, his family working class and of Irish Catholic heritage. He was the first person I got to know, of my own age, whose preference was to listen to classical music rather than the contemporary music which was so important to the identity of other people with whom I was acquainted. I'd never really got much beyond Beethoven's *Für Elise*, despite efforts by my youthful chemistry teacher and scoutmaster, John Reid, to persuade me and my friends that Beethoven's nine symphonies were the very pinnacle of human achievement.

Danny was a much more politically committed person than my other friends. He was of relatively short stature, but with his longish black hair and wispy beard, he perhaps had a slight resemblance to Che Guevara, though I never made that connection at the time. My friendship with him certainly accelerated my awareness of student politics and, in particular, of the politics of the far left, which dominated the debates taking place in Students' Union meetings.

The fractious nature of left-wing student politics, the territory where I supposed, somewhere, my own views would be best represented, bore some resemblance to the schismatic history of the Protestant churches in Northern Ireland. The subdivisions of the faith were exemplified by the number of Protestant church buildings in Newry, despite the fact that it was a majority Catholic town. Apart from the Church of Ireland in which I had grown up, there were also two Presbyterian Churches, a Methodist Church, a Baptist Church, a Unitarian Church, the Riverside Reform Church (where all singing was without accompaniment), and a Quaker Meeting House. I was also aware of at least one non-aligned evangelical group, not easily categorised, and had once attended an event at Newry Town Hall, a showcase for a travelling healer and preacher. I remember feeling acutely disturbed as I emerged from that particular attempt to appropriate my soul. Dr Paisley's Free Presbyterian Church did not have a formal presence in Newry at that time, though I don't doubt that there was plenty of interest. The thing which held all these groups in an uneasy alliance was opposition to Catholicism, which, so far as I could tell, was believed to be a threat to their existence and right to dispute with one another.

In Reading, apart from a small Labour Party contingent, there were the International Socialists, the International Marxist Group, the Communist Party, Maoists and of course, an anarchist group, towards which I gravitated in later years, as they seemed particularly genial, not so given to character assassination and intrigue as others in the aforementioned list. Such groups were male-dominated and slow to provide enthusiastic support for feminists or gay people: such issues would be dealt with after the revolution.

Danny was my go-to person for learning about this tangle of factions. Question: What defined the Trotskyites? Answer: Advocates of permanent revolution; Question: What about the Stalinists? Answer: Advocates of building socialism in one country first. Question: What was the difference between the Maoists and the Stalinists? Answer: I'm still not sure about that one, though probably Mao's cultural revolution was the big break with Stalinism. I was trying to find my own place in this morass of ideas, but the sympathy, even support, for militant Irish republicanism which I not infrequently encountered amongst these left-wing factions, was a real challenge. I was obviously not a fan of unionist politics, but I had no desire to go to war with the neighbours and friends that I had grown up with. In this situation I saw my job as being to argue that militant republicanism was not only morally indefensible, but from a strategic point of view, made no sense, and was entrenching sectarian division rather than creating the conditions for Irish unity. I am not sure that I was particularly successful in promoting this message, but I was listened to with polite respect undoubtedly assisted by the fact that I actually came from the place.

I was eventually, through a friend Jim, from Paisley, near Glasgow, to learn of a tiny group on the margins of British politics, the Socialist Party of Great Britain, who showed no sympathy for the IRA, and who consistently advocated democratic politics as the only way to build a socialist society. They were staunchly opposed to the Soviet Union and Chinese communism — which they judged to be "state capitalist" — whilst nevertheless being very stalwart Marxists. For some years I was a devotee of their austere journal, the *Socialist Standard*, though I never joined the party and remained politically non-aligned throughout my time at university.

This is the End

Patricia invited me to visit her in Holywood on my way home from Reading, via Belfast, for the Easter holiday. On the date of the proposed visit, she told me her parents would be away, but that her older sister would be present. It seemed unlikely to me that her parents knew that I was coming, but I did not delve into this thorny matter.

I made my way to her school where we had arranged to meet. She had been playing hockey, her face, as she approached me, flushed and smiling. She drew my attention to a waiting car. It was her sister Ellen, there to pick us up and take us to Holywood.

Her parents were taking an Easter break and were away for the week. Disconcertingly, from my point of view, a young man, Piers, was waiting in the house. This was unexpected. As far as I could see, Piers was a friend and neighbour who had no evident romantic interest in Patricia. He assumed the role of a court jester, was very at ease with her and not disconcerted by my presence. Patricia's sister was a final-year student at Bristol University. I guessed that she was protective of her younger sister's welfare and might well have been suspicious of my intentions. My hopes that Patricia and I might spend time alone to develop some sense that our connection really had substance, that we might get to know one another a little better in person; all of these hopes were unravelling.

I was well fed and treated with civility yet I struggled to make my mark as the evening unfolded. We looked forward to the summer. I explained my intention was to stay in Reading and to find work. Patricia said that she would be in Cranfield for a month with her family. In no way did our plans intersect and it was beyond me to see how they could be made to do so.

In the company of Piers and Ellen I was stuck in a rut of earnestness and could not compete for Patricia's attention with Piers' unquenchable good humour. It must have been a Thursday night, for *Top of the Pops* was on the television. The Roxy Music single *Pyjamarama*, was in the national chart. Lead singer, Brian Ferry, suave in bow tie and white tuxedo, was a striking and still presence at the front of the band, contrasting sharply with the glam rock styling and dance moves of the other musicians.

There was an uneasy conversation about the merits of the band. Ellen commented on Ferry's handsome face, the straightness of his nose. Piers was clearly not drawn to the performance. Patricia seemed uncertain. I had no particular axe to grind on the topic of Roxy Music and could think of nothing smart or witty to say.

We did not stay up late. Piers made his exit about 11.00pm and not long after, it was agreed that we should retire to bed. By that point I was thoroughly resigned to the course the evening had taken. I was directed to the guest room and did my best to sleep between the clean white sheets of a comfortable bed.

I recall little of what happened the following morning, but with no Piers to liven things up, I imagine the mood at breakfast was down-beat, that I shared with Patricia some of my hopes for what I might be doing during the Easter break — meet up with friends, maybe go for a walk in the Mournes, hopefully get down to Dublin for a day two. The idea that we might meet up seemed even less possible than it had the previous evening.

Whilst I recall no rancour in our parting, neither do I recall warmth, or any concern that whatever friendship we had managed to establish was disintegrating in front of our eyes; I could see no evidence that Patricia was interested in its repair. I knew then that I would not be returning.

Intoxication

Shortly after my final meeting with Patricia, I spent an evening at Declan's flat in Dublin, in Nicholas's company. I didn't labour the details of the dissolution of my friendship with Patricia. We had something else in mind; weed, cannabis, dope, marijuana, whatever you may call it, we were keen to discover what the fuss was about. Declan procured a little block of resin and left us to it. He and a group of friends were going out for the evening. Mixing resin with tobacco and smoking it in a fairly generous roll-up composed of multiple cigarette papers carefully stuck together, was a common way of doing the business but I had never smoked cigarettes and did not want to acquire the habit. We adopted another method, setting light to a piece of resin on a pin contained within a pint glass, and then lifting the edge of the glass to draw the accumulating smoke into our lungs.

We proceeded uncertainly, not sure what we were doing. The main problem was, I did not seem to be experiencing any noticeable alteration of consciousness. I pressed on and repeated the procedure several times. Perhaps if some more experienced party had been present, they would have reassured me: "No, No! You're doing fine." But in the circumstances, I just kept at it until the effects of the drug were not just undeniable, but to be frank, rather unwelcome. I was experiencing odd visual effects, like sparks of light, in the periphery of my vision. I was a little alarmed, believing perhaps that I was never going to descend from whatever cloud I had arisen to, but gradually some sort of perspective returned and I started to observe my surroundings. Hitherto, doubtless on account of my obsession with having the drug experience, I had barely noticed Declan's flat. Suddenly I saw a glossy poster on the wall, its legend, "You can't get away with it in Hollywood." The fact that the Hollywood referred to in the poster was in California and was not the Holywood I had recently visited, did not seem an important discrepancy: I thought the message intended for none other than myself.

It was my intention, on my return to Reading, to write Patricia a letter to make my thoughts clear. I did not wish to strike a bitter note, so when leafing through a copy of the *New Musical Express* I saw a picture of the late Jim Morrison, with the words "This is the end, beautiful friend," I carefully cut it out, folded it and included it with my parting message.

Patricia did not write back.

Solid Air

In the summer term, my friendship with Denise gradually came apart. We saw less of one another and then did not see one another at all; I was to continue seeking friendships in the same kitchen where I had met her despite my engagement with some of the other social options available, such as the Students' Union discos, where I was a willing trier.

The dance floor, however, was not a situation where I felt in the least able to meet girls. The same was also true of the party circuit. Many students in their second, third and postgraduate years, gravitated to shared houses and periodically would throw parties with invitations freely distributed and where, if not invited, it was easy to get in on the coattails of someone else's invitation. The main entry requirement was a bottle of wine or a six-pack of beer. There would be a barely audible hi-fi playing somewhere in the midst of the throng, and not enough room to dance. Occasionally a joint would be passed about, but as these were routinely mixed with tobacco, they made me feel queasy. Alcohol was the drug of choice for these events, but that didn't work for me either. The kitchen in Bridges Hall paid an infinitely better dividend than either discos or parties albeit that I continued to be burdened by the millstone of my virginity.

At some point in these kitchen visits I found my way into a relationship with a beautiful dark-haired Agri-Bot — Agricultural Botany — student. Angie was on the rebound from an affair with a guy who, by her account, had been enormously attractive, but very careless of her feelings. I imagined a kind of Flashman figure. It took me a while to realise that our dalliance was nothing more than balm for the wounds she had suffered in her encounter with Flashman and that she did not consider me serious boyfriend material. Her parents came up from Devon where they owned a farm. We all went out for a meal together. I did my best to sound like a good prospect for their daughter but, I am pretty sure, I was not even close to what they were hoping for in any future son-in-law.

Over the summer vacation Angie, with the help of her department, landed a job in a research institute outside Copenhagen and I conceived the idea of visiting her there towards the end of the summer. She did not discourage me. But first I needed to earn the money for the fare.

There was no point in going home to Newry for work. I saw a hand-written note on the Childs Hall noticeboard, offering a room in a shared house for the summer. I went to see Martin who had put the note up. He had been the student president of Childs Hall during the previous year but now, in his final year, had decided to move out into a shared house. We hit it off immediately and I moved into a room in a little terraced house where, at that time, the only occupants were Martin, his girlfriend Lynn and myself. I found a job in a factory, Gascoigne, Gush and Dent, which manufactured milking machinery. There was space available in the house, so I invited Nicholas to join us. He had a place to study Civil Engineering in Nottingham in the coming year. Without any difficulty he found himself a summer job on the roads and we all settled in for the next couple of months. Though I struck up some warm friendships with my co-workers, my duties were tedious, but in the free time available, life was good. I remember Nicholas, headphones on, deep into Pink Floyd's *Dark Side of the Moon*, the experience enhanced by a little marijuana. For me, the soundtrack of that summer was John Martyn's folk-jazz masterpiece, *Solid Air*. Martin and I talked incessantly. It seemed everything could be interesting. He was an Agriculture student, but with a very lively interest in things outside his university course. He had, for example, started dipping into James Joyce's *Ulysses,* wondering, like myself, how you could get started on such a work. In his research he picked out a resonant phrase for us to chew on, "the ineluctable modality of the visible". We weighed the sinuous quality of these words, thoughtfully, in an attempt to engage with this doorstop of a book, neither of us students of literature, both daunted by the scale of Joyce's masterpiece, not sure how to approach it. There is a photograph of Martin, Lynn and me, which appeared in the next year's Reading University prospectus. The three of us are emerging from the Students' Union that summer, with me clearly in full flow, Martin leaning in to listen and Lynn smiling and looking content.

I haven't really said much about Lynn, for she was quieter than Martin, but I liked her. This became embarrassingly obvious on the thirteenth of July, my twentieth birthday, when we all went to the pub to celebrate. I was plied with alcohol and became very drunk. With some effort I remained upright and, with assistance, steered my course home. The following morning, I felt terrible. As I recovered, Lynn showed me a couple of marks, best described as "love bites," on her upper arm. Apparently, she had been sitting next to me in the later stages of my inebriation and in an amorous moment, I had inflicted these. When reminded, I could dimly recall the pleasure I took in committing the crime. Fortunately, both Martin and Lynn seemed amused rather than offended or upset.

The Market

I flew home for a few days that summer. It was about this time that my mother first began to experience symptoms that would later be identified as multiple sclerosis. My eldest brother, Michael, was working at the Armagh Down creamery, first in Newry, though later he moved to their premises in Banbridge.

My mother had always enjoyed shopping in the Newry Market, but when I was home on that occasion, she sent Michael and I there one Saturday morning for some messages. The market, celebrated in song by Colum Sands, as "the heart of Newry town", was a place where there were bargains to be found in things as diverse as oranges and apples and bolts of cloth which might be turned into curtains, or covers for an ageing sofa. It was really the character of the stallholders which most appealed to Ma. They came from across Northern Ireland for the day. At the fruit and veg stall she might hope for a friendly greeting and, perhaps, a bonus for her willingness to respond warmly: "Ah, there's an extra orange just for you Missus." I liked to watch the theatrical patter accompanying the offer of an unfeasible range of items, literally being sold off the back of a lorry. The trader would orate from the tailgate offering goods, first at a high price and then reducing the price by stages until someone cracked, fearing this great deal might go elsewhere, as there were maybe only one or two available: "Who'll give me five pound for this grand wee kettle," until eventually the "grand wee kettle" was: "Sold to the wumman in the blue headscarf for a pound fifty." Overheard conversations of Newry people were certainly part of the appeal of the market, often framed in a: "Says she to me, Says I to her" interchange. "Says she to me, 'That fella's an eejit.' Says I to her, eejit maybe, but it doesn't stop him always hav'n 'a better idea. Times I could kill him…God lov'm."

The market was not to everybody's taste. I would not have expected my friend Charlie's Mum, to have been a patron. I was wrong about that, for I was to hear her speak memorably about a visit to the market in which she had encountered a British Army foot-patrol.

Such patrols were not uncommon in the Newry streets, mingling with shoppers: a line of soldiers, spaced out so as not to make an easy target for sniper fire, the butt of a self-loading rifle resting over a right elbow, right hand holding the pistol grip, trigger finger extended and ready, and a left hand cradling the weapon close to the horizontal across the soldier's chest. Charlie's Mum would have been a fairly uncritical supporter of the British Army, and for good reason. Her eldest and revered brother had been killed in the Italian campaign in 1944. This esteem for the army perhaps explains why Charlie, when still only nine or ten, was taken to the Savoy Cinema to watch the newest war films such as *The Guns of Navarone*. I'd been with him to watch *The Bridge Over the River Kwai*, early in the 1960s. My parents, in particular my father, had strong pacifist inclinations and were uneasy about my attendance, but allowed me to go. I remember a girl, in the row behind, swooning, when one of the young British Officers appeared in an early scene, I think with his shirt off.

In Newry Market, however, Charlie's Mum witnessed something unexpected and disagreeable, for as the patrol threaded its way through the throng, she found herself a little too close to a soldier who was chewing gum like a disgruntled GI. She struggled to reconcile this uncouth behaviour with her view of the British Army. Her husband, a doctor, was present as she recalled the impression this had made on her. He had served in the Second World War and seemed to have a great deal less difficulty with the idea that an army might contain a few whose graceless manners fell below the standards of the more refined members of society.

I imagine that the character of soldiers who enlisted in the army in the Second World War was, on average, a good deal closer to that British Officer who had made the girl in the cinema seats behind me swoon so readily. By the time the British Army arrived in Northern Ireland, the average squaddie was, not invariably but certainly a little more likely, to be some kind of social misfit, unable to get any other job, or worse still, attracted by the idea of aggression and the menacing power of being in control of a deadly weapon. This said, my own encounters with the British Army were, with the one previously mentioned exception, uneventful, even friendly.

But to return to my visit with Michael to Newry Market that Saturday morning: whatever I was talking about to him as we emerged onto Hill Street, my spirits were high and somewhat under the influence of the conversational mode I had developed with Martin. I failed to notice that Michael was becoming irritated. Eventually he turned to me with an exasperated look. "What's this drivel you're talking about Sunny?" "Sunny" was a nickname Michael had bestowed on me, a droll comment on my disposition. I didn't attempt a reply and seemed to know without further explanation being required that he was making a necessary correction to my unfiltered loquaciousness. That's the kind of thing that older brothers can be good for.

I returned to Reading and continued doggedly with my job at Gascoigne, Gush and Dent so that in September I could take a flight to Denmark. When I arrived in Copenhagen I made my way south to the countryside, open and flat, where Angie was staying and where there would be a room for me. My glimpse of the city was, to be honest, the best part of the experience. Angie seemed less than impressed by my arrival. I did not feel welcome and I began to accept that, however beautiful she was, we had very little in common. I knew it was time to move on.

Sibly Hall

In my second year I attempted once again to take a room in Childs Hall where I had been in my first year but was refused a place, the reason being my participation in a rent strike during the summer term of the previous session. I barely remember the thinking behind this action but no doubt it was related to a demand for a more generous grant. Grants were means tested and because of my father's income I did not receive the full allowance, but my father was always conscientious about paying me the balance. Other students seemed to come out of this deal a lot worse off than I did. Relative to some other students, I didn't spend much money on drink and in general lived a fairly frugal lifestyle, so that at the end of my first year I was able to purchase a Yamaha guitar, costing, as I remember, fifty pounds, a step up in quality, I thought, from my existing instrument. So, what was I complaining about? The rent strike, naturally, was a project of the political left, the main objective, no doubt, to politicise students, bring down the government and to march towards the barricades of the revolution. I was an uncritical dupe of this project, and for this reason found myself blacklisted. The only hall of residence prepared to accept me in my second year was Sibly. This turned out to be a stroke of good fortune.

Sibly Hall was self-catering and situated off campus. I spent two very happy years as a resident. It was a tower block and I had a room on the seventh floor. I shared a kitchen-dining room with about a dozen other students on my wing of the building. We looked out from our domestic eyrie onto farmland, a very large field along the far margin of which ran a line of poplar trees. I became fond of the view and was delighted on one occasion to glimpse a fox winding its sinuous way across the open ground. My co-residents were mostly postgraduates, many of them from abroad; Ricardo and Diego from Mexico; Angelo from Greece, particularly beloved by the ladies who came in to clean our rooms; Sirvan, who was Kurdish, I think from Iraq, but very involved in the struggle for a Kurdish homeland, something of which I knew nothing at the time; Ishmail, from Malaya, who spent a good deal of his leisure time cooking, mostly with offal and other cuts of meat which were not routinely found on the modern British menu. This produced some challenging aromas but was always an interesting spectacle. Then there was Nigel, born in Kenya, his first language Swahili, because that was the language of the nanny to whom his early care had been entrusted. His family however had returned to their homeland of the UK and Nigel was now studying for a PhD. His taste for alcohol was definitely a threat to the success of his postgraduate studies. This cosmopolitan mix rubbed along very happily together.

Trevor

It was in Sibly Hall that I met Trevor, a graduate of the new University of Ulster, who was in Reading to study for a master's degree in English. Trevor was a defiant Unionist, but in most other ways uncategorizable. I was very open about my own hostilities towards unionist politics in general, but this seemed no obstacle to our friendship. Trevor was entirely good humoured and for me, full of surprises. He had attended Orangefield school in East Belfast where Van Morrison had once been a pupil, though this was not a matter of pride where Trevor was concerned. I understood the school to have a strongly working-class character and Trevor's talk of his own background did not dispel that idea. His recollections were full of the activities of the Ulster Defence Association and their presence on the streets in which he had grown up. However, Trevor's interest in literature had developed in an unlikely direction for he loved the poetry of Yeats, the work of James Joyce, in particular *Ulysses*, and had also developed an interest in the Irish language, and in Irish music, especially The Chieftains.

Trevor enjoyed talking about his subject to anyone who would listen, and more than anyone else on that wing of Sibly Hall, I was ready to be his audience. Joyce's *Ulysses* was not even a book I had properly attempted at that stage in my life, but Trevor seemed able to talk about it in ways that I found intriguing. Perhaps I already understood how the narrative followed the adventures of the Greek hero Odysseus, that the hero of Joyce's book, Leopold Bloom, was Jewish, but Trevor explained other mysterious layers of complexity and how the different organs of the human body were woven into its structure.

Ann

Sibly Hall for all its cosmopolitan allure was not a place to meet girls and from there, once again, I threaded my way to Bridges Hall kitchen. Briefly it seemed as though I was going to become involved with a lovely girl, Lori. Fairly quickly though she decided that her existing boyfriend was probably a better option and we stopped seeing one another. It was then that I met Ann, who was to become my first serious girlfriend, someone I valued and cared for and who seemed to have similar feelings for me. We were to spend the best part of the next five years together. I took her home to meet my parents during the following summer vacation. I showed her round all of my favoured haunts, the lighthouse strand at Cranfield and from there, round the rocky headland to climb to the Coastguard station and beyond to the white timbers of the house where I had stayed with Nicholas and Philip.

4: In Search of a Profession

Centre Lane

Sliding down the centre lane
I watch the world through a smoked pane,
The radio plays in my ear,
Says "Tomorrow's world's already here,"
And life and death seem nowhere near,
And I look on without fear.

I let the world wash over me,
As I become nobody.
I take the road that's straight ahead
With all that matters in my head,
Don't care to hear what's left unsaid,
Don't care if I'm alive or dead.

The minutes pass the hours fall,
It seems that I just don't care at all.
I'll drive on through pouring rain,
I'll drive on while there's no pain,
I'll drive on while I've got the cash
Just waiting for this car to crash.

Written in Reading in 1979, after a car journey with Peter Coombes at the wheel, though he should in no way be held responsible for this result.

Summer Jobs

In my second summer at Reading, I found a job on a farm. Had I been a student of Agriculture, this would have been unremarkable, but for a Sociology student, was an odd choice. The idea of working outdoors had some appeal. I had memories of the Truell's farm on the Commons outside Newry and a romantic vision distilled from the small farms I had seen in the West of Ireland. From these glimpses I had acquired an ill-conceived notion of what the farming life might be. The fact that I went to school with the sons and daughters of farmers should really have corrected this, for what I did recognise in my school friends who came from a farming background, was a kind of buccaneering spirit, a physical toughness and an unsentimental approach to their livelihood. The boys, in particular, rarely had any other objective than to work on the farm and, from their earliest years, whilst I was at play, had been doing useful work; as soon as their legs were long enough, they were driving tractors, as soon as they had the strength, they were carrying bales of straw or hay.

I answered an advertisement in the *Farmers Weekly*, and went for an interview a few miles outside Newbury, a little under twenty miles west of Reading. Keith, the farm manager, welcomed me. He was clearly desperate for help but deeply sceptical that I was up to the job. Part of the interview involved being walked into the midst of a herd of lively cattle. I knew this was a test but put my faith in his judgement that this was a reasonable thing to do and that they would not trample me underfoot. I did not flinch visibly and I got the job.

On the first day I was put into a line passing bales of hay from a trailer to a barn where they were to be stacked. Truly, I was not ready for the demands of this work. I struggled with the weight of the bales. The twine cut into my soft hands. I could barely keep up with the pace of those with whom I was working. At the end of a long day, I was exhausted, my hands blistered. I was lodging with Keith and his wife Veronica and I am sure that, when they saw the state I was in that first evening, they must have had serious doubts as to whether I would last the week, but I got up the following morning, not exactly a new man, but at least ready to have another go.

My first job of each day was to feed the pigs. This was a fairly easy if somewhat unglamorous start, after which I would breakfast with Keith and Veronica.

About once a week the pigs were weighed and marked to identify those which were ready for slaughter. There was no allowance for sentimentality in this task. The pigs, not always cooperative when being put into the cage to be weighed, were cajoled, shoved and, if necessary, kicked on the backside to get the job done. Those that made the grade were marked with an aerosol spray so they could be readily picked out when the lorry came to fetch them for the abattoir. This job complete, I was once again put to loading and unloading bales. Quite how I survived the first fortnight I am not sure, but gradually I seemed to toughen up and even to enjoy the experience, pitchforking bales from where they lay in the field onto the back of a trailer and then unloading them into the barn at the other end.

Late in the summer I was baling up a field of straw, left by a combine harvester which had brought in a crop of wheat. A Land Rover appeared and a man got out and announced himself as the owner of the farm. I had never previously met him. In fact, he owned this and two other farms of about a thousand acres each. He casually walked over and tested the weight of the bales I was making, and then approached me to say that they were "too light", rather as if I had set the baler deliberately to make my life easier. He made some adjustment and then left. I continued baling up the field. This intervention might have gone unnoticed had it not been for a heavy shower of rain whilst the bales lay unprotected awaiting collection. This of course doubled their weight, leaving Keith and I the unenviable task of clearing them. Keith was not happy with what the farm owner had done, but he was small, wiry and strong. He could manage the bales and lift them to the trailer. I however struggled. I think by this point Keith was more amused than annoyed by my inadequacy for the task. I had established good relations with him and with Veronica, and he was prepared to excuse my failings in this particular instance.

Ann came to visit me on the farm at weekends to stay over on Friday and Saturday. I was doing a good deal of overtime but there was some opportunity to go walking in the countryside around and even swimming in a canal which ran across the farm. There was no doubt that over that summer I did take pleasure in the wide-open landscape in which I was working and, in occasional moments, even to glimpse something of the farming life that I had been seeking. But in general, my conclusions were negative. This was no rural idyll. The animal husbandry was industrial in its character. The hours were long, the work more physically demanding than I was fit for in the longer term. I did not regret the experience but knew this was not where my future lay.

The next summer I spent gathering up biscuit orders in the Huntley and Palmers factory in Reading. This was not a joy to me. In truth I found very little job satisfaction in any of my summer jobs. On the other hand, I was generally able to get on with my fellow workers and there was usually one or two with whom I would strike up a particularly friendly rapport. An exception to this was a lady with whom I crossed paths in the Huntley and Palmers' warehouse. She was from Cork, and so I was disposed to think well of her, but she took against me for some reason which seemed connected with my social class and perhaps my Protestant Irish heritage, though quite how she detected this I am not sure. I imagine her to have been a person of some intelligence, possibly suffering some of the negativity which working class Irish people were liable to be subject to at the time, something which I never encountered directly at all. Whilst I have always retained an Irish accent, my manner of speech is moderated by class and education in ways which have generally worked in my favour. Her future no doubt lay in dull and poorly paid jobs such as the one we were both doing in the gloom of that vast biscuit store. She will have known that, for me, Huntley and Palmers was a temporary stop off on the way to something more bearable; perhaps that was a source of resentment. It was really the only occasion in England when I encountered any open negativity regarding my background and odd that its source should have been someone Irish.

By contrast, I also worked for a while on the building of a link road from the M4 to the town of Reading. In this case many of those I was working with were Irish, mostly so far as I was aware, from Galway, Mayo, Sligo, and Donegal. When my period of work was over, I was, together with a number of others who were finishing up, invited to go out for a drink with the gang. This was daunting for I knew that I didn't really have the constitution that would be required for that kind of drinking, but of course I went. Moderation proved impossible. When the pub had closed, a point at which I thought I might decently withdraw, I was invited back to the house where a number of the men were staying. This was no family home and we gathered in a sparsely furnished room, bereft of pictures on the walls or ornaments on the mantelpiece, illuminated by a single bare lightbulb hung from the ceiling.

When a mug full of vodka was handed to me, I realised that the evening had just begun.

Despite the austerity of the setting there was a convivial atmosphere, with occasional singing. I felt called upon to contribute, though none of my usual repertoire seemed fitting. I had, however, been working on a version of *She Moved Through the Fair*, a song I had first heard played by a Dublin rock band who had been one of the guests at an open-air concert in the Newry Showground, an event no doubt inspired by the example of Woodstock. I would have to say, for the record, the crowd attending was sparse and no free love or drugs were in evidence. Still, that version of *She Moved Through the Fair*, which was in some rather marvellous way fused together with Tim Hardin's song *How Can We Hang on to a Dream*, caught my attention. Inspired by this early instance of Irish folk-rock, I had learnt the song and, swaying gently, without feeling any need to excuse or introduce myself, I launched into the opening verse:

> *My young love said to me, my mother won't mind*
> *And my father won't slight you for your lack of kine,*
> *And she went away from me and this she did say:*
> *It will not be long love till our wedding day.*

The company were clearly not unused to such impromptu performance and turned to pay respectful attention. Sadly, it was about the end of the second verse that I lost my way and ground to a halt. I have always struggled with remembering song lyrics, though the embarrassment of forgetting has never stopped me from having another go. Without any apparent need to commiserate or encourage, the company reverted to their conversational mode and closed round me. It is possible that such incomplete performances were familiar to these men but I was determined to complete my act and before long and once again without feeling any need to call for attention, I set off on the final verses which I had managed, in the intervening moments, to dredge from my memory. I do not remember great applause at the conclusion but I felt nevertheless that my effort had been appreciated and that I had made some slight connection with these men who came from such different circumstances to my own. The following day, I suffered greatly for my excess.

It might have been a year or two later that I entered a pub near Reading's Cemetery Junction, not far from where I was living at the time. Quite why I was there I cannot remember for it was not an establishment frequented by any of my friends. True, there was a fashion amongst some of us for seeking out pubs distinguished by their traditional and unimproved character, but this pub was not of that type. Indeed, it had no character that I could discern, either traditional or modern. It was just a place for drinking. As I looked over to the corner, I noticed a man sitting on his own, who I recognised from the gang of navvies with whom I had been working. Before him, a pint glass, he sat in a blur of alcohol, lost to this world. He could have been thirty years old, or much more than that. I have seen a few drunks in my time, some happy, some very annoying, some aggressive and unpredictable. On one occasion some years later when I was living in Ballycastle in Co. Antrim, a very drunk man had turned to sing to me, I thought rather tenderly, as I attempted to order my own drink from the bar. The man in the pub at Cemetery Junction was in a different category, someone clearly in search of oblivion. I could not help imagining that it might have been better for him had he stayed in Galway or Mayo or Sligo or Donegal or whatever place it was from which he had been cut adrift.

Graduation

In the summer term of 1975, I sat my final exams and managed a second-class degree in Sociology. It was not a great achievement, disappointing even, but having no particular ambitions, neither did I have a sense that doors were closing in front of me. Still, it was no longer possible to think of the world of work in terms of summer jobs. I needed to earn a living, perhaps even, as my parents no doubt were hoping, settle on a career. In my haphazard pursuit of this objective, I was to continue to be based in Reading for a further six years.

Whilst I had been a student, in addition to my grant, I was able to claim money for three journeys home in each year and had taken full advantage of this. Without this subsidy, I went home less frequently, though always at Christmas. I was, however, content with my life in Reading, with no plan to return to Ireland and, to tell the truth, little that could be considered a plan of any kind. And yet 6 years later, I was to find myself in Ballycastle in County Antrim. I had been invited to work there for a year.

My invitation to become a volunteer in an innovative project for young offenders, run by the Save the Children Fund, came out of the blue, but things had happened in the intervening years which do make some sense of how that offer came my way and I will digress a little on the subject of what happened during those years that I spent in Reading. One of those years was spent as editor of the Students' Union magazine. I had never seriously thought about being a journalist but the job was available and I saw an opportunity to promote some ideas, in particular on the subject of education. I had fallen under the spell of a book which was in vogue at the time, *Deschooling Society*. The title alone is a mark of just how radical its themes were. The position of editor came without any salary and I supported myself for that year on the proceeds of a part-time gardening job. I spent much of the following year at a teacher training college just outside Liverpool and despite my scepticism, managed to gain a Post Graduate Certificate in Education, perhaps not the most sensible career move for someone with no plans to become a teacher. That PGCE proved useful later on. Though the course was in Liverpool I would return to stay with Ann during the holidays and we would manage to meet up from time to time in the interim. She had not yet completed her degree, and indeed progress towards that end was interrupted when she had a serious accident, being knocked off her bicycle and fracturing her skull. Thankfully, she made a full recovery from this and was eventually able to complete her course of study.

Easy Rider

On my return to Reading from Liverpool, I managed to acquire the tenancy of a house and persuaded Ann that we should move from the perfectly agreeable house where she was renting a generous room, close to the university campus, to what was objectively a less appealing dwelling in Woodley, a few miles out of Reading. There, I imagined, we might establish a household committed to a cooperative model of living, though in reality I didn't have a very developed idea of what that might be. My old friend Nicholas, from school, had expressed an interest in joining us. Ann, who was a graduate of Horticulture, had shown some interest in the fairly generous garden which came with the house and was going to grow herbs. I was full of optimism.

Since leaving home I had lodged in several types of accommodation from a single room in a hall of residence to shared houses. None of these were communal in any formal sense though some aspired to a degree of cooperation with regard to household tasks, meal preparation and shopping. Where this did occur, I enjoyed the experience of eating as a household and the conversation and convivial feelings which seemed to arise and had managed until that point to avoid some of the less than happy outcomes which can occur when a group of young people find themselves sharing a living space.

If a vision of communal living had entered my soul this inclination had been sparked when I went in the summer of 1969, with my brother Michael, to see the film *Easy Rider.* I have a vivid recollection of walking from our home on the Belfast Road to the Savoy Cinema where it stood at the junction of Merchant's Quay and Monaghan Street. It was a beautiful sunlit evening and both of us were in a state of exhilarated anticipation. The aura of the film, with its music and free spirit, had in some way intoxicated our small-town state of mind, and that was before we had even seen it.

Looking back on this move to the house in Woodley, I can see that Ann's enthusiasm for the experiment was muted. What is more, it was becoming apparent that during the year I had spent in Liverpool she had been getting on with her own life in ways which involved different interests and different friends than my own, and though none of this caused any immediate problem between us, what bound us together seemed less substantial. In the midst of our resettlement in Woodley however, we were to be faced with a new challenge — a family challenge. Michael was, unexpectedly, to become an integral part of our life together.

Around about the time of the move to Woodley, Michael, had disappeared from home in Newry, his whereabouts completely unknown for a couple of weeks, until he turned up in the village of Dorchester-on-Thames, not far south of Oxford, where he had stumbled into work as a dishwasher in the White Hart Hotel. The job came with a room across a courtyard from his place of work. It was pretty basic accommodation, but for a while it seemed as though he might be able to use this as a place to settle until he could think clearly enough to plan what he should do next.

In his late teens Michael had experienced what was initially described as a "breakdown" though which came subsequently to be diagnosed as schizophrenia. He spent time in the Downshire Psychiatric Hospital in Downpatrick, where he was prescribed medication and given shock treatment

— Electro Convulsive Therapy. It was a bleak experience both for Michael and the rest of the family. The period of his recovery was a challenge to all of us, but in particular to my mother whose own health was beginning to suffer.

In trying to understand and support Michael my family were not at all at ease with the drug and ECT treatments which he had been given when he was a patient in the Downshire Hospital. These seemed crude responses to his anguished state of mind. Alternative treatments however were unavailable. It was in response to these events that I first became interested in the ideas of R.D. Laing, who was to challenge conventional thinking on psychiatric illness. His book, *The Divided Self*, offered the novel idea that schizophrenia was less to do with anything lacking in an individual and more a problem of the world with which they were having to contend. It was an analysis which I thought fitted very well with Michael's situation.

Following his discharge from Downpatrick and, after a few false starts, Michael began to build a life at home with our parents, working initially in the Armagh Down creamery in Newry, and then commuting to their premises in Banbridge. He seemed to settle to this work and to become a valued member of the staff who got on well with his colleagues. After a time, he was offered the job of storeman, but he declined. He was not confident that he could cope with the additional stresses the job would bring.

Michael had a good friend, Elsie, and each weekend they would go off to dances at the Ballymascanlon Hotel over the border. Elsie and Michael plainly got on well but Elsie's real interest, I eventually concluded on the basis of a few things Michael said, was in finding a rich farmer at one of these dances to which he was taking her. Still, Michael never complained and was completely loyal to Elsie, apparently happy to accompany her on whatever journey she was on, but no doubt there were times when this life, living at home with his parents, going out with Elsie, working at the creamery, began to test the fragile stability he had established. Whilst I do not see the background of the Troubles as being the cause of Michael's difficulties, the unrest in Northern Ireland was not something with which he was at all at ease. On at least one occasion previously, he had left without warning and my parents, anticipating his intention to go to England, intercepted him boarding a boat in Belfast. He was on his way to try to work out something new for himself over the water. On this most recent occasion, which had brought him to Dorchester-on-

Thames, his departure had gone unremarked until his disappearance was complete.

Why did he not discuss such matters with my parents? I think because he knew how insubstantial his plans were. He had no ready answers for the good sense with which he knew he would be confronted and this good sense would trap him in the rut he was stuck in. Whatever his frame of mind, whatever the risks, he felt compelled to leave.

I was the proud owner at the time of an A35 van, purchased at a very reasonable price from a friend who had some itinerant plans in the offing which made this possession an encumbrance. By this means, Ann and I visited Michael at Dorchester-on-Thames. He was very pleased to see us, but like someone recovering from a hallucinatory excess, remembering only fragments of what had happened to him in the intervening fortnight. He had been sleeping rough much of the time though appeared to have been the recipient of some kindness from the lorry drivers who had given him a lift along the road to London, his intended destination. He spoke of other locations and encounters, some in London, some further south. There was a hint he had been trying to get to the continent. All of this was recalled as though from a dark and unsettling dream.

He clearly had the capacity to do the kitchen job he had fallen into, but his employer and his working conditions were less than sympathetic. He became restless but with no clear idea how to move forward and, as seemed inevitable, he eventually moved into the house in Woodley to which I had acquired the tenancy. Whatever insight I believed I may have had into Michael's troubled state of mind, it did not provide a way of supporting him in this time of difficulty. When he moved in it quickly became clear that he was very ill at ease, sleeping little and obviously disturbed in his manner. But this was just the beginning of difficulties in the household.

Nicholas, having decided upon some other course, was not going to be joining us. I sublet rooms to a couple of young lads, Anton and Sean, both local boys who were starting out as house painters. They were likeable guys but naively I had not foreseen that all of their friends, who were still living at home, quickly came to view Anton and Sean's new accommodation as a place they could party, free of the constraints of their parents. It became a routine experience to get up in the morning and to step over the sleeping bodies of people we had never met, on the way to the kitchen for breakfast.

With increasing disorder, it did not come as a complete surprise when Ann told me that she was going to move out. Whilst the problems of the household, I felt sure, accelerated her decision to do so, I knew that she had begun to question whether our relationship had a future. When faced with the reality that she was going to leave, I did not resist; yet I cannot say that letting her go was an easy thing from my point of view and I was aware also that our parting would not come as good news to my parents; they had become very fond of her.

Unreliable Tenants

Not long after Ann's departure, I got a job as an ambulance driver, to be clear, not an ambulance with blue flashing lights and a siren. My ambulance was adapted for the transport of a group of people with disabilities who came each day to a workshop where they were provided with tasks for which they were paid a modest sum. At the end of the day, I took them all home again.

I was paid £45 a week, which even in 1977 did not seem a great deal of money. During the day I would generally work alongside the staff and clients in the workshop, though, from time to time, I would be expected to collect goods which were to be organised or packaged, from various businesses in the town. Once this work was complete, I would gather up the finished products and return them. The manager in the workshop was a taciturn man who seemed happiest behind his desk, but his deputy, a Welsh lady, was very sociable and determined to establish a warm rapport with everyone involved. I got on well with her.

Back in Woodley I was trying my best to sustain some kind of order in the household. There was still a room available and this was eventually sublet to a Turkish student, Istam. Though on the surface of things Michael and I had little in common with Istam, we both liked him. He was a big guy, quiet, a little louche in his manner, inclined to dress for his day-to-day affairs as though he was just going out to a nightclub or a disco. He was a student of Engineering, though study did not form the basis of our conversations. He had a gently philosophical turn of mind and he and Michael got on well together. Shortly after his arrival he came home with a brand-new hi-fi.

Together we unboxed it and set it up in the front room. Ian Dury and the Blockheads had just released their album *New Boots and Panties* and this dominated the playlist and seemed to please all members of the household, including Anton and Sean.

Istam's stay in the house was short lived, for he was arrested and taken to Pentonville Prison, pending deportation back to Turkey. We were never to discover the precise nature of the crime with which he had been accused but the rumours were that he had made inappropriate sexual advances to a girl in one of the student halls of residence. Based on what I knew of Istam, this did not seem impossible, but both Michael and I felt that his macho presentation masked a sensitive, thoughtful and gentle individual. It soon became apparent, however, that there was to be no trial in the UK and no opportunity for him to plead his case.

Istam's only significant possession was his hi-fi and Michael and I decided that we should make every effort to return it to him. Our first step was to visit him in Pentonville Prison and we drove to London, stereo in the back of the van, in hopes that we might meet with him and return it to him. He was pleased to see us but it soon became apparent that a simple transfer of the package into his possession was not going to be possible. Various strategies for ensuring his precious system went back to Turkey with him were considered but nothing was made simple by the authorities in the prison. Whatever arrangement we did finally agree, I had no real confidence that Istam would ever see his hi-fi again. Still, we wished him well and parted with sadness.

Istam's vacant room was re-let shortly afterwards to another character who should probably have been rejected at the interview stage. This was Richard. He always had money on his person, a wad, not just enough for a drink or two. It was obvious that he had an entrepreneurial streak and I suspected that, apart from planning his business future, he was probably supplying cannabis, possibly other drugs, to his fellow students. He didn't spend a great deal of his time in Woodley but he was always agreeable when present and, most importantly, he paid his rent regularly and in full.

Sean and Anton, on the other hand, had begun to falter in this department. This was no doubt a consequence of a certain decadence that had seeped into their lives since arriving in the house. Together with their friends they were keeping late hours, drinking a good deal, having girls around, smoking cannabis and experimenting with LSD. I suspect that it was Richard who was supplying them with the latter. LSD was a drug I was wary of because its hallucinatory effects were so powerful and, from time to time, resulted in terrifying experiences. I suspected I might be susceptible to these LSD terrors. I could see that Michael was a little fascinated by the possibilities of LSD, perhaps even seeing it as having a therapeutic potential and I was concerned, imagining that he would be an even less suitable candidate for the drug than was I. Sean and Anton showed some sensitivity regarding this concern and took care to shield Michael from the drug; however, so far as they were concerned, the consequences of taking LSD seemed benign, indeed a source of excitement and fascination to them. Drugs in general are an experience of the moment; of pleasure, excitement, sociability, but the impact of LSD that I observed was as much about reflection on the experience afterwards. This could incline the LSD adventurer towards a philosophical, even a spiritual turn of mind, and so it was with Sean and Anton. Sadly, this impact had yet to evolve into a system of belief which might have emphasised the importance of the disciplines of work and the necessity to pay one's bills.

But worse was to come. Whatever redemptive path Sean and Anton may have been on, they could not stem the flood of neighbourhood humanity which coursed through our sitting room, and some of this was particularly unwelcome. Things were going missing, for example, my painstakingly acquired set of tools, a vital asset in my struggle to keep my van on the road as, with a Haynes manual in one hand and a box of spanners in the other, I nursed it from one MOT to the next.

The house was becoming notorious in the area. Mr Honor, the landlord, turned up to have a word. The police had paid him several visits to keep him updated on their suspicions regarding the crime wave they believed to be centred on his property. He had decided his only resort was to terminate the tenancy. In short, we had a month's notice to vacate our quarters.

The previous tenants had told me what a gentle soul Mr Honour was and so far as I was concerned, he had been a good landlord. It may have crossed my mind that I had some right to object to this summary treatment but, if so, I quickly concluded that the game was up and that it was probably best for all concerned.

For Sean and Anton this bombshell presented no serious challenge; they returned to their respective parental homes. Quite how Richard solved his accommodation problem I am not sure, but it never seemed like an emergency for him and I imagined that, as he came with benefits, there were many sofas out there on which he could crash in the interim. For Michael and I, however, this really was a crisis.

Bulmershe Road

Michael's state of mind continued to be a concern. He appeared to have lost all sense of purpose and resolution. The fact that I, his younger brother, did appear to have some grasp of how we might steer a way through the mess we were in appeared only to increase his sense of powerlessness. Relations were tense; but there was no alternative than that I find accommodation for both of us.

I had started to look for flats and rooms that might meet our requirements. I went to view a few places, all of which seemed depressing, unsuitable and over-priced. I was explaining all of this one morning to Roger who, as part of my daily routine as an ambulance driver, I took to and from his job for Berkshire County Council. I never knew exactly what Roger did but I imagined him working in an office managing a staff team. He was, however, reliant on a wheelchair for mobility, hence the need for my services. When I transported Roger, there was never anyone else in the ambulance and so we had plenty of opportunity to chat. When I explained my plight to him, he was not only sympathetic but also, to my surprise, able to offer a solution. The house in Bulmershe Road where he occupied part of the ground floor, had three storeys which had been subdivided into flats, one of which had just become vacant. Entry to this was via a side door, along a narrow passage to a staircase, which rose to the front door of the flat. At this level there was a sitting room, a bathroom and a small kitchen. A further steep, winding stair led to an attic storey with two surprisingly generous bedrooms. Given the other properties I had been viewing this seemed like luxury accommodation.

Bulmershe Road had clearly known better days but the area was pleasant, tree-lined, relatively traffic free and yet close to shops, pubs, a library and a cinema. Roger said he could provide me with the landlord's address and also that he would be happy to give me a reference. There was just one obstacle: an interview with the landlord would be required. Captain Album insisted that his tenants should be married, or at the very least engaged. Roger assured me that as the Captain had a large property portfolio, as long as my rent was paid regularly and I was not a source of trouble, following a successful interview, I would never have to meet him again.

A friend generously agreed to play the part of my fiancée in this subterfuge. Everything went as planned and so, by this stroke of good fortune, Michael and I moved to our new accommodation. I was to continue to live in Bulmershe Road for the remaining years that I spent in Reading.

I was hopeful that our new home would offer a well-ordered setting in which Michael might stage a recovery from his troubled frame of mind. It fairly quickly became apparent that his ability to forge a path for himself in Reading was not helped by the fact that he had no social life separate from my own and was, in effect, living in my flat. To say that he was ill at ease in the midst of this would be an understatement.

Finding employment offered a route to greater independence, a basis for making his own friends and eventually moving on to living in a place of his own. He did in fact start a couple of jobs but neither lasted more than a week. I knew that he could sustain employment but something was going wrong at the outset of these jobs and I felt unable to provide support, indeed probably betrayed unhelpful frustration at his failures. We settled into an uneasy coexistence.

While Michael floundered, I continued to get by happily enough in my job as an ambulance driver and at the workshop. Each week a Berkshire County Council bulletin was circulated and I studied the job opportunities that were being advertised. In June 1978, I spotted an intriguing job offer: Detached Youth Worker. The position advertised involved getting to know young people informally and on their own territory and, on the basis of these encounters, providing support that might be relevant to their needs. The post was seconded to No5, a youth counselling service and the premises of this service would be the base from which the Detached Youth Worker would operate.

I decided to apply and was invited for an interview. The most challenging aspect of this was being asked to spend a little time in the company of a group of young people, who I believe had been invited from the mean streets of Reading to take part in the exercise. Their opinions of the various interviewees were to be considered when deciding the best candidate for the job. I should have anticipated something of this kind, but I did not. My response to the challenge, as I remember it, was halting and uncertain, but I understood that listening to the young people and showing a respect for their interests and concerns was a more important objective than attempting to impress them with what a great guy I was. I dare say this insight had something to do with the fact that I was offered the job.

I was delighted but fairly quickly started to feel a little like someone who had been employed to fix the boiler despite not having any experience of plumbing or being provided with any of the tools necessary to do the job. I was going to be working with young people, typically dropouts from education who had experienced deprivation, or were from broken and troubled families, or might have suffered abuse. None of this was any part of the sheltered world in which I had grown up. As far as bread and butter problems of employment and accommodation were concerned, I would have little or no power to assist with such difficulties and when it came to helpful information about welfare benefits and rights, I knew next to nothing about how to navigate these systems; yet a month later, having worked out my notice in my previous employment, I turned up at the No5 Youth Counselling Service ready to do whatever I could and as things turned out, I was to discover that my general performance as a Detached Youth Worker would be judged more generously by other people than by myself. I worked as a Detached Youth Worker for two years, but eventually became discontented due to a conviction that my job was a sticking plaster remedy to problems which merited a more radical solution. That is something I would like to say more about, but not in the context of this memoir. I decided to resign my post and for the remaining time I lived in Reading got by on the basis of casual employment.

Football Hooliganism and the Sash in Dundalk

Despite my decision to resign, there were many things I had liked about my job as a Detached Youth Worker, not least the people with whom I was working. My day-to-day encounters were always interesting and some of the young people I met were very ready to talk to me about their involvement in football hooliganism, which was a significant problem at that time. There were two lads, in particular, I spoke to on this subject. I thought them both articulate and intelligent, capable I felt sure of doing something admirable with their lives, but equally capable of malign behaviour: my inclination was to believe what they told me about their exploits and that the hazards and excitement of street fighting with opposing fans was their primary release from otherwise tedious lives. These fights were between individuals who, had they met at an England game, could have been best friends. Were other factors of difference such as race and religion to have been added into the mix of these invented football conflicts, there was, I couldn't help feeling, a potential for escalation into something much more toxic and intractable. This reckless impulse to stir a pot that was already close to boiling point, was not unfamiliar to me. Boredom and frustration is often at the root of the problem and I witnessed a tangentially football-themed instance of such behaviour in July 1966. I had just turned thirteen years old and was returning with the 1st Newry scout Troop from a camp in Bray, just south of Dublin, where we had spent a very enjoyable week, singing songs around the campfire and trying to catch glimpses of Carita Jarvinan, Finnish-born actress and model, who was starring in a film, *The Viking Queen.* This epic production was being made in the Wicklow Mountains, the cast being billeted somewhere close to where we were staying.

Much of the bus journey home was taken up with listening to the World Cup Final on the radio, allegiances being roughly divided between the finalists, England and West Germany. Radio reception declined as we left the Dublin area and, as we progressed north and the game entered extra time, we lost the signal entirely. Passing through Dundalk on the final stage of the homeward journey, the mood on the bus was one of exasperated ennui. It was at that point that some wag started singing the opening verse of *The Sash My Father Wore*. Everyone on the bus knew instantly this would be a reliable irritant to the residents of Dundalk, our neighbouring town, situated just south of the border. Before anyone could so much as ask "Might this offend?" a jubilant chorus joined in. I was immediately uneasy. There may have been others who shared my misgivings, but they were as stunned into silence as I was. Not even the scouters, who surely must have recognised that this was behaviour unbecoming to a scout troop, appeared able to raise a serious challenge to what was happening. I imagined that if we were to be stopped at some traffic lights, the doors would be burst open by an angry mob which would enter the bus intent on tearing us to shreds. In fact, little notice was taken of this impromptu and high-spirited rendering of *The Sash*, though I do recall a moment when the traffic, which set the pace of our passage through the town, slowed to a standstill and, what I believed to be an apple core, struck the side of the bus.

My fellow boy scouts just could not resist this opportunity to pass the time by making mischief and I felt myself alone in fearing this trivial incident might have an incendiary consequence far outreaching the fun intended. I am pleased to say, about the time Geoff Hurst scored his disputed but clinching "they think it's all over, it is now" goal, that we made it to the northern side of town without triggering an international incident, possibly involving our dismemberment.

Happy Christmas Your Arse

Whilst a significant proportion of the young people I had come to know through my work were engaging routinely in illegal or antisocial behaviour, I was with them in circumstances when such activity was merely spoken about; it was certainly not behaviour I witnessed. A memorable exception to this erupted in the unlikely setting of the General Post Office on Reading's Broad Street.

I was well into my second year as a Detached Youth Worker and someone had tipped me off that Thursday morning, about eleven o'clock, was when claimants with what were deemed to be, "unsafe addresses," came to collect their giro cheques. It was obvious that the lives of people living at those addresses were in some degree of disorder. This seemed, from my professional perspective, like a phenomenon worth exploring. I had only been to the Post Office on a few occasions on previous Thursday mornings and indeed don't recall these outings being especially productive in terms of building relationships with those attending, but I persisted. This particular occasion was the final Thursday before Christmas and the large rectangular concourse which lay between the main entrance from the street and the long Post Office service counter, was packed. Into the midst of this crowd came a group of half-a-dozen young people, two girls and four young men. One of these stood out, being more heavily built than his friends, an imposing figure. In some way I formed the impression that he was under the influence of barbiturates. He had a glazed and fierce look on his unshaven face. I was immediately wary but also interested enough to pick up that he and his friends were from Belfast. "Desi" I heard them call him.

Not long after this group entered, another group, this time exclusively young men, spilt in through the door from the street. They were in high spirits, had obviously been for a few drinks, and were singing in unison: "We are English, we are English." What had brought on this burst of national pride was not at all obvious to me, but then, why not? We were in the heart of southern England.

Whatever dazed frame of mind Desi may have been in, he was immediately alerted to this celebration, and was not pleased by it. He lumbered towards the leader of the revellers and, without pausing to introduce himself, head-butted the guy full in the face. This piece of savagery unleashed some pent-up reservoir of anger in the assembled mass, and within ten seconds, half a dozen fights had broken out, spreading across the floor of the Post Office concourse. My personal safety was obviously an immediate consideration, but it also flashed through my mind that I had some professional obligation in the circumstances to be a peacemaker. As it happens, I could see that Desi, the instigator of this mayhem, having disposed of his prime irritant, was looking unsteadily about, intent on finding someone else worthy of his displeasure. I moved cautiously in his direction and, when I thought myself close enough to be heard, I did my best to open dialogue. "It's not worth it Desi," I said, hopefully. He turned towards me, his face darkening, if that were possible, and made some attempt to focus, like a bull trying to get a fix on his tormentor. He started to lumber towards me with gathering rage and I quickly concluded that the peace talks were dead in the water, and I melted into the crowd, leaving Desi to find someone more willing for the contest.

Not everyone in the Post Office was there to pick up a giro cheque and so there were quite a few present unused to this kind of impromptu brawling. One of these was a little lady, respectably dressed, hatted, in her sixties maybe. Having come in, I imagine, to buy a few Christmas stamps for the final posting, she suddenly moved centre stage and finding a small space in the battlefield, raised her hand and pointed to heaven. "In the name of God, stop!" she declaimed in a ringing voice. I admired her courage and determination to take action, but sadly no one, apart from myself, paid any attention to her whatsoever.

At about this stage I noticed that Desi's friends were gathering around him and clearly persuading him that this might be a good moment to move along and, together, they slipped quietly out through the door onto the street. Not long after, the police turned up, no doubt called by someone on the other side of the counter. Several arrests were made but, so far as I could tell, none of those involved in the original upheaval were anywhere to be seen. I retired for lunch.

Michael

When I started at No5 Michael was, in theory, still trying to find work, but this quest was not going well. When he did find a job, he rarely lasted more than a few days, a week at the most. I knew that none of the work that came his way was to his taste but also believed that in many circumstances, given the chance, he could become a valued and trusted employee. He could drive, was physically capable, could be articulate and personable, was numerate and had an ability to express himself in the written word with some elegance and in a fine cursive script. But in the state of mind he was in at that time, these talents and qualities were obscured beneath his uneasy and unsettling manner.

I dare say I betrayed some frustration with this cycle of failure and that of course was not helpful. We were not communicating well. When I brought friends home, he did not welcome them or put them at ease, rather the contrary in fact. On one occasion I brought a woman friend home, someone I had recently met and with whom I had hopes of becoming more seriously involved. Michael must have been aware that this visit was planned for he had prepared a meal, murky soup which he served to us explaining that, amongst other ingredients, it included a sprinkling of earth from the garden. Certainly, the taste of this brew suggested that earth might indeed have been the principal spice. We sat together and ate our meal in silence, the curtains drawn, though it was still early on a summer evening.

Sometime later, I came home to be met by Michael in a state of obvious distress. Without words he ushered me upstairs to my room and following a gesture that might have been used to direct my attention to some work of art he wanted me to view, I saw my guitar lying on the floor smashed beyond any possible repair. This was not something that made me at all angry, for I knew that he regretted what he had done and that his anguish in the circumstances was greater than mine. This destructive act was further evidence of what I already suspected: the small success that I, his youngest brother, was enjoying in life, threw his own failures into stark relief and this made him susceptible to negative feelings towards me.

After we had been in the flat for about a year, something terrible happened, which nevertheless was to offer me some sense of hope. As I departed for work one morning, Michael was nowhere to be seen. I knew that his pattern of sleep was very irregular, but I would expect to see him before I set off, restless, the strain of facing another day clear on his face. When I returned from work, he had still failed to show up. It was a worry, and yet such disappearances were an occasional feature of his behaviour when he was particularly disturbed. I thought maybe that he had set off to try his luck in London, or perhaps even to cross the Channel to France, both ideas that occasionally seemed to appeal to him. Neither of these destinations, in my opinion, were a good idea, but it was equally obvious that his life in Reading had become a torment to him. I assumed he would eventually get in touch and this would be the correct moment to pass on news of developments to Ma and Da.

On the third day of his disappearance, he showed up, bruised and battered, having discharged himself from the Royal Berkshire Hospital. On the first night of his absence, he had gone for a walk in the early hours of the morning and had encountered a gang of youths. In some way he had provoked them and they had attacked him and beaten him badly, breaking several of his ribs. A passerby had come to his aid and, with the help of this good Samaritan, an ambulance had been called. The extraordinary thing was that, though Michael recalled little of the actual assault which had taken place, he was in other respects in a very rational frame of mind. He was certainly subdued, but glad to be home, evidently pleased to see me and grateful for the meal I prepared for him. In the weeks immediately following this trauma and, as he recovered from the physical injuries he had sustained, he was relaxed and companionable. He made an effort to tidy up and clean the flat, to help with the shopping and to prepare meals. This awakening of his former self lasted for about a month but with his full physical recovery he began once again to slide into a disordered pattern of behaviour.

It was hard not to conclude that the shock of what had taken place had in some way been helpful to him, breaking up obsessive and self-destructive patterns of thought which were preventing him from sleeping and in other ways destroying his ability to function coherently. I also suspected that his injuries had given him temporary respite from the pressure he felt to seek work and pay his way in the world.

There was to be a court case arising from the attack. The person who had come to his aid had provided information leading to some of his attackers being arrested and charged with assault. The thought of the court case, however, was not at all congenial to Michael, who understood that he would be obliged to attend, when really, he would have preferred to let the matter go. Pressures were once again unsettling his equilibrium.

What these events made absolutely clear to me was that, given the right circumstances, Michael had the potential to live a productive and contented life. He remained with me for a few more months until he once again disappeared without warning, this time turning up several days later at our parents' home, which was now in Warrenpoint, my father having retired. I am sure that this homecoming will in some ways have felt like a defeat to Michael, but it must also have been a relief. It should in addition be said that, for everything that was wrong with Northern Ireland, from which he might have wished to escape, he had also experienced important friendships there; with Elsie, with his former colleagues in the creamery, with Mrs Ferris who came to help my mother, through chance encounters. He is not the only person I know of who went to England to escape terrors, but who found it an alien place and chose to return home.

A Small Drama

Becoming a playwright had never really featured in my plans, but an idea came to me which I thought could best be expressed in theatre. The idea was simple: to imagine a group of young people who decided to use vandalism in a politically organised way to demand things that might make their lives better. The model for such a campaign was terrorism though, in the story I wanted to tell, there was no place for violence against or intimidation of people; yet, undeniably, my plan was to make a case for illegal politically motivated activity in circumstances where there is a democratic deficit.

Sometime in 1979 I'd been to see a production of Dario Fo's *Accidental Death of an Anarchist* at the Half Moon Theatre in London, and no doubt this satire, based on the death in police custody in 1969 of a Milan worker, Pino Pinelli, falsely accused of being a bomb-throwing anarchist, had seeded the idea in my mind, that theatre could be exciting, funny and provocative. I was only a very occasional theatre goer. I had attended one or two Shakespeare plays in the hope of self-improvement but had always found the experience difficult. I might even have said, with reference to the entire Shakespearian cannon, that it was "full of sound and fury, signifying nothing" — now who was it wrote those words?

The last time I trod the boards myself was in that production of *The Mad Hatter's Tea Party* when I was in the Prep School in Newry. It was a limited theatrical outing but, putting aside the inadequacy of my qualifications or any thought of what I might do with a play once written, I set to work.

Subtenant

I had adjusted to living alone in the flat but my employment situation, following my resignation as a Detached Youth Worker, remained uncertain. It became obvious that I should sublet the room which Michael had vacated. Pete, who took the room, was a friend. He had recently started work on an MA in Contemporary European Studies and had a part time job, driving a van, to earn money to finance his studies. At an early stage in his tenancy, he expressed interest in the play I was writing. That proved to be a great asset.

It had always been my intention to seek the actors for the play from some of the young people I had encountered as a Detached Youth Worker. My instincts drew me to a pub I had previously known as a gathering place for the local punk scene. I don't think a single one of those I approached responded negatively to the idea that they might take a part in the play, though none of them spoke of having any previous theatrical experience.

The theme of urban decay, the anger, boredom and frustration embodied in acts of vandalism, would, I was confident, interest them, but the campaign in favour of votes for under 18s which I had written into the play, as the chief objective of the miscreants, I didn't imagine would be met with much enthusiasm — why not a lower age for drinking alcohol, or better recreational resources for young people? That, however, never became a point of argument outside the context of the play.

There was a small cast, four main characters and a couple of police officers, one of whom Pete was enthusiastic to play. There were no auditions for the other parts. Indeed, it felt a little as though I was auditioning for the part of a playwright and was still uncertain as to whether I'd convinced anyone that I could play the role credibly. We got the cast to come round to the flat, the only place we had available to rehearse. I watched anxiously, listening for negative response from these newly minted thespians, but none came and, suddenly, it all began to seem possible.

The four whom I had recruited from the pub, Russell, Helen, Joe and Davey, were all fans of the Clash who, I thought, struck a more self-consciously political note in their work than some of the other punk bands. I didn't assume however that this would translate into a disciplined approach in our company: attending rehearsals, getting down to work, learning words; it all seemed a challenge. I was confident that Pete and I, with the help of some friends, could solve other problems of staging and production, but if the actors did not commit, then the rest would be thrown away. I needn't have worried.

They were all there at the rehearsal the following week. The atmosphere was relaxed, and we were getting on well. It seemed important to put a fairly tight framework in place for the production and with that in mind, we set a target date for performance a couple of months ahead, even though at that point not even a venue had been agreed. A target date towards which to work was the only discipline that was applied other than a certain amount of cajoling to learn lines as the date approached. The cast knew that success was reliant on a combined effort and those who were better at learning their lines pulled the others along.

As regards production of the play, the DIY values of punk rock were definitely an influence. No attempt was made to stage it in a theatre. Instead, we found a pub on Reading's London Road, The Marquis of Granby, with a basement function room. We booked this for the purpose.

A good friend, Mal, who lived across the road from us was a fine art student and was happy to paint a couple of street scenes, one on either side of a free-standing frame across which a canvas had been stretched. This was our backdrop. It could be transported in Pete's van and easily turned about when in situ to provide the required backdrop for the drama as it unfolded.

In the run up to the big day of the performance I cycled about the meaner streets of Reading, with my camera, in search of graffiti, decay, broken windows and any kind of urban decline or neglect that I thought resonated with our theme. From the resulting photographs a set of slides was produced which was to be projected onto a wall in the gathering-time before the play got under way. There was also a soundtrack, *White Riot*, The Clash; *If the Kids are United*, Sham 69; *Alternative Ulster*, Stiff Little Fingers. I can't really remember what was on that tape, but there was plenty to choose from that resonated with our message.

As the scheduled night approached, tensions ramped up, mostly in relation to the learning of lines, but we did seem to be getting there, by the skin of our teeth. Advertising was entirely word of mouth and our expected audience, a mix of friends and friends of friends, who were intrigued enough to be drawn in.

There was no dress rehearsal. Mostly the cast were costumed as themselves, but we did acquire prison guard attire to serve as police uniforms. Pete remembers changing in his van parked near the venue and passers-by greeting him with "Evening officer," as he walked from his "changing room" to the door of the pub. Better still, when he came into the packed room where we were staging the play, he shouted something like: "Alright, you lot! The police are here! Now pay attention, sit down and don't move." This directive had an immediate impact on those present and proved an effective way of getting the play started. It was not the first instance of improvisation which distinguished the evening.

I dare say I started to relax a little as the night unfolded but I was too wound-up to properly enjoy what was happening. Pete, however, reports: "It was a HUGE hit! And for one night only! We had sound, breaking glass, and slides. At the time, I thought to myself: 'Maybe I could be an actor?' The buzz was something I don't think I'd ever felt before or since. And being part of a drama gang was fun, too."

As the play rolled on, I noticed that Russell was introducing unscripted swearing. He admitted to me later that he had been nervous and, consequently, had taken an amphetamine tablet shortly before going on stage. In the event, swearing found its way into his lines. It was getting laughs, which encouraged him to swear even more. What could I say? I would prefer to have believed that the audience were responding to the lines that I had written, but it can't be denied that the anarchic energy of the cast was a big part of the success of the evening.

In the afterglow of this small triumph the question of what we should do next, naturally arose. There had however been such a complete focus on this single performance that no additional performances had been considered. There was some discussion about further shows but I could sense that the success we had enjoyed was more of a relief than a spur to further action. We could hardly believe what had happened.

As I look back on this, I can see that the absence of a plan to build on our success was a missed opportunity. It was not a great play. It was, in truth, not even a particularly good one. But there was a provocative idea at its centre, and a cast and production team that was fresh and energetic. If we had taken things forward, we would have got better and more confident, improving the script and our production as we went. I don't imagine we would have won any awards at the Edinburgh Festival Fringe, but I am sure we would have found an audience that liked what we were doing; sadly, the cast drifted off and got on with their lives, and this opportunity was missed. Pete continued with his postgraduate studies and I was left without much clue as to what I should do next. I certainly wasn't thinking of myself as a playwright, but then, what was I? Into this hiatus was to come an offer that, though it did not provide an answer to that question, at least took care of the immediate future.

Invitation to Ballycastle

I answered the phone one day and a voice I did not recognise, having confirmed my identity, asked me if I would be interested in working in a recently established project intended as an alternative to custodial sentencing for young offenders. The venture was sponsored by the Save the Children Fund and was based in Ballycastle on the north coast of County Antrim. Needless to say, the vacancy was not "Officer in Charge". What they were looking for was a volunteer. It was made clear that this position would come with forty pounds a week and bed and board. I was interested and was invited to come over so I could take a closer look at the programme and, of course, so they could take a closer look at me.

Where did this offer come from? I dare say this was all explained to me at the time, but I didn't really pay much attention. I imagine that there were networks established around courses and conferences, at which individuals who knew of my work and resignation from my job as a Detached Youth Worker would encounter other people, perhaps giving a presentation on this new project in Ballycastle and, later on at the bar, my name would come up as a possible candidate for a position they were having difficulty filling.

I made the necessary arrangements for my visit. All my costs were covered. I travelled by boat and train as far as Coleraine, was met at the station and driven to my destination in the project minibus. The staff in Ramoan seemed like the kind of people I could get on with and the values embedded in what they were doing, I felt I could support. My questions were answered. I answered their questions.

It was agreed that I would start my new position in the coming August and that I would have a room in the old rectory, where the project was based. Before I returned to Reading, I managed to fit in a visit to my parents and Michael in Warrenpoint.

The decision to go to Ballycastle coincided with my growing feeling that my time in Reading had run its course. I felt a need to relocate to the north of England or the south of Scotland to be closer to my family. My brother Peter and his partner Deirdre had settled in Dumfries and had taken out a mortgage on an old house there which they were renovating. This became an obvious base to which I might move my possessions. I could easily return there following my year in Ramoan, and then follow through on some of the travel plans which were forming in my mind.

Making My Escape

My final days in Reading were often spent in the company of Pete and our mutual friends, Heather and Linda. On the 29th of July 1981, shortly before I left for Ballycastle, we went for a walk together on the Ridgeway, not far north of Reading. The day in question was a national holiday to mark the wedding of Prince Charles and Lady Diana Spencer. The weather was perfect.

Whilst intending no slight to the royal couple, our plan was designed to take us into a space we knew would be blissfully free of the day's jamboree.

The Ridgeway follows a route used since prehistoric times. Our walk took us along the top of a chalk escarpment with a great sweep of southern English countryside stretched out below us, the haze of the metropolis just visible in the distance. We had walked there before, taking sandwiches and a flask of tea, or stopping off somewhere at a country pub. We did not set ourselves any taxing objectives. That evening we ended up back at Heather and Linda's, as was often the case. The kitchen cupboards were thrown open and a meal assembled from what was to be found there. Mostly this was Linda's doing, but we were all liable to be drawn into the preparation. Garlic bread seemed an almost obligatory component of these meals. The preparation was as sociable as the meal to come, all of it accompanied by a glass or two of wine. Once we settled down to eat, our conversation would continue until, at some late-ish hour, Pete and I would take our leave and wander back to our own flat.

What did we talk about on that particular evening? The hunger strike in the Maze Prison was edging towards its inevitable conclusion. Six of the ten on strike had already died, most recently on the thirteenth of July, Martin Hurson. We all believed that Mrs Thatcher's steely determination not to bend in the face of this slow-motion tragedy, whatever its appeal to her supporters, was storing up a problem for the future. But not all was well elsewhere in the kingdom. That year there had been inner city riots across England, from Brixton to Toxteth.

I don't imagine the royal wedding figured greatly in our conversation, for we were of one mind where the monarchy was concerned. Years later I wrote a song, at least one verse of which owes something to my imagination of what was happening in London on that day.

Who do you trust Charlie?
Are there a chosen few?
Allowed to look you in the eye,
To tell your confidences to.
Here in the crowd,
A flag in every fist,
A people pressed against the rails.
By a force that they cannot resist.

In 1991 or thereabouts I submitted that song for inclusion for the fourth in the tape series, *Songs from Under the Bed*. I'd had a couple accepted for the third in the series, but this more recent offering was declined and returned to me with what I thought was something like contempt for its "sympathetic" take on the plight of the heir apparent. I thought my reviewer missed the hint that all that adulation for British royalty was really just suppressed anger.

Round every corner
Cheats and sycophants await,
The subject nation
That is your estate.
As the cameras aim
And the onlookers gape,
Do you ever wish, Charlie,
That you could make your escape?

A few days later I was to make my own escape. My departure from Reading was a low-key affair with Heather the only person who came to the station to bid me farewell. I've never been back.

5: Ballycastle

The Rising of the Moon — updated

Oh, then tell me Sean O'Farrell tell me why you hurry so
'Hush-m'buachaill, hush and listen,' and his cheeks were all aglow
'I bear orders from the Captain, get you ready quick and soon
For the pikes must be together at the rising of the moon.'

At the rising of the moon, at the rising of the moon
With your pikes upon your shoulder at the rising of the moon.

Henry Joy McCracken, Robert Emett and Wolf Tone
Called the dispossessed of Ireland to take what was their own
And with a signal token whistled up a marching tune
Take your pikes upon your shoulders at the rising of the moon.

At the rising of the moon, at the rising of the moon
With your pikes upon your shoulder at the rising of the moon.

Well they fought for poor old Ireland and full bitter was their fate
Yes there was pride and there was sorrow, they still sing of '98
But the memory has been tarnished by those still marching to the tune
For they kneecap lads and break their legs at the rising of the moon.

At the rising of the moon, at the rising of the moon
It's thugs that rule the streets now at the rising of the moon.

All That Guff: Updating songs from the Orange and the Green traditions for the modern era.

Management Consultant

It's August 2022 and I'm watching a video podcast in which Oliver is being interviewed regarding his career in coaching senior executives. He's pretty much as I remember him, though with less hair. Solidly built, with powerful shoulders, he had been a champion swimmer in his youth. I remember him saying that his real strength was in the butterfly. That's a stroke which I've tried a few times but am unable to get past a couple of turns before giving up exhausted.

In the video podcasts I watched, Oliver has a couple of good stories to tell about his early days as a Social Worker in the late 1970s; the time he had to take a child into care from the Divis Flats in West Belfast and the requirement to negotiate with the Provisional IRA in order to do this whilst also working closely with the police and the army, and another occasion when he was again somewhere in West Belfast with a client and there was a gun battle going on outside. Oliver's transport at the time was an old post office van which he had painted yellow. As he rose to leave, his client said to him with some concern: "You'll not be going away in that yellow van of yours?" Oliver looks puzzled, and the lady helpfully explained that one of the gunmen had been seen earlier driving a yellow van, "just like thon one of yours." How Oliver made his exit from this situation we are not told. Under cover of darkness? Or did he just take his chances, a kind of Russian roulette? Anyway, the picture was clear: there was jeopardy working as a Social Worker in the 1970s in Belfast, and Oliver was in the thick of it.

I'd have liked more of these stories, but clearly, they would have been hard to justify in a discussion about leadership and coaching senior executives. What I thought there surely would be, however, was some mention of the period in which Oliver managed the team at Ramoan in Ballycastle where, for just a year, from 1981 to 1982, I had worked as a volunteer. Ramoan did get a mention in the podcast notes where it was made clear that Oliver's "First leadership role was [as] founder of the Ramoan Centre, Save the Children, [which had been established in 1980] the first direct alternative to custody for serious and persistent young offenders in Northern Ireland."

My recollection of the team I joined in the summer of 1981, was that, in addition to Oliver, who was the boss of the operation, there were another three individuals employed to work directly with the lads. Each of them made a distinctive contribution to the project. To Oliver's credit, he seemed to command respect from his disparate team and to manage their diverse energies in a relaxed and collegiate manner whilst leading a project that was — given the background of civil unrest and conservative values — innovative.

Every member of that team was to go on to do something distinguished. There was Phil, who was himself to become a management consultant; in his X (Twitter) profile he describes himself as, amongst other things, an "Artist, Sailor, Adventurer." Should you think that may be a somewhat overhyped sales pitch for his management consultancy business, then I would point out that, when I knew him, he was already an art school graduate and in 2007, long after I had lost touch with him, a little internet research tells me that he sailed single handed across the Atlantic. There was Colin, the Assistant Director, who was in 1990 to become Centre Director for Corrymeela, a community dedicated to building constructive cross community relationships. Colin was to gain much additional distinction in his subsequent work. Then there was Mervyn, with an extraordinary personal story to tell, who had spent time as a prisoner in Long Kesh. He was to become Dr Mervyn Love, a respected academic who, in 1995, published his book: *Peace Building Through Reconciliation in Northern Ireland.*

There is no denying that these male personalities were central to the Ramoan project, but there were also women playing a significant role in making the wheels of the organisation turn. Lynn, Phil's wife, had responsibilities caring for the animals when the lads were not in residence to do this work. Volunteers from the local community also came to help out. There was a clerical assistant, whose name I have forgotten, who ran the office; small, smiling, energetic and very competent. Her husband was a farmer, a slighter figure than his wife, but industrious and obliging, an extremely useful connection where practicalities such as the supply of hay and straw for the animals were concerned. There were regular visits from probation officers, for of course all of the lads who came to Ramoan were on the books of the probation service. Some of these officers must have been men, but the ones I remember best were women, strong personalities, able to hold their own in the male company of the Ramoan team.

If I had been the interviewer on that podcast, I would have probed Oliver until, as it surely would have done, the story of Ramoan all spilt out, its challenges, its inspirations, its failures, its disappointments, its successes. But in that podcast, it was as if none of it had ever happened or it had been overwritten by a successful business promoting and selling what seemed to me a shadow of the inspiration and originality I think was embedded in Ramoan.

The Devil and the Deep Blue Sea

Lads came to Ramoan in groups of about eight, aged from fourteen to an upper limit of seventeen. They stayed for a month, then went home for a month after which they returned for a further month. In that intervening month arrangements for the succeeding group were being put in place. None of the crimes committed were political in character, so I imagine they were mostly thieves of one kind or another, though perhaps vandalism or fighting may have featured in their back stories.

Despite my experience when I was a youth worker and not infrequently attending court with young people, whose primary objective was to avoid a prison sentence, when I arrived in Ramoan, I knew little about the standard punishments dealt out to young offenders. Brendan Behan's autobiographical experiences of imprisonment in *Borstal Boy* was my main source of knowledge as regards what this might mean. I'd also fairly recently read Jimmy Boyle's *A Sense of Freedom* which told his story of growing up in the deprivation of the Gorbals in Glasgow and becoming something of a gangster in the 1960s. He became part of a very dark criminal underworld and went on to serve a fifteen-year sentence for a murder — which he has always said he did not commit. The book tells of his many battles with the prison authorities, the bleak times he spent in solitary confinement, but then goes on to describe his journey to a new life in the experimental Barlinnie Special Unit. It was the Special Unit which gave Boyle the opportunity to develop his talents as a writer and a sculptor.

I didn't imagine that Ramoan in any way reassembled the Special Unit, but undoubtedly what attracted me to it was its rehabilitative rather than punitive intentions and the fact that I could see this was so important to all those who

Ballycastle and Rathlin Island — Extract from Ordnance Survey half-inch sheet 2, North-east Northern Ireland, published in 1968. Full map image available from Wikimedia.org.

were to be my colleagues. In the time I spent there I was never witness to any cynicism about what we were doing.

In practice young people were offered the opportunity to come to Ramoan at a point when a more conventional lock-up sentence was on the cards. If their crimes had not been political and their probation officer thought they might be suited to what Ramoan had to offer, this possibility was explored. If the young person decided in favour, then Ramoan was proposed to the court as an alternative to more conventional incarceration. If this seemed like a choice between the devil and the deep blue sea, then, for those miscreants who chose Ramoan, the deep blue sea was the North Atlantic Ocean, which crashed in on the beach at Ballycastle and where we would often go with a group, swimming and canoe surfing.

Ramoan was not run in the least like a young offender institution. There were no uniforms, no jangling bunches of keys, no barbed wire, no secure perimeter fencing. In practice the boys could walk out at any time, though inevitably this would be a breach of their probation order and would have resulted in a return to court and a review of their sentence. In the time I was there I only remember one occasion on which this happened and even that I judged to be an accident of sorts. In practice the boy in question, Sean, did not leave on foot. I suspect he may have been struggling to establish his status within the group of lads he was with. He was a diminutive figure and boasted of joy-riding — that is, stealing cars and taking them for a drive. Perhaps that had been his crime, but the other lads found it difficult to take seriously his claims to having cruised the streets of Belfast in stolen cars. That was a highly dangerous activity given the likelihood that a joy-rider might encounter a British Army checkpoint and be faced with the choice of arrest or driving through at speed and being shot dead. Sean obviously felt it necessary to prove that he could hot-wire a car and when everyone was looking the other way broke into Mervyn's Ford Cortina — which was probably open — successfully started the engine and set off down the drive. That's really as far as Sean got. Perhaps the gates were closed. I don't remember the precise humiliation that concluded his escape bid. He may have stalled the car or realised that he just didn't know the way home. Inevitably he was returned to court for review of his sentence. We were all sorry to see him go but felt there was no other choice.

Mucking Out

Ramoan had originally been a Georgian rectory for the parish of the same name, a rambling two-storey detached house, set in substantial grounds, on the Novally Road, just half a mile south-west of Ballycastle. When I first arrived, there were no boys in residence and so I was able to familiarise myself with the layout of the house. The front door opened into a generous hallway, to the left of which, was the office and, to the right, a very spacious sitting room, with television, couches and, the ubiquitous asset of any facility designed to cater for teenagers, a pool table. Being able to hold one's own in a game of pool was an important way of establishing one's place and I worked hard at improving my skills.

To the rear of the main house was a yard surrounded by a set of stone outbuildings, such as one might find in a traditional farmstead. These buildings were home to goats, hens, a rabbit and two pigs named Stan and Ollie, though they were both female. The pigs had been a gift to Ramoan from a friend of Colin's and Stan — or was it Ollie? — with a little outside help organised by Phil and Lynn, produced a litter of piglets whilst I was there, a momentous event in the life of the community, both for the staff and the lads. The animals were an integral element of the rehabilitative philosophy of Ramoan and their care formed part of the daily routine for the boys when they were in residence. Phil, in particular, made it clear to all, including staff, that dereliction of this duty would not be passed over lightly. I have a memory that on at least one occasion I realised I was being firmly corrected for my sloppy approach. I knew of course that there was no argument against this requirement for exacting standards. It was a responsibility before which we were all equal and it seemed to me that the boys who came to Ramoan instinctively understood this duty, did not argue with it and, mostly with good grace, accepted the daily rituals of feeding, watering, and mucking out.

All of the lads that I can remember came from towns and cities and so were not versed in the farming culture that in large part defined the character of Northern Ireland in that era. It was not all about duty however, and in the time I was there, the stars of this menagerie were the piglets, a sight to soften even the most cynical of hearts, an ever-present anxiety being that the sow would inadvertently crush one of these innocents with her great bulk. Some boys naturally responded more warmly to the animal care elements of their routines, but I remember no one who seriously resisted their obligations in this aspect of life at Ramoan.

Mervyn

In talking about Mervyn, I am conscious, more than with others to whom I refer in this memoir, that I am trespassing on someone else's story. What he told me about himself seemed to say something of importance, not just about the recent history of Northern Ireland, but also spoke of something indelibly positive in the character of its people. My retelling, given the passing of time, is inevitably an imaginative reconstruction of what was said.

Mervyn was discreet about his personal story in his work with the lads. Nevertheless, that someone who had served a sentence for terrorism-related crimes, was working with "serious and persistent young offenders" might, for many people, have seemed a cause for concern. It didn't take long for me to decide, however, that Mervyn was the most dedicated of a dedicated team. He loved his work. He took an interest in the lads regardless of their background. It was not just a job for him.

Mervyn had in a previous life been a civil servant. Following his imprisonment for terrorism-related offences, his introduction to Ramoan had come via an encounter with Colin in the Corrymeela Community. He had been brought to Corrymeela by a good friend of Colin's, Tom Foley, who was working for the Peace People, an organisation with which my own parents were to become involved. From this point of contact, Colin had approached Save The Children and persuaded them that Mervyn would be a suitable candidate to work as a volunteer at Ramoan, the same role that I was myself to take on. As Colin remembers it: "This was no easy thing for them to agree and Chief Executive of Save the Children, Alan Gillespie and the Deputy Director, John Quinlivin and Oliver deserve real credit for trusting us to do this. Mervyn was still on licence. We were taking on a 'convicted terrorist' but he was soon an incredible part of our small team."

As I got to know Mervyn, he began to share more of his personal story with me. Many of his anecdotes were domestic in character, a rich source being snippets from his visits to his hometown of Portavogie on the Ards peninsula; how a visiting minister from the family's Free Presbyterian Church had attempted decorously to eat the biscuits and drink the tea which had been proffered whilst the family dog, with persistent ardour, wrapped itself amorously round his leg. Such incongruity was a source of amusement to Mervyn. Another, darker instance, involved a second family pet, this time a budgerigar, which was ailing. The vet was called. On arrival he drew the bird gently from its cage and examined it carefully. The family stood round, anxious, no doubt prepared for a gloomy prognosis. The vet paused thoughtfully and then, without ceremony, took the bird into his right hand, announced to the company that nothing could be done for it and with an extended thumb, before any protest was possible, pressed the bird's head firmly against the adjacent doorpost. Whatever he may have felt at the time, Mervyn clearly delighted in this story of unfiltered farm vet manners so unsuited to the more sentimental world of family pets.

Long Kesh

Why had Mervyn ever become involved with a terrorist organisation? Given the perspective I was coming from, his explanations were never going to seem satisfactory; I did not cross-question him on the matter. From what he did say, his motivations had been to defend the loyalist community which he believed to be under threat. In the opening stages of the Troubles, people were being burnt out of their houses on both sides of the religious divide and there was fear amongst loyalists that they were going to be "sold down the river" by the unionist establishment. It was, I imagined, in just such a moment of disorder, that Mervyn had been drawn in; but from everything he told me I believed his concerns had been defensive rather than aggressive. He was clear that, even when a member, he believed the violent sectarian acts which characterised much of what came to be understood as loyalist terrorism were not simply wrong, but counterproductive. He had tried to persuade others in the organisation of this reality.

Mervyn's arrest and subsequent sentence were, as I understood the matter, a direct consequence of his membership of a proscribed organisation, though he did talk about learning to make weapons and so he may have been in possession of such illegal ordnance and also paid a price for this offence.

His arrest and interrogation had clearly been a traumatic experience and he had been subject to many of the questionable techniques of sleep and sensory deprivation used in the arrest and detention of republican terrorists. These were being applied equally to loyalist terrorists. Eventually his case came to court, and he was sentenced for his offences. I don't recall what that sentence was, but I believe that he served five years in Long Kesh.

It was clear that, having served his sentence, he had turned his back on the organisation of which he had been a member and set himself on an entirely different track. Despite this, he had a remarkably nostalgic view of his prison experience. He spoke of a feeling that developed between his comrades in Long Kesh, a feeling which did not exist in the friendships of his previous life.

He suggested that the men he had been confined with became close to one another, supported one another through their difficulties and were able to express a sensitivity in their nature that would have been seen as unmanly in the world that existed beyond the prison wire. Some of the men of whom he spoke would, I imagined, have committed grievous crimes. Mervyn never talked about that reality. I expect he thought their actions more a product of the political context in which they were living than of a failure in their individual character.

Mervyn had served his sentence as a special category prisoner. This category had been removed in March 1976 and the restoration of special status for politically motivated crimes was to be the central demand of the IRA hunger strikes which were to follow. One can understand that those close to the victims of terrorism have a harsh view on the way perpetrators should be dealt with. Withdrawal of political status was widely supported by loyalists and people elsewhere in the United Kingdom. Many politicians, pre-eminently Margaret Thatcher, saw that there was political capital to be made from taking an uncompromising line on the matter. Nobody bothered to look at the culture which emerged under the special status for terrorist crimes which had originally been in place. My impression, from what Mervyn told me, was that the impact of political prisoners being allowed to associate freely with one another and to engage in educational and recreational pursuits was benign and civilising, led to self-education, a better understanding of history and a more thoughtful approach to solving the problems of Northern Ireland.

In prison Mervyn, like many of his comrades, started to take a wider interest in literature and the arts and began a course of university study. He made it clear that in many other ways the men with whom he associated were discovering unexpected qualities and abilities in themselves. Each Christmas, for example, a group of men would put on a pantomime for the entertainment of their fellow prisoners. They wrote the script themselves; they made all of the costumes and the scenery from whatever materials they could lay their hands on. Men happily stepped into the female roles which had been written. Great ingenuity was deployed to make the production a success. It was a labour of love, and yet, typically, these men did not have any previous experience of the theatre.

Although I understood Mervyn to be locked up with other loyalist prisoners, he also told me that there were, on occasion, opportunities for him to associate with prisoners from the other side of the political divide and that these meetings were cordial, an opportunity to better understand one another's point of view, an opportunity that simply did not exist in any other context.

A compelling instance of this came towards the end of his sentence, at a moment when Mervyn was allowed home for weekends in preparation for his release. The prison authority clearly believed their part of this arrangement was complete at the point the prisoner stepped out through the gate in the perimeter fence; how a man on weekend furlough made it from there to his own front door and back again in the allotted time was his problem. In practice the terrorist organisations had a welfare system which transported men to home and back in accordance with the rules which had been laid down.

On one occasion Mervyn found that no one from his organisation's "welfare" had turned up to take him home for the weekend. There were of course men from other organisations waiting for the same service from their own support systems and, one of them, a member of the IRA, noticed that Mervyn had been marooned. He came over: "We could take you into the city" he suggested. "You'd be on your own from there." In the circumstances it was a good offer, and Mervyn accepted. A car arrived and Mervyn took his place in the back seat, I imagine along with other members of the IRA. There was some good-humoured back and forth on the topic of what was just happening, but Mervyn reported no sense of threat. It was all friendly. Eventually the car arrived in West Belfast and stopped outside the home of the man who had first offered Mervyn a lift. He turned to Mervyn: "Do you fancy a cup of tea?" And so it was that Mervyn found his way into the house of an IRA man, being introduced to his family and offered tea and biscuits as if the entertainment of members of loyalist terrorists in this household was a daily occurrence. The details of how Mervyn found his way from this unlikely stopping point to his mother's home in Portavogie did not form any part of the story he told. Even Mervyn, who had been in attendance, found it hard to believe this surreal tea party in West Belfast had ever taken place.

Such experiences clearly changed Mervyn's views of what was best for Northern Ireland. I am equally sure, however, that it gave him the belief that every young person who came to Ramoan had within them a potential to do something positive with their life.

Phil

Of all the staff team at Ramoan, I thought Phil closest to being a kindred spirit, yet spending time in his company was a bit of a workout, both physically and mentally. Were we to be out on a hike in the hills I was struggling to keep up with him, but he also had a sharpness of wit that could be bracing. I felt better for spending time with him but pleased when the session had come to a finish and I could relax in less demanding company. If I had done something slipshod in the course of my work, Phil would be sure to notice it and let me know, doubtless with good humour and yet with a distinct edge that could not be ignored.

My job in Ramoan as a volunteer did not require me to be an innovator, but if I happened to have a promising idea I was listened to respectfully. There was a board in the office with maybe a dozen keys on it to various cupboards and rooms where important resources were kept secure. Frequently one came to this board and found that the key one sought was missing. Who was in possession of it was the obvious question and the only answer was to find people and ask them. That could be time-consuming and sometimes fruitless if the miscreant had gone off site with the key. At a staff meeting I suggested that beside the key board there should be a second board with name tags for each member of staff and then, when a key was borrowed, the staff member would put their name tag on the empty key hook. This system was immediately implemented.

Designing systems has always been something I have enjoyed and perhaps even have a knack for it. I felt pleased with myself. Unfortunately, use of systems, whether designed by myself or others, is not something that comes so easily to me and I was one of the first to be found, not just with a key in my possession, but having left the building, completely forgetting that I had it. My friends from Reading, Linda and Heather were visiting and I had just returned from a fine walk along the beach with them. Predictably, it was Phil who, like a Native American tracker, caught up with me and crashed into my good mood by pointing out that I had the missing key in my possession. He did not forget to let me know, in so doing, the details of the inconvenience that had resulted from its absence. There was no case for the defence. I was bang to rights.

So far as I was aware Phil had no previous professional experience of working with young people, but he got on well with the lads, and was respected by them I thought. He gave no quarter. Physical competence and quick wits are a great asset in working with challenging young men and Phil had both.

What had he done though, before coming to Ramoan? What I learned was that he and Lynn had, for a few years, lived in what I imagined to be a small-holding in the hills above Carnlough, further down the Antrim Coast. It was there they had developed their knowledge and skills in the care of animals which were such an important part of the Ramoan regime. As I got to know Phil better, I came to see that the importance he placed on responsibility for the animals and the disciplines required to care properly for them were connected to a belief that taking on such responsibilities could help to ground a person both morally and psychologically. Perhaps he would not have put it that way, but that is how I saw it and it made sense to me in the context of the work we were doing.

So far as I was aware, neither Phil nor Lynn had any family connection to the land, but I did read into his occasional comments on the traditional farming life an admiration for the qualities required to prosper, or even just to survive in agriculture. In one such conversation we were reflecting on a time before the advent of farm machinery when so much on the land was done manually. Phil concluded with what I took to be a humorous comment on the soft and undemanding lives we lived in the modern era: "Ah, in the days when men were men." There was something about the emphasis he placed on masculinity that I thought told only a partial story and I felt moved to add: "And when women were men," meaning simply that the lives of women had been equally tough. He laughed and did not object to my correction.

On one occasion Phil and I took a group of lads camping in Donegal. We all piled into the minibus, towing a trailer full of canoes and kit. The plan was just to turn up in Donegal and find a place to pitch camp in some likely spot. This proved a little more difficult than anticipated, but eventually we spotted an open space just large enough to accommodate us, at the foot of a steep escarpment rising sharply, about 150 feet, to what may have been a plateau beyond. It was starting to get dark and there was a fresh breeze blowing. We began to unload the tents when we heard a voice shouting from above. It was a man, presumably the owner of the land on which we had decided to spend the night. His manner was not welcoming. Beside him was a dog. In his hand was a shepherd's crook which he was waving wildly above his head whilst continuing to berate us at the top of his lungs. Dark clouds were swirling in the sky which framed him. None of his words could be heard above the wind, but we got the general idea of what he wanted to say.

Phil took stock of this calmly and then dropped whatever it was he was carrying and started very steadily and without any attempt to engage in the conversation, to climb towards the source of the hostility. Meanwhile the stick waving and shouting continued unabated. As Phil reported later, it was only when he got within about twenty feet of the man that his manner began to change dramatically, and for the better. As the distance closed between them his demeanour softened and suddenly, he was making us welcome, couldn't have been more helpful. "Stay as long as you want!"

The following day we found a better spot close to one of the magnificent empty beaches which are to be found all along the coast of Donegal. This one was a crescent encircling a sheltered bay, where the boys were able to go canoeing safely. Trailing a line of feathered hooks, they landed enough mackerel to feed us all and, that evening, we cooked them over an open fire. I remembered my mother's frequent rejoinder where mackerel were concerned: they should be eaten fresh. These ones certainly were, and it was a glorious experience for all of us.

Colin

Colin was the Assistant Director and had been prominent in the design and development of the programme. He had been influenced by the radical ideas in Ivan Illich's *Deschooling Society* and Paolo Freire's *Pedagogy of the Oppressed*, both books which had shaped my own thinking. He was the only member of staff employed as a teacher, so his role was an important one, for all of the lads who came our way were obliged, whether they wanted it or not, to receive a daily dose of education. I took no part in the formalities of this process, but my impression was that Colin carried this task off without making enemies of his pupils. The classes were small, some of the lads were, if not academic, clever. Few of them will have brought to Ramoan a positive idea of what education could offer. Colin took on his charges with a belief that, regardless of their previous school performance, they could progress and prosper in their education, and it was only a matter of striking the right rapport to start building a new attitude to their learning. Was the time of their stay in Ramoan sufficient to do this? I doubt it very much but equally it would not surprise me if in a good many cases Colin encouraged his pupils to revise their view of their own capabilities and in a few instances turned their attitude around. Though much of Colin's teaching was classroom based his training had been in physical education and together with Phil he had developed the adventure learning parts of the Ramoan programme. This, with the care of the animals, gave a very distinctive character to what was on offer to the lads whilst they were in residence.

Colin was a quieter presence than the other members of staff, but I found him a supportive colleague. He noticed, for example, the trouble I was having with Kevin. Kevin was clever but he was wary of authority and, like many lads dealing with such a situation, alert to weaknesses in the staff he encountered. An uneasy mixture of mildly homophobic or misogynistic comments is not uncommon amongst wayward adolescent boys. To this day, unambiguous heterosexuality is generally the safest identity for a young man still trying to find his place in the world. When I heard the kind of comments so often used to claim this heterosexual male territory, I would feel some obligation to challenge them. Kevin noticed and could not resist raising questions as regards my own sexuality. I would respond ambiguously. Trying to deal with Kevin's "curiosity" by asserting my own heterosexuality would not, I thought, have been an appropriate way to respond. This was not always an easy line to take.

I expect other members of staff noticed what was happening, but Colin was prepared to have a conversation with me about what he observed and I found this helpful, though really there were no simple solutions. Kevin was well-liked by the other lads. He was not a bully. Indeed, I thought there was a spark of something in his character which in another context might have found creative expression, but he was in the meantime just trying to survive in a tougher world than the one in which I had grown up.

Barriers

To establish some basis of respect with the boys at Ramoan it was helpful to be able to hold your own in a kickabout or play a reasonable game of pool and certainly I got plenty of opportunity to practise the latter. More important was to be able to connect on some other level, to discover an interest or a talent, which a young person was quietly keeping to themselves, something they were shy of disclosing. Perhaps it might be a lad who kept pigeons, or who helped his Granda with his garden, or his Ma with the cooking, or maybe was good with his hands, fixing things or making things; in short, the kind of thing which might reveal a sensitivity not easily displayed in the unforgiving world of adolescent banter.

One of my jobs was to ferry lads to and from their homes in the minibus and I remember being rather touched by a lad, Gerard, from Omagh, who confided that he would prefer to be dropped off at his granny's rather than at his own home; in all of his family it was she to whom he felt closest. It meant something that he felt able to say this to me.

Another young man, Geordie, had brought a flute with him to Ramoan. It lay uneasily in his belongings until noticed by one of the other lads. At home Geordie was a member of a flute band and I imagined one day would graduate to adult membership of the Orange Order. The potentially divisive character of his interest was ignored and he was asked to give us a tune, the Catholic boys just as intrigued as the prods. After a few bursts from tunes he might have played on the twelfth of July, it was Mervyn who asked him to have a go at something more neutral; John Denver's *Annie's Song* was suggested. It's a love song, written by Denver for his wife. No problem, said Geordie and, without pause, rattled off a version until someone pointed out that he was playing with a swagger which suggested marching rather than romance. He paused for a moment and had another go. With his second attempt he achieved something more like the romantic lilt we were familiar with.

Gerard, who I mentioned earlier, was a Catholic, but his best friend at Ramoan was Alex, a skinhead from Randalstown and someone I assumed to be a supporter of the Orange Order and an undiluted loyalist. Yet these two guys struck up a friendship, I think in part because they were the smartest in the group and had a mutual respect. None of the young men who came our way were promoting the activities of the paramilitary groups which were undoubtedly in the background of their lives and it is probable that, as repeat offenders, their relationship with paramilitary authority in their areas was an uneasy one. There was never, that I can recall, any political strain arising from the different traditions from which they came.

Observance

Religion was not in general a subject of discussion amongst either the staff or the lads. There were no daily prayers or religious rituals at Ramoan. However, on a Sunday, it was expected that all the young men in our care would either go to mass or to a church service of the denomination to which they were affiliated. It was a staff duty to supervise, and I took my turn. In general, I preferred going to the chapel, simply because it was something I had not done previously other than attending a funeral on one occasion. In Ballycastle Mass was always full to overflowing, standing room only. Those attending did not appear to feel it necessary to dress up for the occasion. I liked this informality, preferring it to the Sunday best on display in the Protestant churches, the men in suits, the women in their best outfits and, always, hats, something I remembered well from the times when I used to attend church with my parents. I was told, however, that in Belfast things were quite different and, that there people got dressed up to go to Mass.

Some of the lads it seems were curious and saw an opportunity that did not normally come their way. As far as the Ramoan staff were concerned, I was not aware of any objection to the idea that, if they expressed a wish to do so, the Protestant boys might attend Mass on a Sunday and the Catholics attend a church service, either Presbyterian or Church of Ireland. It was an idea that came entirely from the lads and was not promoted in the least by the staff, though, my own view was very much in favour. How many times this cultural and religious exchange occurred, I cannot say, but some parents became aware of what was happening and were not at all happy about it. At the conclusion of the resulting rumpus, we were instructed absolutely not to facilitate this in the future.

Take Me Home to Mayo

At the foot of Ballycastle's Ann Street, where the Glenshesk River spills into the Atlantic, a fine sandy beach stretches eastwards for more than half a mile from the harbour. This finally gives way to rocks at the eastern end. It is then a scramble over these outcrops to advance towards the bulky headland of Fair Head with its sheer cliff rising above a scree of boulders. Beyond is visible the coast of Scotland, its nearest landfall, the Mull of Kintyre.

Just six miles out across Ballycastle Bay is Rathlin Island, which could be reached by a ferry from the harbour. Looking north beyond Rathlin, on clear days, I could see the Scottish islands of Islay and Jura. I had in my childhood been to Portrush and Portstewart which lay just a little over ten miles west of Ballycastle and I had taken much delight in their brash tourist offer, but their setting bore no comparison with this dramatic panorama.

Ballycastle was largely untouched by the Troubles and the town had a relaxed atmosphere, a contrast to Newry, where bombings and shootings were a looming threat and the presence of police and army much more in the foreground of daily life. Ballycastle in general felt like small towns I knew in the Republic of Ireland and this no doubt reflected the fact that a majority of the population were Roman Catholic and happy to embrace their Gaelic identity. But there was a significant Protestant presence and people lived harmoniously alongside one another so far as I could tell. A little research tells me that when I arrived in Ballycastle it had experienced two significant terrorist events. In August 1973 loyalist paramilitaries left a car bomb outside the Roman Catholic church, timed to explode as Mass-goers left. The service ran late thwarting what could easily have been a massacre. Fifty people were injured, three of them seriously. I can only imagine that this botched plan was hatched by men who had no familiarity with Ballycastle or appreciation of what it had to offer. The IRA had also taken their turn at stirring up disaffection in Ballycastle and in 1979 had bombed the Marine Hotel, seriously injuring a Protestant guest who died from his injuries three weeks later. My personal experience however was of a town untroubled by such conflict and where I felt secure.

Though I was gradually getting to know my colleagues at Ramoan a little better, they were not the source of my social life outside of work. Oliver and his wife Rosie were based in Belfast, Phil and Lynn were both friendly, but when not engaging with Ramoan preferred to keep their own company, or that of more established friends. Mervyn and Colin had strong attachments to the Corrymeela community.

Corrymeela was situated on an elevated platform overlooking the sea just east of the town. Whilst I was very respectful of the values of reconciliation that I knew were at the heart of Corrymeela's activities, I shied away from what I perceived as its religious ethos and my atheism discouraged me from exploring the community beyond what I could learn from Mervyn and Colin. In these circumstances I was happy to take whatever opportunity was available to explore Ballycastle's social offering and there were a number of pubs which seemed interesting. One of these, which I visited on a Saturday night, was always packed, standing room only. The main attraction, so far as I could tell, was the fact that singers were welcome to perform and yet very few of the patrons seemed to pay much attention to the brave souls who stepped forward. There was one young man with a mellifluous tenor voice, who regularly took his place at the microphone. His repertoire was just one song, *Take Me Home to Mayo,* and this he intoned every week. His performances, for all their insistently repetitive character, resonated with me, not only because of his fine tenor voice but also, I am sure, because of the men I had worked with on the roads, who came from those western counties of Ireland, though I was later to discover that the song in fact concerns Michael Gaughan who had been a member of the IRA and had died on hunger strike in Parkhurst Prison in 1974. This detail was lost on me at the time, and I understood only the mournful refrain.

Take me home to Mayo, across the Irish Sea,
Home again in Mayo where once I roamed so free.
Take me home to Mayo, and let my body lie,
Home at last in Mayo, beneath an Irish sky.

An audience which pays no attention can be unrewarding, but it is less intimidating than an audience which actually listens. I couldn't resist having a go myself. I generally used my own song, *All this Rain,* as an opener and this is the first verse for any souls present who may have strained to hear it.

All this rain is worrying me,
Another series of depressions rolling in across the sea
Everywhere I cast my weather eye,
Big black clouds fill the sky.
Could it be a sign from above?
Could it be the end of love?
On such things do I philosophise
As I wait while my washing dries.

I wasn't really surprised that this drew no more attention than *Take Me Home to Mayo*, but I was back the following week, and I had another go with another song.

Another place I visited a few times hosted traditional Irish music sessions, about eight or ten guys who sat around, all with fiddles that I can remember, though maybe there was a bodhran. They all played along with one another and were perfectly harmonious but there wasn't a great deal of ambition in what they were doing. It certainly wasn't the Chieftains, complex arrangements and virtuoso playing. Nevertheless, it was a novelty. Growing up in Newry I was unaware of any Irish traditional music in the local pubs and so far as I could tell from what was advertised on hoardings and featured in the *Newry Reporter*, it was showbands and country and western singers which were most celebrated in the town, though at the time I considered these genres distinctly uncool.

Country and western had a strong following on both sides of the religious divide. Gradually my view of country music shifted. No doubt Bob Dylan's *Nashville Skyline* released in 1969 had done something to challenge my view that the genre was irredeemably sentimental and shallow, although the discovery of singers like Emmylou Harris, Linda Ronstadt and Bonnie Raitt had helped to open my mind a little. This education continued in Ballycastle. I got a bit of a surprise when Oliver produced a Willie Nelson album and was happy to declare himself a fan. He seemed to suggest that Willie was an artist to be taken seriously. I made a note, but it wasn't until years later, sitting in a pub in the Scottish Borders that I was convinced. Willie came on the jukebox singing *Always On My Mind*. I think of it now as the definitive version of that song, and it distresses me to hear people saying how great a version Elvis does when I think his slightly operatic take lacks the finely-grained emotion of Willie's sensitive and beautiful singing. Still, Elvis did have a few other tricks up his sleeve.

Locals

My colleagues at work were not natives of Ballycastle, but I was lucky enough in time to make the acquaintance of a few locals. Jack was a Glasgow Catholic but had married a Ballycastle girl and was clearly pleased to be living there. He was an electrician. He let me know that he had a source for poteen. In later years I was to purchase something labelled "Poteen" from an off-licence in Dublin; it was strong stuff, but a disappointment. Poteen in my mind was a spirit which, by definition, came from an illicit still. Jack was very discreet about his own source but, in due course, a bottle of clear spirit was produced, and a sum of money exchanged. The mythology surrounding poteen suggests that, given the unregulated circumstances of its production, it can be very rough, even dangerous, so I sampled with care. I am not someone able to distinguish one malt whisky from another or who can tell the difference between a four-star and a five-star brandy, but what Jack had given me seemed very good indeed, smooth and, I would be tempted to say, with a fine finish — whatever that may be. With the passing of time, I have wondered if the "back door" through which this quality article had been obtained was that of the Bushmills Distillery which lay just along the coast. It is not hard to imagine that there was a local trade in the raw spirit, a quantity syphoned off before the bulk of it was placed in oak barrels to age and mature. Still, I prefer to believe that what Jack had provided had been lovingly collected from a hand-crafted pot-still concealed in some secluded part of the Antrim hills.

On one occasion I was introduced to a young woman who had grown up in Magherintemple House, a grand residence which had been the ancestral seat of the Casement family and the home of Sir Roger Casement. In the early twentieth century, Casement had been a diplomat in the British Foreign Office. In 1911 he had been knighted, having gained distinction for his investigations into human rights abuses in the Congo and Peru. None of this was known to me at the time; however, I was aware of the more notorious fact that Casement had been executed for treason in 1916.

My limited knowledge of the Casement story derives a great deal from the fact of a caravan holiday my family had taken in the late 1950s, to Ballyheigue in County Kerry. There my mother had encountered an old man who spoke warmly of Casement. The old man remembered the occasion of Casement's arrest on nearby Banna Strand. Casement had been coming ashore from a German U-Boat with a cache of arms, intended for the 1916 Rising. My mother passed no judgement on Casement as she related this story and I think was more interested in the fact of this oral history and the evidence it provided of the continuing regard local Kerry people had for him.

Cushendall Road

Living-in at Ramoan was fine, but when Mervyn acquired the tenancy of a sizable house on the Cushendall Road, I gladly accepted his offer of a room. It was generous accommodation with a large kitchen and living room. The decor was not really to my taste, but this didn't seem at all important, particularly so, given the fine location. It was within walking distance of the town centre, easy cycling to and from Ramoan and had a lovely open aspect with windows which looked north across a golf course to the eastern edge of the Ballycastle beach.

Joining us was a new member of the Ramoan team, Terry. He was a teacher and was also very at home with the outdoor pursuits aspect of what Ramoan offered. As a household, I think Mervyn, Terry and I functioned well together. Without the need for complicated rotas, we kept quite a tidy house and happily took turns at cooking and washing up. Mervyn and Terry might have their own stories to tell on the strains of our coexistence, but so far as I was concerned the arrangement suited well.

Valentia

In late July of 1982 I got an invitation from a probation officer friend to join a group who had taken a holiday cottage on Valentia Island, just off the coast of County Kerry. Though it was in a part of the country with which I had some familiarity from childhood holidays, I had never been to Valentia and yet it was a place which had acquired a certain poetic resonance as the weather station situated on the island provides storm warnings which often feature in the litany of the BBC's shipping forecasts. Holiday cottages formed no part of my earlier recollection of this part of the world, but they were on their way to becoming a staple of the tourist industry in the West of Ireland. After the long drive, we crossed the bridge to the island and were pleased to find ourselves comfortably accommodated in something a little more than a traditional cottage.

The mood of the party was relaxed and, as it happened, the conditions were perfect for a boat trip to the Skelligs, two rocky pinnacles which rise dramatically from the Atlantic Ocean just over eight miles west of the mainland. The taller of these two spikes, Skellig Michael, reaches up to just over 750 feet. Apart from its visual drama and the teeming birdlife, it is the location of a remnant of a Christian community which was established there in the sixth century, a monastery in fact, though quite unlike any other. On this inhospitable crag the monks built little domed dwellings, beehive cells, made entirely from the stone to be found lying at their feet. In these cells, many of which remain intact, they lived, getting their sustenance by fishing or trapping sea birds and collecting rainwater by whatever means. One does not have to be religious to feel something like a spiritual response to this evidence of belief sustained in the face of such extreme physical challenges. George Bernard Shaw visited Skellig Michael in 1910 and wrote to a friend that it was "An incredible, impossible, mad place … I tell you the thing does not belong to any world that you and I have lived and worked in: it is part of our dream world …"

The weather on the day of our visit could not have been better, the sky cloudless, the sea a perfect calm and with just the slightest of swells our landing was an easy one. We had plenty of time to climb the stony path, to run our hands across the stonework of the dwellings and to absorb the evidence that this inhospitable place had once sustained a human community.

Later that evening we managed to fit in a visit to the Fisherman's Bar in Portmagee, just over the bridge from the island. We fell in with another group on a holiday visit. They were from Dublin. Fintan, had a guitar and was an accomplished musician and singer. Though the songs he performed were in the tradition of Irish music, they were not rebel songs, either in celebration of a previous era or of more recent events further north. Unlike that pub in Ballycastle where I had listened to a weekly homage to a hunger striker, Fintan's repertoire was more out of the Horslips catalogue, songs you could take anywhere in Ireland without causing an uproar.

I was no match for Fintan's talent but in these kinds of impromptu sessions there is a generous tolerance of the amateur performer. I sang one of my songs. Ah, joy. They asked me to do another.

Tourism

One of the advantages of my new accommodation was that I could more easily entertain friends than was possible when I was living-in at Ramoan. My old friend Nick, at that time living and working in Dublin, came up and we spent a day on Rathlin. The weather fair, we walked the length and breadth of the Island, caught sight of puffins close to the lighthouse on the western tip, and went looking for seals on the rocks on the island's northern margin.

Heather and Linda, my friends from Reading, came over for a few days. I was scheduled to take a group of lads home from Ramoan during the period of Heather and Linda's visit and, a little to my surprise, it was agreed that they might come along for the ride. This resulted in a more edgy tour of Northern Ireland than they might have been hoping for as we found our way through some of the more politically expressive parts of the country, housing estates with red, white and blue paving stones on the one hand and unabashed display of Irish tricolours on the other.

1982 was not really a high point for the tourist industry in Northern Ireland and yet the number of attractions clustered around the stretch of the North Antrim Atlantic shoreline where I was living, was impressive. Most famous of all was the Giant's Causeway but, however astonishing, I was more drawn to some of the less celebrated features of that ragged coast with all of its cliffs and rocky coves.

The Carrick-a-Rede rope bridge offered just enough security for me to dare to cross the 100-foot-deep gap which separated the cliff top on the mainland from the tiny Island of Carrick-a-Rede, with its single cottage and salmon fishery. The rope bridge was a fascination for lads who came to Ramoan, a challenge which could produce some surprises as to who would make the crossing and who decided, maybe, not this time.

Another striking feature of that coast is Dunluce Castle, ruinous, perched right on a cliff edge, looking north past Rathlin, to the Scottish islands. The story of how, many centuries ago, the entire kitchen had fallen into the sea during a banquet with the loss of all the honoured guests, was a favourite with the lads. At the time I never questioned this excellent tale but there is no evidence that it ever happened. Such are the wishful dramas that emerge from the Chinese whispers of orally transmitted history.

I was to learn that Dunluce was an important stronghold of the Kingdom of Dalriada which encompassed a good part of what is now north Antrim, all of the Scottish islands and the western part of what we now think of as the Highlands of Scotland. There is some dispute as regards the origins of the

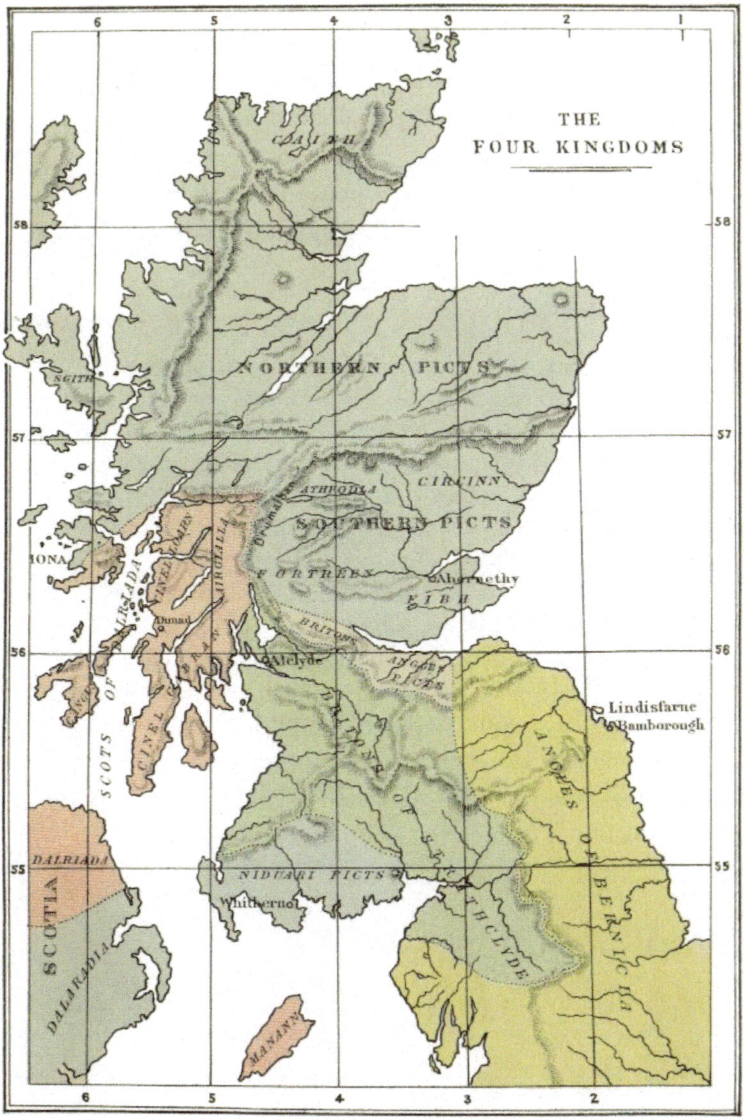

Map originally from "Celtic Scotland: a history of ancient Alban" (1876) showing the Kingdom of Dalriada, image available from Wikimedia.org.

Kingdom, but what seems undeniable is that it was associated with the spread of the Irish language to the Scottish islands and beyond.

With the collapse of Dalriada in the eighth century, the language in Scotland evolved along a separate path leading to what is now known as Scots Gaelic (pronounced Gallic), a very prized part of Scottish culture. It is a curious irony that, with notable exceptions, many who identify as Ulster Scots have been inclined to think of Irish as an alien tongue and are happier to acknowledge their connections with the lowland Scots of Robert Burns.

Some Ulster Scots claim Burns as part of their cultural heritage but there is not the same passion for Burns' poetry and his radicalism as may be found amongst Scottish people.

> *What though on hamely fare we dine,*
> *Wear hoddin grey, an' a that;*
> *Gie fools their silks, and knaves their wine;*
> *A Man's a Man for a' that:*
> *For a' that, and a' that,*
> *Their tinsel show, an' a' that;*
> *The honest man, tho' e'er sae poor,*
> *Is king o' men for a' that.*

There is no doubt that in some parts of Northern Ireland the influence of the lowland Scots language can still be heard, or even seen, as in the case of a parcel that arrived in Ramoan one day with the informal inscription "Save the Weans". That was a reference to Save the Children, the charity which was sponsor to the Ramoan project.

For Want of Funds

At some point I became acquainted with a couple, John and Margaret. They had a young son, Connor, just two or three years old. I never got to know them well, but they struck me as a little out of the ordinary for that part of the world. Margaret was a quiet but determined feminist, John a bit of a daydreamer. They lived in a tiny house, a part of a terrace of three, which sat out in the middle of some heathland not far west of Ballycastle. The row of houses was set back from the coastline, half a mile or so, but when the skies were clear, the gentle fall in the ground, looking north, afforded panoramic views across to Rathlin and beyond.

I was interested when they let me know that one of the houses in the terrace was vacant and going on the market for just £600, which even in 1982 seemed a very tempting price. I didn't have £600, but my father had let it be known that there was some surplus cash which could be made available for any reasonable project. I knew that he would take a good deal of persuading that the purchase of this tiny house in the middle of nowhere was a sound idea. How could this be sustainable? The kind of casual work that had kept me in the latter stages of my time in Reading just wasn't available in that part of the world. There was a Barnardo's home in Ballycastle, and I thought, if I were patient and got lucky, I could land a job there. My father listened to what I had to say on the matter, but he was not impressed. He said "No." With that decision one of the possible futures I had been considering was neatly foreclosed.

Kevin

My preferred journalism during that year in Ballycastle was *Fortnight* magazine. It seemed to offer the sanest of commentary on what was happening in Northern Ireland. Its editor at the time I was reading it, Andy Pollock, has described it as a "small, impecunious, left-of-centre magazine." Those were certainly some of the qualities that appealed to me. I took an interest, however, in a range of literature from right across the political spectrum and on visits to Belfast would find my way to bookshops on neutral territory which were prepared to offer sometimes rather primitive literature from the more extreme ends of the political spectrum, both loyalist and republican. My small library of such rough material was not something I would have felt appropriate even to have brought through the door of Ramoan but when I moved to Cushendall Road with Mervyn and Terry I made no attempt to conceal my interest.

On one occasion we had a couple of visitors in the house and I was, perhaps a little carelessly, reviewing a pamphlet which was clearly propaganda for the Provisional IRA. It contained a picture of a British Army Saracen vehicle in the Bogside in Derry. Visible in the back of the vehicle was a little boy, aged about six years old. The caption read: "The Brits take another prisoner." Kevin and Chas were guests of Mervyn and had come across from Derry for a break in Ballycastle. Kevin had previously spent time at Ramoan, his stay, I believe, falling in one of the earliest intakes. He and Mervyn had remained in touch after Kevin's sentence was complete. Chas was Kevin's friend. He walked on crutches and had been kneecapped by the Provisional IRA for alleged offences against their code of behaviour. "Kneecapped" doesn't really do justice to the injuries he had sustained. Bullets had passed at an oblique angle through both legs. Chas did not expect ever again to be able to walk without support.

Both of these lads, aged about sixteen or seventeen when I met them, were from Derry's Bogside. Kevin noticed the pamphlet I was looking at and leaned in to take a closer look at the picture of that wee boy. "That's me," he said. "On Bloody Sunday." It was a startling revelation and I immediately had questions about the story behind the picture. Kevin told me first of all that he had witnessed the British Army shooting unarmed civilians. At the time he was speaking, this version of events was not widely accepted amongst the unionist and loyalist community. "But Kevin," I asked, "If you saw that happening, why don't you like the IRA in Derry?" It was a stupid question really, particularly so given what the Provisional IRA had done to Chas. Still, his response was an interesting one.

He described a situation, a few years previously, in which many of the young people in the Bogside were at loggerheads with the Provos. Kevin characterised himself as a "hood," which I understood to be a corruption of the word "hoodlum" implying that he and other hoods engaged in what might loosely be called anti-social behaviour. This anti-social behaviour drew unwelcome attention from the local IRA who believed that in "Free Derry" it was their job to maintain order. The fact that Kevin had served a probation term in Ramoan is some evidence that his hoodlum activities had also come to the attention of the RUC, but that was not the aspect of his experience which was of interest to me. He explained that, for a time, the hoods had growing support amongst the young people in his area and that they were openly writing anti-IRA graffiti on the walls of the Bogside.

Could this really have been true? Kevin's stories seemed extraordinary and yet there was good reason to believe them. The Undertones, whose members came from Creggan and the Bogside, had emerged in the mid-seventies, their *Teenage Kicks* album being recorded for a John Peel session in 1978. The Undertones' material was not conspicuously political and yet they were clearly associated with punk rock music, which was instinctively rebellious against any authority and in Free Derry, it was the IRA who represented authority. But if, as Kevin implied, the hoods had been such a growing force in Derry, why was he now running scared of the IRA. Kevin had told me that both he and Chas had been forced out of the city and had, for a while, gone to England. Their exile hadn't been a success. Nobody understood them. They were homesick and had slunk back to make some kind of life in their home city. Kevin's answer to the question of what had turned things against the hoods and had renewed the dominance of the Provisional IRA, was a simple one: the Hunger Strikes. With each death that had taken place, it became increasingly difficult and then nigh impossible to be critical of the IRA.

Years later I wrote a song about Kevin's story and called it *Witness to Brutality*. The song doesn't really spare anyone from criticism, other than the witness of the title: the British Army, the Provisional IRA, the Thatcher government are all included in the litany of shameful conduct. The opening two verses will suffice to summarise what he told me.

Six years old in Derry
A stone in his hand
Picked up by the Brits,
And put in a Saracen.
He saw the soldiers raise their guns,
Saw them fire into the crowd,
Saw bodies tumble to the streets,
And drawn a bloody shroud.

A witness to brutality, he saw the soldiers' shame,
And he knew the reality was not the justice that was claimed.

He grew up on Bogside streets
Where gunman's rule was law,
Where stones were toys and foul-mouthed boys
Came to take them on the jaw.
But he saw friends were beaten
By this side and by that
He saw corruptions twisted face
And gangsters getting fat.

A witness to brutality, to mobsters and to sharks
When honest men who'd taken arms were blind or in the dark.

One of Kevin's claims was that the IRA were nothing more than gangsters, lining their own pockets. I have no doubt that the IRA's own historians would contest this bitterly, but I was witness to some evidence of Kevin's version of events. This occurred when I drove Kevin and Chas back to their homes in the Bogside at the end of their stay. I was scheduled to pick up another lad to take back to Ramoan. As we closed in on his home street, I drew Kevin's attention to a BMW motor car parked outside a house otherwise indistinguishable from the rows of plain houses past which we drove. "Who can afford that car in this area?" I wondered aloud. "Ah, that's one of the boys," was Kevin's reply.

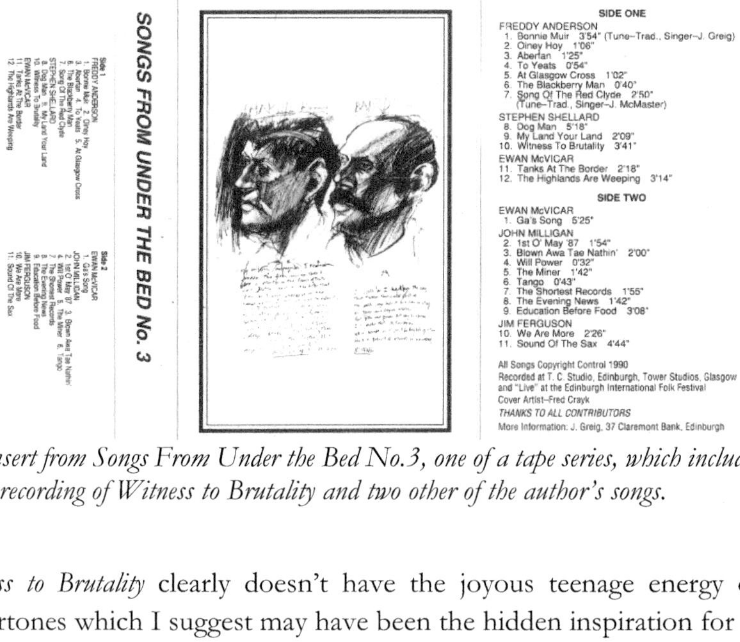

Insert from Songs From Under the Bed No.3, one of a tape series, which included a recording of Witness to Brutality and two other of the author's songs.

Witness to Brutality clearly doesn't have the joyous teenage energy of the Undertones which I suggest may have been the hidden inspiration for Kevin and the hoods, but the song does tell an interesting, perhaps even important story, of hoodlum rebellion against the IRA in Derry in the late 1970s. I thought it so significant that I sent a copy to the BBC with a detailed explanation of what lay behind the narrative. I thought it might make an interesting radio script. I love the BBC, but they never wrote back.

Last days

When my father declined to help me purchase that little house in the middle of nowhere, my immediate ideas as to what I would do on leaving Ramoan had begun to crystallise around travel. Phil and Lynn shared with me some details of a vineyard, near Avignon, where I could get work in the autumn, picking grapes. They had been there in previous years themselves and did not hide from me the fact that the work was hard and the accommodation primitive. On the other hand, the pay was the going rate for such seasonal work and they spoke warmly of the Patron. The wine that he made, Gigondas, was of high quality, and the countryside in that part of the world, beautiful.

I had a second plan which was a little more elaborate. My friend Heather had moved to Hamburg where she had friends, I think from her school days. What she told me of her experience there encouraged me to believe that I might travel to West Berlin and there be able to find work and a place in a squatted house. I thought that if I were to spend a year in such accommodation, apart from having an interesting experience, I might learn German.

One of my nagging ambitions during that era, when the Cold War was at its height, was to cross over and get some sense of what life was really like on the other side of the Iron Curtain. I knew from a relentless diet of news commentary that it was grey in colour, that supermarket shelves were never full, that there were queues for any remotely desirable consumer goods, and that speaking your mind could be a dangerous business. Still, I felt the need to investigate the matter for myself. East Germany seemed the obvious place for such an enquiry, and so learning a little German an important part of this project. The fact that I had a tin ear for languages did not discourage me. Total immersion in the language, I felt sure, would deliver the result I was looking for.

As far as my longer-term plans were concerned, I had decided to move to my brother Peter's house in Dumfries where he lived with his partner Deirdre. I thought I might use it as a base from which to find work there, or perhaps more likely, in Carlisle, just over the border in the north of England.

When my last day at Ramoan finally came, there was a gathering of staff to mark the occasion. John Quinlivin, the lead officer of Save the Children in Belfast, attended. He was a friendly, gregarious, good-humoured man. He said a few words to thank me for the contribution I had made to Ramoan and in so doing reflected on his meeting with me when I had first arrived in Belfast: "When Stephen first walked into our office …" he hesitated for a moment. "Obviously, a nice chap from a nice family, but I just wasn't sure he could connect with the kind of lads we work with in Ramoan. I had doubts. Maybe we hadn't got the right person." There was a further pause. "But now I see a changed picture, someone who has grown into the work and who has become a valuable member of the team."

This was a generous conclusion. Still, I'd have to admit, I felt slightly patronised by his description of me on arrival. I can't remember what I said in response. I hope I said, "Thank you!" I hope I said: "Working at Ramoan has been an unforgettable experience. I am so glad I came." My colleagues gave me a present. It came in the form of a small, red, tin box. Inside was a little brass primus stove. The idea had come, I am sure from my sharing with them the details of a camping trip I had made to Donegal with a friend. I had turned up for the trip, somewhat under-prepared, without even bothering to bring adequate means for the making of a cup of hot tea. This resulted in a few tensions in the early stage of the expedition. I love that stove, but unfortunately owing to an incident when, one hot dry summer, several years later, I nearly set fire to a Scottish hillside whilst trying to light my beloved primus, I have not, over the years, been given much encouragement to make use of it.

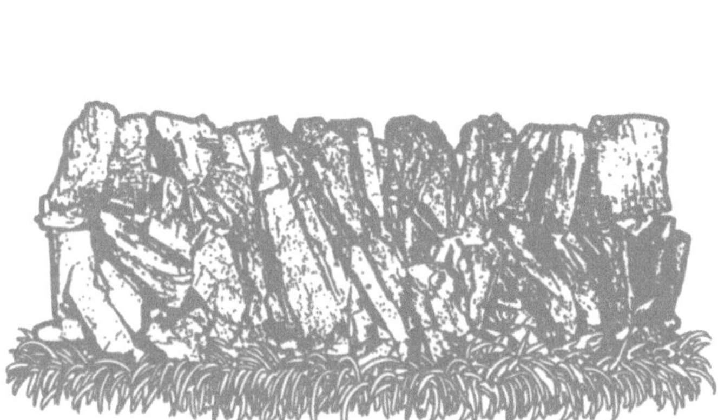

6: No Direction Home

Modern War (Extract)

When Cain first felt his anger rise
And slew Abel in the field
His hand held no dagger
And Abel held no shield
And God said onto Cain
"Thy brother's blood cries out from the ground"
And Cain became a fugitive
In flight from that bloody sound

Now soldiers strut in ignorance
Of what they're fighting for
Believe in Ulster or the Falklands
That they've seen modern war
As if these bloody conflicts
Are not a tragedy enough
They're really just a sideshow
To make our soldier boys feel tough

This country has an army
An army of technicians
Prepared to fight an enemy
Known by dreams and superstitions
We all shelter behind missiles
Playing with our latest toy
And let lesser mortals hunger
For the peace that we enjoy

1985

The Sinking Ship

I earned a little money picking grapes in the south of France and then made my way back to Peter and Deirdre in Dumfries. They were renovating a house and doing a good deal of work on the project themselves. There were always things to do and it was easy to make myself useful, painting usually, but odd jobs were my speciality. I was intending to travel to Germany early in the New Year. It was during this interlude that I met Elaine. She was originally from Dumfries. On leaving school she had attended Stirling University and then worked for a few years in Glasgow, before returning to her hometown to work at the local museum. Deirdre and Elaine were both volunteers for Women's Aid. Elaine was a member of the Campaign for Nuclear Disarmament. Peter and Deirdre were also members. There were of course social and fundraising events associated with these causes. I found myself in her company on a couple of such occasions. I must have expressed some interest in the local folk club during one of our early encounters, so I was pleasantly surprised when she rang up to say that she was going to the Dumfries Folk Club the following week and was wondering whether I might also be interested in attending. Definitely! I soon discovered that our respective record collections took in more than folk music and overlapped a good deal, always a good sign.

Margaret Thatcher had become Prime Minister of the United Kingdom in May 1979 but there was to be a General Election early in June 1983. In 1980 Michael Foot had won the leadership of the Labour Party. A somewhat shambling and yet charismatic figure, he was a genial, cultured man, celebrated for his oratory, his journalism, and his books on literary and biographical topics. He was, however, considered to be on the extreme left of the party. Doubtless because of this, four prominent members of the Labour Party had cut loose and formed a new party, the Social Democratic Party which, in alliance with the Liberals, hoped to win the centre ground of British politics.

In the early part of her first term in Government, Margaret Thatcher had become deeply unpopular, not just with Irish republicans but with working class people across the United Kingdom. Unemployment was rising, the economy was in recession. Future electoral success for her seemed improbable, the emerging story being the contest between the Social Democratic Party and Labour.

But then everything changed. In 1982 a British Protectorate in the South Atlantic, which few British people knew even existed, was invaded by Argentina. Initially things looked even worse for Mrs Thatcher. Her Foreign Secretary, Lord Carrington, was obliged to resign, acknowledging a failure to ensure the islands were adequately defended. However, against what appeared impossible odds, Mrs Thatcher decreed that a Task Force should sail to the South Atlantic and retake the Falklands, a mad idea it might have seemed but, as things turned out, a political game changer.

Despite its loss of Empire, the United Kingdom was unquestionably a superior military power to Argentina, but to send the Task Force was an audacious and risky strategy; yet the campaign was a triumph. One should not overlook the fact that in a mere 74 days of conflict, 907 lives were lost, of which 255 were British Servicemen and three, citizens of the Falklands; yet Margaret Thatcher's star was suddenly in the ascendant.

The reason I bother to set the scene for the election of June 1983, is to make it clear that Elaine, who had had come in from the fringes of left-wing politics to join the Labour Party, regarded my plan to go and spend time in West Berlin at this critical moment as nothing less than dilettante. Nevertheless, when I suggested we might remain in touch whilst I was away, she did not dissent. I made a careful note of her address.

Kreuzberg

It was early in February 1983 that I hitched down to London, dropping in briefly on some friends in a squatted house in Vauxhall, before making my way to Hamburg via Harwich. There I was to stay for a few days with Heather and her friend Reiner. They had some knowledge of the squatting scene in West Berlin where a good deal of residential property had been left to moulder by speculators and then been occupied by people who might not otherwise have been able to afford to rent an apartment. These squatters argued they were doing something worthwhile by expanding the housing stock available for the less well off. The arguments were similar in London, squatting often initiated by politically motivated individuals. This vanguard opened opportunities for an assortment of others. From Heather and Reinier I got addresses of places where I might be welcome and armed with this information, I set off for West Berlin hoping I might for a while become part of the squatting ragbag.

Following the end of the Second World War, West Berlin became isolated within that part of eastern Germany which had been overrun by Russian troops. Berlin itself, as the capital city, had been carved into four sectors, Russian, US, British and French. The Russian sector was eventually integrated into communist East Germany whilst the American, British and French sectors coalesced into the enclave of West Berlin, a defiant free market symbol at the very heart of the Cold War. There was a transport corridor through East Germany by which one might access this outpost of western freedom, or capitalist decadence, depending on your point of view. I stood at the entrance to the corridor, put my thumb out, and got a lift. There were no stop-offs. A single hop took you the whole way into West Berlin.

I had settled on an address to go to that first night. There, I imagined, I might be offered at least temporary accommodation. It was dark as I entered Kreuzberg, an area largely untouched by allied bombs, but nevertheless, crumbling. As I approached 43 Willibald-Alexis-Strasse I felt growing anxiety for I did not really know what to expect. I found the door indicated on my scrap of paper and with assistance from some of those coming and going through it, I found my way up a broad staircase into a large room, a kitchen, as I learned, where there were perhaps a dozen people present. I explained, in English, that I was in search of a room. "Do you speak any German?" someone asked. "Ein bisschen," I replied, meaning that I spoke "a little," though it didn't take me long to conclude that this was not much better than a lie. The seriousness of my linguistic deficiency was thrown into sharp relief by the very thing that was to slow my progress in getting a grasp of even the basics of the German language: most people in the house spoke passable English, and they were all keen to improve.

A room was available, and the terms of the contract explained to me. I would pay so much a week and would then become a member of the household and free to take a share of the breakfast which was laid out every morning in the kitchen and also to take my place at the same table for an evening meal. These meals were prepared on a rotational basis by members of the group who used the kitchen. I would be expected to take my turn at this daunting exercise in due course but, in the short term, my obligations seemed very acceptable, and I made my down payment for the first week.

The house itself was made up of a number of generously proportioned apartments arranged around a central staircase. The first room I was offered was on the ground floor, its furnishing simple though very adequate for my purpose. In the corner stood a substantial edifice, which turned out to be a stove, though that was not at all obvious to me as it was covered with white porcelain tiles. I was told that if I wished to use it, I should purchase "braunkohle" for the purpose. This fuel was widely used in Berlin at the time and was cheap. I thought braunkohle resembled turf (or peat) briquettes and that indeed is exactly what it is. In an urban context it is considered highly polluting. Berlin winters could be cold, so that was the least of my concerns. I made myself comfortable.

If I was to stay for any length of time, I had to find employment. This is where a contact Heather had provided for me proved exceptionally helpful. Ricardo was Spanish and fairly recently arrived in Berlin with the intention of perfecting his German. He already spoke a lot more than "Ein bisschen Deutch" and indeed was an accomplished linguist. He assured me that he could speak four other languages. In the course of our conversation, he told me that, following an argument, he had just walked out of a job as a dishwasher at a large hotel on Berlin's Kurfürstendamm. I didn't know it at the time but Kurfürstendamm is one of Berlin's great commercial thoroughfares. My interest, however, was in the job which Ricardo had so recently vacated. His parting with his employer had not been on good terms, and so a reference from him would have been of doubtful value. Instead, he suggested that I just turn up the following morning at the hotel and ask if they had any work. He assured me, they would be desperate for my services. I arrived at the Hotel Mondial not long after the first shift of the day began, and inquired innocently if there were any jobs available. The plan worked like a dream, and by five past seven I was in the kitchen and hard at work as "spüler," a job at which I stuck doggedly for the next five months.

The dishwasher, though a vital role in a busy kitchen, was not the most respected position. I was on the receiving end of a fair amount of impatient harassment when pots were needed in a hurry, or I had not polished the cutlery adequately. At peak times things were frantic, and I could understand why someone like Ricardo, who plainly knew himself to be the smartest person in the kitchen, had tired of such treatment. But I also understood that, just by turning up and doing the job reasonably, a more generous attitude towards my presence would develop; and so it did.

The high point of the early shift, for me, was following the breakfast rush, when we would all retire from the kitchen to enjoy our own breakfast, set out on a long table in an adjacent room; rolls, cold meat, cheese and coffee and an atmosphere punctuated by much high-spirited conversation, which I couldn't follow, apart from the occasional "Wunderbar!" Still, the mood was relaxed and I looked forward to that oasis of calm each morning shift.

The chefs were all young, well-travelled and generally spoke, at the very least, French, German and English. In quieter moments they treated me very civilly. I became friendly with a couple of them, particularly Uwe. He told me that he was in Berlin as a means of avoiding West German National Service. He seemed to discern that I might be destined in the long run for something other in life than dishwashing and he took an interest in me and what I was up to so at quieter moments, in the ebb and flow of orders from the dining room, I had a friend with whom I could pass the time.

Christina

As in the case of Uwe, Berlin was a draw for many people who were not from the city itself. That was true of the residents of the house where I was living. They came from all over West Germany and beyond. I don't think a single one of them was from Berlin itself, though given that I never worked out how many people were living in the house — it could have been forty or fifty — I cannot be certain of this. What was clear is that the other occupants of the house defied easy categorisation. There were some who I might have identified as punks, a few as hippies but others who could not so easily be pigeonholed. Some of them were squatting for political reasons, others were simply using the house as an economical way of furthering some personal objective, typically study. Some were there just to work out a personal problem they were experiencing. One such was Christina.

I formed the idea that Christina may have been from quite a well-to-do family but had become estranged from her parents. Perhaps this was because of the young man she had fallen in love with and who had jilted her. Following the break-up of her relationship, she had attempted suicide, taking an overdose of paracetamol which, even though it did not kill her, had resulted in damage to her liver. Her health seemed fragile. She was thin and pale. She took an interest in me not particularly because we had much in common, but because she could see that few people in the house had the patience to help me improve my German, and she decided to take me on as a project.

Christina, still struggling to recover her mental and physical health, had not yet returned to work or study. She had a passion for reading Agatha Christie novels in translation. I learnt that these were popular amongst young German people. Christina was quick to anger at the behaviour of others in the house and had a special animus directed towards a few residents who kept dogs and allowed them to soil the stairwell. It wasn't just the owners that angered her; she really didn't like the dogs either and occasionally her frustrations would boil over into a rant. A key phrase which stays with me from these outbursts, "Die scheisse hunde!" She spoke good English but enjoyed making me struggle to express myself in her mother tongue. We spent a lot of time together. Inevitably her sense of mission to improve my German would slip from time to time and allow a more expansive conversation in English.

Someone in the house was kind enough to pass me a guitar that was lying unused, perhaps left behind by a previous resident. It was not a great instrument, but I was grateful to be given it. I was working on a song at the time and played a first draft of it to Christina. I didn't think of it at all as a song about her, but maybe I was hoping its essentially optimistic message would lift her spirits.

Suddenly I find my head
Is filled with hopes that I once thought were dead
You could say that I had been reborn
You could say that I had ridden out the storm
But I don't really understand
The things it takes to make or break a man
You've just got to take your chances
Whatever way your fortune dances

It's so good to be awake
Good to give as well as take
I've known my energy misplaced
And felt to struggle was a waste

But at this moment I have found
That something's turned my fortunes round
You've just got to take your chances
Whatever way your fortune dances

She listened politely as I sang. "Hmm," she said, and returned to her Agatha Christie. I'd hoped for something better and have been slow to try that song out on anybody else, though I have continued to polish it a little over the years.

When eventually, near the end of my stay, we were evicted from the house by the police and the residents dispersed to a variety of locations, I lost touch with Christina. I think some other residents of the household may have felt that she was not really a suitable companion for me, but I did not think that and hoped that the time we had spent together had been of some value to her, as clearly, it had been to me.

Food

I mentioned how much I enjoyed the breakfasts I took at work, but breakfasts in the house were still more lavish. The table was loaded with a superior selection of German bread, cheese, and salami. Coffee was served from huge pump action flasks and people would just wander in at their leisure and take what they wanted. Evening meals, also, could be interesting. For the first time in my life, I watched as a couple of residents made pasta from semolina flour to go with the sauce they had been preparing. Apart from the very German character of the breakfasts, the main culinary influences were Mediterranean but whether it was Italian food or just plain old "kartoffelsalat und wurst" — potato salad and sausage — it was fine with me. My contribution to meals at that stage was clearing and washing up which, despite the fact of my day job, I was very happy to take on in the sociable atmosphere of the kitchen in Willibald-Alexis-Strasse.

Once I was reasonably settled in the house and had some sort of story to tell I did my best to offer this up in a letter to Elaine. A little time elapsed but a reply came eventually in an envelope addressed in rather beautiful italic handwriting. The letter itself was set out in similar style, so, not like the letters from some of my correspondents, which were hard work even to decipher.

The content offered up enough news and interest in my doings to persuade me that a reply, in due course, would not be unwelcome.

Nightlife

As the year wore on, some kind of life outside of the house started to develop for me. I understood that Berlin had a club scene full of curiosity and idiosyncrasy, which I imagined owed something to the cultural legacy of Berlin in the 1920s, but I was barely to scratch the surface of that demimonde. I was invited along to several very busy discotheques, but I wasn't so drawn in as to return regularly. There were lots of interesting bars, often looking like repurposed shops, where what was happening within was framed by plate glass windows and lit by brightly coloured neon. Our local bar, further along Willibald-Alexis Strasse in Chamissoplatz, was less exotic, but I could generally find someone I knew from the house drinking there.

When at home, my cohabitees were a sober lot. There was probably more beer than wine in evidence, but nobody got drunk. Once or twice, I saw a joint being passed around but, apart from this, there was little evidence of drug-taking or indeed any kind of illegal activity. Nevertheless, after I had been resident for a couple of months, we were raided by the police, the house searched, the residents turned out on the street, quizzed as to their particulars and then, just as suddenly, allowed to re-enter. Apparently, there had been a suggestion that the house was being used for handling stolen goods. Nobody was arrested on that occasion, and I never saw any activity of that kind. The residents that I knew just seemed to be getting on with their studies or their work or whatever other projects they had underway. Hucky, for example, was working on his VW camper van and had floated the idea of a summer trip to Greece. That sounded interesting.

Hucky was friendly, keen to improve his English, always happy to invite me as a passenger in his camper van on any expedition through the city which he was undertaking. These often seemed to involve transits along roads running parallel or close to the Berlin Wall, with tantalising glimpses of the barbed wire corridor and the armed guards that separated us from East Berlin. He knew the city well and I benefited from this.

Bedrooms, Sex and Swimming

The bitter cold of winter gave way to milder weather and then, in May, we began to get some real heat. I was pleased to be invited with a group of my housemates to the remains of a gravel pit situated somewhere to the west of the city, where we could swim. It was completely informal, and many people gathered there for a dip, costumes optional, but mostly not worn. That such places existed in West Berlin was a surprise to me and warmer weather offered more opportunity to explore and uncover what lay hidden. I had imagined West Berlin to be an entirely built-up environment, punctuated by a few parks. However, not only did I discover the Tiergarten, close to the Reichstag and the Brandenburger Tor, but with the help of my friends from the house, I found my way to the extensive wooded spaces and lakes of Grunewald on the southwestern margin of the city, where one could get views over to Potsdam. It was there, in July 1945, that Stalin, Churchill and Truman had met in conference to agree the post-war order.

At some point I was offered another room looking out over the central courtyard around which the house was built, and I moved my few possessions to this more desirable location. One night I was awoken by the sounds of a couple making love. Their pleasure in the experience echoed around the well of the courtyard, so loud that I might have suspected it to be a deliberate broadcast, perhaps assisted by intoxicants. More likely though it was just a combination of a warm quiet night, windows wide open and the rather fine acoustic of the courtyard which my room overlooked. It was a rare instance in my sojourn in West Berlin of intimate behaviour becoming, in some degree, a public event.

I kept to my own room for sleeping but I was aware that others chose to sleep in what were referred to as "schlafzimmer." These were in fact dormitories where anyone, male or female, might make their sleeping quarters. There were established couples in the house, but they invariably shared a room together and were not part of this communal arrangement. When, to everyone's surprise, we were evicted from Willibald-Alexis-Strasse on the 1st of June, the alternative accommodation I was then offered in another house along the street involved sleeping in one of these schlafzimmer. I dare say such an arrangement would seem shocking to many people of a prudish turn of mind who might have predicted that it would inevitably lead to sexual incontinence, but that was not my perception. The room in which I was billeted was large with space for perhaps twenty or thirty people who each had a single bed, in fact a mattress, on the floor. In these dormitories it was very natural to become relaxed about dressing and undressing in front of others, regardless of sex and seeing others do the same, but there was no sexualised behaviour arising from this; if anything, I thought, probably the opposite. The large number of people using the rooms provided some element of protection from anyone with a predatory tendency. Indeed, it occurs to me that women may have felt less vulnerable in these schlafzimmer than if they had been sleeping in a room of their own. In a schlafzimmer, there were always others present, or likely to enter.

There are always exceptions and one night I retired early to my bed intending to rise in good time for work the following morning. Shortly after my head hit the pillow, I became aware that a couple had come into the room. One of them was Bernt, who I knew a little, a bit of an old-fashioned political activist I thought, definitely not tuned to the politics of Die Grünen — The Green Party — who were just starting to build their support amongst younger people in West Germany and, I supposed, were the coming thing. Bernt and the girl he had come in with lay down together. Either they hadn't noticed me or they chose to ignore me, for it was not long before I began to hear gentle moans of pleasure coming from their corner of the room. I thought it best to roll over and go to sleep leaving them to their lovemaking and have never thought the matter worthy of mention until this moment, when it seemed necessary to put on record that schlafzimmer were not entirely sex-free zones.

It is pretty clear from what I have said so far that the sexual behaviour which I was noticing fell very much into a heterosexual category. The house in which I was living, the bars and discos to which I was a visitor, did not represent a time-shifted out-post of Weimar Berlin, a cabaret of ostentatious behaviour, dress and makeup which challenged the conventions of sexual orientation and gender identity. And yet, I understood that young people who came to a city like Berlin and a household such as the one in which I had taken up residence often did so in search of the freedom to express something hitherto buried in their identity, so perhaps I was paying insufficient attention. The first direct challenge to my thinking on this matter came when a new group moved into the house, I believe because they had been evicted from another squat elsewhere in the city. There was a ground floor area of number 43 Willlibald-

Alexis-Strasse which was unoccupied, and they were invited to take this over. What was initially remarkable about their arrival was the speed and skill with which this group of ten or twelve individuals created a rather lovely living space out of a previously derelict fragment of the house. At the centre of this was a simple but beautiful wooden table, which members of the group had crafted themselves. I gathered that one of their number was in the business of repairing church organs, and I daresay he was at least one source of the woodworking talent on display.

Though they had their own living space, this new group quickly became integrated into the existing resident community and so I had plenty of opportunity to observe them. I soon realised that two of the men were gay. I saw them kiss openly in the street outside their front door, a kiss on the lips, not just quick and affectionate, but lingering. When I was at Reading University, I had known people who were openly gay but it is doubtless evidence that I had lived a sheltered life that I had never seen two men kiss one another so publicly and with such unrestrained affection.

I have a further memory of one of these two men, nothing to do with his sexual orientation or behaviour, but striking. As I think of him, I picture someone whose appearance was a little like Garry Kasparov, the great Russian chess champion, as a young man. This image is certainly a distortion which nevertheless has propagated in my mind over the years. There is a simple explanation for this. He and a group of others had been sitting in the main kitchen of the house. He had been playing chess with another member of the group, but the game was finished, and the board lay idle. I enjoy a game of chess. I suggested that we might play. I don't recall him speaking much English, but the look he gave me was not encouraging. However, he agreed to the contest, and I set the board out and opened the game. The distinguishing feature of his approach was that, when it was his turn, he took only a few moments to assess the state of the board before decisively making his move and then, very pointedly, returning to conversation with his friends. I was left to puzzle over the conundrum he had left me. The game moved inexorably in the direction of my defeat, if not humiliation. I thanked him for his trouble but did not bother to ask for a rematch.

Fritz

Someone I had got to know early in my Berlin adventure, was Renate. In the first week of my stay, she had invited me to join other members of the household to view a theatre production put on by a company of which she was a part. This took place in a kind of warehouse setting. I couldn't understand a word, but I was happy to recognise the originality in the way the production was staged and said as much. Renate showed interest in my situation, what I was doing in the house, and became someone to whom I could refer when I was struggling to understand what was happening around me.

I continued to be on good terms with her right to the conclusion of my stay in Berlin and like my parting from several others in the household, we spoke, no doubt over-optimistically, of possible future meetings and, with this thought in mind, exchanged addresses. I did eventually receive a letter from her. In this she told me that she had decided that she wished in future to live as a man and was now called "Fritz".

This took me by surprise, but from knowledge of Renate's earnest turn of mind, I knew that it was not a joke. I found it difficult to respond. I have never returned to Germany, still less to Berlin, and we were never to meet again. I should have liked to talk to Fritz about what this decision really meant. Did he want simply to experiment with a male identity on an occasional basis or was this a more fundamental attempt to be the male person he really felt he was. The woman I had known seemed unquestionably female, and so the revelation of this letter was disorienting, troubling even.

Let's Dance

Perhaps I would have been better attuned to these nuances of identity had I paid more attention to the importance of David Bowie in the mythology of Berlin. His early work, as is well known, consistently made a drama of his own identity, in ways that gave others the courage to examine the possibilities of who they might be. But Bowie's artistry and playfulness with identity and gender was not the complete explanation of his mythic status in Berlin; his connection with the city was personal, for he had made three of his most recent albums in the city and had released a German language version of the album, *Heroes*.

The album, *Let's Dance*, was released in April of 1983, the title song part of the soundtrack to my Berlin adventure. In June 1983, Bowie was to play a concert in West Berlin. I became aware of extraordinary interest in this event amongst my acquaintances. A couple of the chefs at Hotel Modial had secured tickets. The outdoor theatre, the Waldbühne, where the event was to be staged, seated over 20,000 people, but those tickets were hard to come by and I certainly didn't get my hands on one.

Apart from Bowie, I was eavesdropping on a great deal of other music, some of this, no doubt, the ephemera of the time. Berlin had its own homegrown punk band Einstürzende Neubauten; Nena had her hit *99 Luftballons* in that year, but to be honest, these are not representative of what I recall most vividly. There was a particular track by the Italian singer, Gianna Nannini which was played a great deal. She had a bluesy voice, a kind of Italian Janis Joplin. I have tried hard to find the song in question on the internet, but without success. I'd never heard of her before I turned up in Berlin and I never heard her music again after I left. Much of the music which people played in the house came from British or American bands though it was British bands with which I was not at all familiar that seemed to feature most. The Cure for example and, in particular, their song, *Object*, from their album *Three Imaginary Boys*; it was on repeat.

Objection

Speaking of objection, it was in the month of May that I was encouraged by my friends at Number Forty-Three to attend a street demonstration. I cannot recall the cause. It could have been one of many where I felt comfortably in alignment with my housemates, for example objecting to the deployment of US cruise missiles on European soil. Elaine and Deirdre were involved with demonstrations supporting the Women's Peace Camp at Greenham Common protesting against the delivery of US nuclear armed cruise missiles. The day of the Berlin protest was fine and there was a good turnout. For me though what was memorable was my encounter with a young Turkish man. I fell in step with him as I walked towards the gathering-point for the planned protest. Though he spoke no English, in some way it became clear that he too was demonstrating. He had been living long enough in West Berlin to speak some German and, goodness me, we seemed miraculously to be able to communicate. I won't say we discussed the meaning of life or the poetry of

Johann Wolfgang von Goethe. I expect I told my new Turkish friend where I came from, where I was staying, what I was doing and he in turn shared similar details of his own story. It was a thrilling moment; for the first time I had a sense that I was using German to communicate with another person. The fact that the person in question was Turkish hardly seemed important.

There's a Wall, So There is.

Perhaps inspired by this encounter, I thought the time had finally come to take a look at what lay on the other side of the Wall. I recall very little conversation about East Berlin in the house; no one offered to cross over with me for the day to be my guide. Still, one way or another, I had picked up a few ideas as to what might be worth taking a look at.

I arrived early in the day at Checkpoint Charlie which lay within walking distance of Kreuzberg. Having threaded my way through the border crossing under the unwelcoming gaze of the East German guards I emerged blinking into the sunlight with an injunction that I should be back there by ten pm or something inconvenient or worse would result — actually, I don't think any even veiled threats were made, but such was the reputation of East German border guards that there was no way I was going to take any chances.

I wandered into the city and found myself in a wide boulevard flanked by looming grey buildings, architecturally austere and clearly of post-war construction. There was little traffic, perhaps a few Trabants coughing their way along.

At the intersection I had reached there was a bookshop. Although I like to read, I have always found bookshops a little overwhelming, taunting me with so much that I will never read. Given that all these were in a language that I didn't understand, why was I even bothering to enter? I suppose I was hoping to gauge the extent to which this emporium was just a channel for state propaganda. It was in fact easy to find cheap editions of the works of Karl Marx and Vladimir Lenin, but it would be fair to say this was not the sum total of the stock.

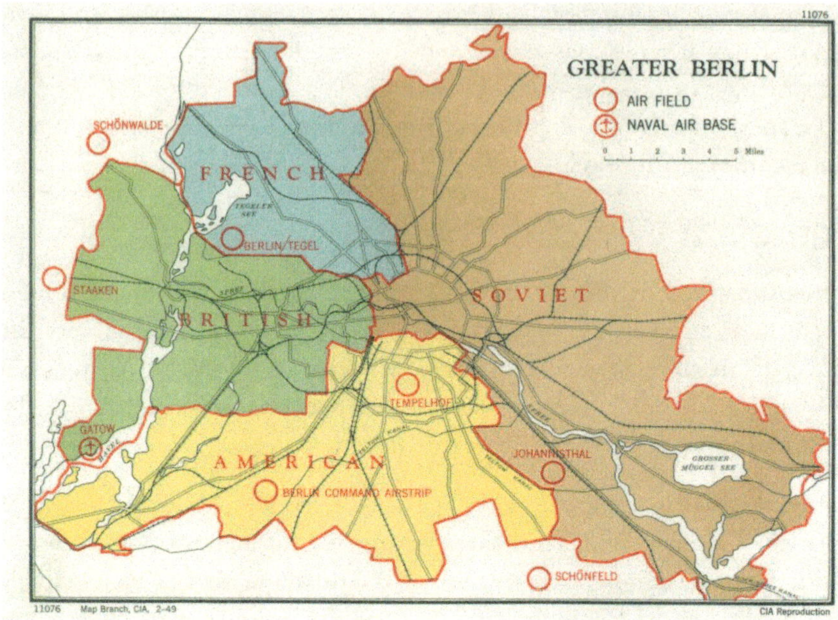

Berlin, as it was divided in 1949. Image available from Wikimedia.org.

Having satisfied my curiosity, I moved on and set out for Treptower Park, the site of the Soviet War Memorial commemorating the Russian soldiers who had lost their lives in the Battle of Berlin in April–May 1945. Whatever one might have thought of the Soviet Union and its allies in the Warsaw Pact, one could only be humbled by the sacrifice made by the Russian people in the defeat of Hitler. The memorial was on a grand scale, a huge sword-bearing Russian soldier looking implacably towards the horizon whilst protectively cradling a child in his left arm, a broken swastika at his feet. As I look now at photographs of that memorial, the heroic gaze of the Russian soldier depicted seems wilfully to overlook the widespread reports of rape, summary execution and pillage which shadow the capture of Berlin by the Red Army. For those in East Berlin the Russian victory was simultaneously a liberation from one tyranny and ensnarement in another, though perhaps that was not how it appeared at the time.

I caught a train back into the centre of the city. It was during this transit that I found myself sitting next to a group of leather clad teenagers who, in their various manifestations, boldly identified as punk rockers: spiky or dyed hair, piercings, torn jeans. I did my best to strike up some kind of conversation and to express my admiration for their very existence. They took a polite interest in me and when their stop came, we parted on amiable terms but don't think I had really managed to communicate just what an extraordinary and hopeful presence I thought they were.

Once back in the city I set off walking and found my way to a district which, like Kreuzberg, had escaped the allied bombing of the Second World War. The tenement style buildings were similar, the most striking distinction being the lack of graffiti, a commonplace on many of the buildings in those parts of West Berlin which were occupied by squatters. I was pleased to find a restaurant for my lunch. I can't remember what I ordered but if I was to say that the menu did not extend far beyond "kartoffelsalat, wurst, senf, und kohl," I wouldn't be far wide of the mark — that's potato salad, sausage, mustard and cabbage: delicious by the way. I ate well and remember the service as friendly.

In the afternoon I visited a museum on Unter den Linden, the grand thoroughfare which one could glimpse through the Brandenburg Gate from the western side. I am inclined to find museums something of an information overload but the fact that the German text accompanying the exhibits was well beyond my understanding allowed me just to wander and soak up the spectacle which I thought offered something impressive, better than the propaganda which I had expected.

On exit, I threaded my way back through a web of streets in the general direction of Checkpoint Charlie, until I found myself in quite a large crowd of people outside a theatre. In this melee, I got into conversation with a couple of lads who, like me, were visitors to East Berlin. They, however, were from the town of Brandenburg, situated a little over fifty miles west of the city. They spoke some English and were clearly as open as I was to our encounter. They invited me to join them for a meal. Over a roast chicken dinner, they shared with me their interest in the books of George Orwell and what they regarded as the deficiencies of the DDR — the Deutsche Demokratische Republik. We had a beer with our meal and the atmosphere in the restaurant seemed relaxed. Other than for the nagging concern that I must leave enough time to return to Checkpoint Charlie, my encounter with those two young men was very enjoyable. I had no sense that the Stasi were listening in on our conversation, but then I don't suppose the Stasi advertised their presence.

However carefree that chance meeting and the meal I shared with those lads from Brandenburg may have been, it was to be another six years before people, on both sides of the Berlin Wall, felt sufficiently emboldened to walk up to it, to clamber on to it, to start chipping lumps from it, to pull down entire sections and, as the world looked on mesmerised, to turn this emblem of the Cold War into a symbol of unity.

Eviction

Once every few weeks throughout the time I was in residence, a "plenum" would take place in the house. That was the name given to a meeting between the residents and members of a church organisation who were acting as intermediaries between us and the owners of the property. The object of these meetings was to establish a legal basis for us to continue living there. The owners no doubt had their eye on a future where higher value tenants would wish to live in Kreuzberg; then the current residents, with their commitment to subsistence, would simply be priced out of the market.

I dutifully turned up at these meetings though I had no real hope of following the arguments which were being worked through. There were long and intense discussions. They seemed amicable and appeared to be making progress. My understanding of what exactly had been agreed and what then happened is far from precise, but I find on Wikipedia a record which quotes from an article in *Der Spiegel*. With reference to 43 Willibald-Alexis-Strasse this reports that: "the Gossner Mission, an institution of the Evangelical Church, wanted to buy the house for the squatters at a price of 675,000 marks. Eyed suspiciously by the Interior Senator, the contract flourished until it was ready to be signed. But then, overnight on June 1st because of 'criminal activity' — Interior Senator Heinrich Lummer had the building vacated." Wikipedia goes on to say that "criminal activity … was obviously not present in Willibald-Alexis 43." Senator Lummer had simply used this charge as an excuse for the eviction. That pretty much fits with my recollection of events, though in fact the eviction occurred whilst I was at my work, and I returned to find the doors barred.

Squatters are a resourceful bunch. I believe many in the household found places in other squats. I was invited to move to a house just along the street. It was a sad and frustrating conclusion for those who had fought hard to create a sustainable framework within which a community might flourish, but no one, I believe, ended up sleeping rough.

Homeward Bound

My new accommodation offered little more than sleeping quarters. Before I had properly settled into this new address, I received a message from my brother Peter in Dumfries. Michael was not well. My parents were struggling. My help was needed at home.

My plan originally had been to spend a year in West Berlin. I was just settling in. And then there was that offer from Hucky and his friends to join them on a holiday to Greece. That seemed tempting. And yet in the end I let all that go and headed for home. The call had come at just the right moment with the breakup of the household and before I had become more seriously embedded in a West Berlin life. I explained my situation to the friends I had made in the house. We said our goodbyes and, as suddenly as I had arrived, I was gone. I'd say that kind of walk-on part was quite a common feature of life in West Berlin in that era.

I made my way to Hamburg, dropped in to see Heather and Reiner and then journeyed north to take a ferry from Esbjerg to Newcastle, and from there back to Dumfries. With a little trepidation I made my way to Elaine's front door and was pleased to receive a warm welcome, but I did not stay long in Dumfries and having touched base with Elaine and Peter and Deirdre, was off again via Stranraer to Warrenpoint.

Michael was indeed in a disturbed frame of mind. It was difficult even to be in his company. Conversation was never straightforward, always a riddle. Even walking with him down the street into town was a challenge. No mutually agreed pace seemed possible. He would not make eye contact. Gradually though, this more acute phase of what was happening to him seemed to run its course and by September something more like a settled pattern of behaviour became established and more productive conversations were possible. I never really did get a clear idea of what had precipitated his most recent difficulties, just a few clues about a friendship with a local girl that had not worked out as he had hoped.

In the July of that summer, it was my thirtieth birthday and a package arrived to mark the occasion. It was from Elaine, a pair of gloves that she had knitted for me, but not just any gloves. These were knitted in a Sanquhar pattern, midge and fly to be exact. Sanquhar is a mining community situated about thirty miles north of Dumfries. It has a very distinctive set of traditional knitting patterns, built up from a grid in which are contained a variety of motifs, the finished article, generally in black and white, and in the case of gloves, with the initials of the intended owner set into the inside of the cuff. There they were: SPS. I was touched of course, but really it was my mother who was most impressed and that, in turn, gave me cause for thought.

When I was about six years old, my mother had taught me to knit. There is a photograph of me sitting back-to-back with Alan Masterton, who lived just down the road in Balmoral Park, both of us knitting with intense concentration. I don't know what Alan did with this skill, but for me it was a passing interest, and an ability which I lost. My mother clearly thought that the maker of those Sanquhar gloves deserved due respect. I was eventually to wear them out but regret sometimes that I did not take more account of my mother's judgement of the matter and put them in a frame on the wall.

A Legend in Blue and White Stripes

In August 1983 Michael's frame of mind was sufficiently improved for us to set off to watch a pre-season friendly between Newry Town and Shamrock Rovers. As a teenager I had occasionally joined the small crowds which went to the Showgrounds to watch the Town play. Regardless of their lowly status in the B-Division, I knew that my footballing talents would never win me a place in the team but that didn't prevent me from daydreaming occasionally that I might become their manager and lead them to promotion to the Irish League and then eventually glory in Europe — but let's not get carried away with this fantasy.

The real thrill of the match in question was that, in the twilight of his career, George Best had been inveigled, for that game only, into playing for Newry Town. It seemed hardly believable but, on a lovely summer evening, Michael and I turned up at the appointed hour to watch as Shamrock Rovers warmed up at one end in their green and white hoops and at the other end in the blue and white stripes of Newry Town was George, swapping passes with his temporary teammates. He was perhaps carrying a little more weight than in his heyday and who knows what he had been doing earlier in the day by way of match preparation, but he seemed in good shape.

I have searched hard on the internet to see if I could find the result of that game, but though the event is noted in various places, I have been unable to confirm a final score, suggesting, perhaps, that was the least of anyone's concern. Surely the man from the *Newry Reporter* was there? My own recollection is 3-2 in favour of Shamrock Rovers, with the Town's first goal being scored by George from the penalty spot. But maybe I am just imagining that.

What I do remember was that in the second half George's progress towards goal was halted by an over-enthusiastic tackle just outside the right-hand edge of the penalty area, not far from the touchline where Michael and I were standing. The whistle blew for a free kick. It was a position where a shot at goal would have been possible, but a little too close to curve a ball over a wall of defending players. George had another idea; almost in the same moment the kick had been awarded, he had taken it, gliding the ball across to a player in blue and white who stood loose at the other corner of the box and who had time to calmly fire a shot low into the back of the net past a wrong-footed defence and a bemused keeper. It was an unspectacular assist but nevertheless a little piece of magic which I felt privileged to witness.

* * *

As the summer progressed Michael started to play his guitar again and one day, when Mrs Ferris was in for her weekly visit to help my mother with the household chores, we asked him to play for us. We sat in the kitchen as he gave us his version of Earl Montgomery's *One of These Days*. It is a song full of self-doubt and anguish yet suffused with hope for a better future, for peace of mind. It was very hard not to imagine that Michael was singing about himself. Suffice to say, he had many trials still to endure and yet he did eventually find something that seemed very much like peace of mind in his life. I will say more about that in due course.

7: Dumfries

Small-Town Loner

The small-town loner has struck again,
He's a cowboy on the loose
A foot soldier to the end
And he takes orders from nobody,
Or maybe someone
He'd like to be.

Standing in the doorway he reloads,
In his battleground
His head explodes.
There among the fragments of the innocents,
Scattered on the playground,
The evidence.

The paper shows a picture
Of his high school class,
As we search for his future
In his past,
Just a quiet boy
Maybe a little strange,
Dreaming of a life
Out on the range.

No one noticed
As he entered by the gate,
Just a small-town boy
With no enemies to hate,
But he's the soldier
In your street
And he marches
To his heart beat.

1996

Whereof One Cannot Speak, Thereof One Must Be Silent

When things had at last settled in Warrenpoint I returned to Dumfries, initially living with Peter and Deirdre and helping out with the refurbishment of their house. The interest rate on the mortgage was high at nearly 10% and the project under stress but it wasn't until a year or two later that they were obliged to sell up and move somewhere more affordable.

I had no thought of returning to Germany and began to look for work, preferably something that might form the basis of a career, though I still lacked any clear idea as to what this might be. In the autumn of 1983, national unemployment was running at over 19% for those under 25 years old and over 8% for those over 25. In a small rural Scottish town such as Dumfries, the situation was, if anything, bleaker still. Whilst signing on, I decided to look for voluntary work, perhaps supposing this might open up other employment opportunities. I started visiting a home for people with physical disabilities, run by the Leonard Cheshire charity. It was in a former country house, Carnsalloch, not far from where I was staying with Peter and Deirdre. Once a week I would cycle there and spend the afternoon doing whatever small tasks were asked of me. When there was nothing for me to do, I was encouraged to socialise with the residents. Over the weeks, however, I became aware that there was a resident, Craig, who was not coming out of his room into the communal social areas. He was studying with the Open University and, it seemed, preferred his own company, though it later became clear to me that he was quite well-connected with the Carnsalloch residents, indeed an important spokesperson for their community.

One day I was approached by a member of staff and asked to go to Craig's room and replace a lightbulb. I was pleased to have the opportunity to find out a little more about this mysterious recluse. On arrival in Craig's room, I introduced myself and explained why I was there but took the opportunity to ask him about his studies. He was taking a degree in Philosophy. I had studied Philosophy for a couple of terms at Reading, and so was bold enough to quiz him further about what he was working on at the time. Our conversation went on for the rest of my shift and, in subsequent weeks, I just went to Carnsalloch to visit Craig.

Craig had been an aircraft engineer but had broken his neck in a motorcycle accident. Though he still had some use of his upper arms, his dexterity had been damaged. Before his accident, he had played the piano, but that ability was lost. He had learned, however, to work the computer which sat in front of him. Typing an essay was not a simple exercise but this did not prevent him from eventually being awarded a first-class honours degree.

Dumfries and Galloway — Extract from Ordnance Survey quarter-inch sheet 8, Solway Firth, published in 1966. Full map image available from Wikimedia.org.

Craig eventually moved to a flat in Dumfries, but whilst he was still living in Carnsalloch I continued to visit him there. He was a member of a whisky club and had accumulated quite a collection of bottles, each with a green and gold label stating the alcohol content and the provenance of the contents. Part of the ritual of our weekly meeting was to sample one of these. He would pour me a generous measure and our talk would range untidily over whatever had taken our interest in the world of philosophy, politics, literature, music and trivia, though I was probably more interested in trivia than Craig. After one of these sessions, I would climb aboard my bicycle and sail home in a state of mild euphoria. The afternoon drinking tailed off eventually, but it was pleasing while it lasted.

Though he did not necessarily share enthusiasm for some of my more eccentric ideas, Craig was to become a significant ally in the development of various schemes which seemed important to me at the time, whether it was a submission to the *Opsahl Commission on Northern Ireland*, published in 1992, or my belief that updating songs from the Orange and the Green traditions might be a useful contribution to the deflation of the mythologies they continued to support. I called this project *All That Guff*, a title inspired by Hamish Henderson's cycle of poems, *Elegies for the Dead in Cyrenaica.* Henderson had served as an Intelligence Officer in the North African campaign of the Second World War. It was during this period he wrote his *Elegies.* He had lived in Germany before the war and was a fluent German speaker. In the opening elegy he speaks of the German dead whose effects it was his job to process:

> *There were our own, there were the others.*
> *Their deaths were like their lives, human and animal.*
> *There were no gods and precious few heroes.*
> *What they regretted when they died had nothing to do*
> *with*
> *race and leader, realm indivisible,*
> *laboured Augustan speeches or vague imperial heritage.*
> *(They saw through that guff before the axe fell.)*

Craig, in turn, would attempt to explain to me the challenges of the mind-body problem in philosophy, the importance of Daniel Dennett's contribution to this and other such thorny matters as "*Why We Have Free Will Even if Determinism is True.*" I still have the pamphlet he wrote on that subject including an epigraph from Kris Kristofferson's *Me and Bobby McGee* with its memorably brief definition of freedom, nothing left to lose. Ludwig Wittgenstein was Craig's philosophical hero. I can't say I ever really got to grips with Wittgenstein, but this was not for want of instruction on the matter.

Craig was a big chap, physically strong, but his health had obviously been compromised by his accident and he was vulnerable to respiratory infections. His death, following a short illness in October 2006, was a shock and a great loss to me personally.

Keeping Nithsdale Tidy

So far as paid employment was concerned, I was ready to try anything, and a few opportunities did come my way in the years that remained of the 1980s. A couple of these were to prove significant in the longer term. The first was what passed for an environmental project in the UK of that era. It was called

Keep Nithsdale Tidy, Nithsdale being the administrative district of which Dumfries was a part. It involved teaching primary school children the benefits of tidiness in the public realm. The watchwords were "Reduce, Recycle, Reuse." This was something I could endorse, even if the messaging trailed quite a long way behind that of the German Green Party in which I had become interested whilst in Berlin. I was ready, however, to set aside my reservations about the teaching profession to accept this offer of work and would have to say, the experience was an enjoyable one. I made good friends in the team in which I was working and would even admit to having some fun in the classroom.

An initial obstacle to my employment was the Middle School teaching qualification I had gained in England which was judged by the General Teaching Council for Scotland to be unworthy of the Scottish system. The concept of Middle Schools, with an intake spanning the upper primary and lower secondary age-groups, had never caught on north of the border. This summary rejection of my qualification was oddly reminiscent of my mother's experience when she sought to use her teaching qualification from the Republic of Ireland in the North. When I was old enough to go to school, she tried to return to teaching. The Northern Ireland Education Authority refused to recognise her qualification. This problem was never resolved and so in the end she took on work supporting the home schooling of a little boy. Though less lucrative, this proved rewarding in other ways. Adrian had spina bifida, wore callipers on his legs and could only walk with the aid of crutches. At the time, there was no provision in the local primary schools for his education. Though his family did not have a history of high academic achievement, his elder sister Margaret was a talented linguist, and he too clearly had the potential to go far academically. Eventually he went away to a special boarding school, but he had ongoing health problems. Years later, as my mother became unwell, Adrian's mother started coming weekly to help with the household chores. That was Mrs Ferris who was to become an important friend of and support to our family.

* * *

Following my return from Berlin to Warrenpoint, Mrs Ferris told me a story intended to explain the strength of her religious faith. In his early teenage years Adrian became unwell and was taken into hospital in Belfast. Mrs Ferris planned to visit him, travelling to the city from Newry by bus. During her journey, she started to feel unwell and to experience a very acute abdominal pain. The pain got worse. She felt she could not bear it, feared she might collapse, but she carried on and made her way to the hospital. As she approached Adrian's bedside she was in desperation, not wanting to meet with her son in this distressed state. It was at that moment of extremity that she involuntarily uttered the words: "Dear God! Take this pain away!" Immediately, as she told the story, the pain disappeared and she was at Adrian's bedside, able to comfort him as she had wanted. What moved me about this story was not the benign intercession of the Almighty, as Mrs Ferris understood the matter. I saw only the power of a mother's love for her son.

Adrian's death, when he was still a teenager, was a shock to us all. I remember the morning Mrs Ferris came to tell us the news, her grief as she arrived at our front door, audible to me in the upstairs room where I sat, like a tearing of the clear air of the morning.

Ho mo leannan bhoidheach!

On my return to Dumfries, Elaine and I started to see one another regularly. Sometimes she would stay over with me at Peter and Deirdre's house in the countryside just north of Dumfries. Sometimes I would stay at her flat in the town, and often at weekends we would go up to Glasgow to visit her friends there. It was probably on one such adventure that we went to see Runrig, and I shared the unique intoxication of being part of an audience joining in with Donnie Munro as he sang *Loch Lomond* in his peculiarly beautiful tenor voice, the floor of the Barrowlands Ballroom seeming to bounce gently, and a little alarmingly, under the rhythmic sway of the packed audience. To imbibe the full experience, I needed Elaine to explain the meaning of the song and the story of the two Scottish soldiers imprisoned south of the border, one of whom, the singer, knows that he is dying from his wounds:

> *You'll tak' the high road and I'll tak' the low road,*
> *And I'll be in Scotland afore ye.*

And then there's that Gaelic chanting that Runrig add to the middle section — *Ho mo leannan bhoidheach* — Oh my beautiful sweetheart. It was a powerful brew, and I drank it deeply.

Life was good and worries few though lack of steady employment remained a nagging concern. Elaine seemed prepared to forgive this deficiency. It wasn't long before we decided to amalgamate our record collections and I joined her in her flat in town.

At that time Elaine owned a Sony Hi-Fi system, the components of which were arranged on shelving contained in a glass-fronted cabinet. I was impressed and moved to write a song about this important piece of our furniture, but mysteriously the words have gone missing. I can only remember the chorus:

Let me turn on the lights of your stereo,
It's a small town this, but I can't think of a better show,
We could stay at home and just watch the glow,
Here in the dark, with the lights turned low.

No doubt the fact that I was committing to a life in Dumfries had some influence on my parents' decision to leave Warrenpoint and settle in Castle Douglas, eighteen miles west of Dumfries. They had lived in the Newry area for over thirty years and had many friends there. Given my mother's declining health, their decision to move was not taken lightly, but there were obvious advantages. An obstacle was that Michael had started to train as a piano tuner in Belfast, but eventually a comparable course was found in an Edinburgh college. He succeeded in getting a place there and so relocated to Scotland with my mother and father.

Work in Progress

Keep Nithsdale Tidy was just a temporary measure, and I was obliged to cast about for other ways of earning my keep. Opportunities of various kinds came my way. I took advantage of the Enterprise Allowance Scheme promoted by the Thatcher Government. This offered £40 a week for a year to assist an individual with a plausible business idea to get their enterprise off the ground, and so for a couple of years I was a self-employed gardener. I lacked the green fingers to do the things that proper gardeners are capable of but there were plenty of customers near at hand who simply wanted their grass cut, their flower beds tidied up regularly and a little occasional tree pruning. Mostly they were used to such work being done by pensioners who were happy to accept pocket money for the privilege. This competition made it difficult to earn a living wage, but I kept at it for a couple of years before moving on to several other employment options. For a while I was a support worker in a residential home for adults with learning difficulties, many of whom were being moved out of institutional settings into homes in the community as part of Margaret Thatcher's Care in the Community programme, a fine idea I thought, had it been adequately funded. I liked the work, but I was only filling in for someone on a maternity leave and so, soon enough was once again an unemployment statistic. I wore a badge at the time to declare myself "One of the Three Million," this being the number of people on the dole between 1983 and 1986, about 10% of the UK population. Other opportunities did come my way, however, and I established some kind of stability of income and employment when I took a job as a Special Needs Auxiliary in Elmbank, a unit which took in young people excluded from secondary schools in the region. My experience as a youth worker and as a volunteer at Ramoan in Ballycastle clearly had given me relevant experience for this kind of work. The fact that my colleagues were teachers and significantly better paid did not trouble me even though I had a comparable level of training. I worked happily there for three years until the logic of making better use of my teacher training qualification became impossible to ignore.

Ma

Michael's adjustment to the move was troubled, but eventually he settled into his piano tuning course and completed his training. My father was not slow to build networks of support for my mother and to establish a new life for himself in Scotland. Influenced by my Uncle Bill who I had visited in Canada, my mother had become a Christian Scientist, a religion which makes a strong link between religious faith and physical health. My father, as usual, kept his own council but always supported my mother in what she was doing and enabled her to take part in the Christian Science community in Dumfries. They kept in touch with old friends and family; however, my mother's multiple sclerosis was progressing and she was now in a wheelchair. Worse though, her hearing loss was preventing her from properly making new friends. Even within the family she was finding it difficult to follow the conversations going on around her. Perhaps as a compensation for her isolation from such casual exchanges, she began to express more of an interest in music than previously. Indeed, she was apt to burst into song, mostly the same song, I would have to say, *Danny Boy*. She had never sung like this previously and I think may have felt inhibited by the mythology that all musical talents in the family came via the Shellard line. Ma compensated for her lack of repertoire by demanding that Michael and I should sing something, anything really, but apart from *Danny Boy*, the song I most remember her calling for was *Passing Through.*

I saw Jesus on the cross on a hill called Calvary,
"Do you hate mankind for what they done to you?"
He said, "Talk of love not hate, things to do — it's getting late
I've so little time and I'm only passin' through."

Following a dip into the Old Testament and a meeting with Adam as he leaves the Garden of Eden, the time travelling singer recalls further encounters, with Franklin Roosevelt and George Washington. Each of these notables offers a distinctively quirky message, but always with the same chorus:

Passin' through, passin' through
Sometimes happy, sometimes blue
Glad that I ran into you
Tell the people that you saw me passin' through.

Jackie Copeland

I didn't usually sing songs that I had written myself for my mother, but there was an exception. In 1986 I listened to an interview on BBC Radio 4 with a veteran of the Somme from Northern Ireland. He reflected on how he and his friend had joined up to fight in France aged sixteen years old, and how his friend had been killed at the Somme. The fact that he himself had gone on to live a long and happy life made him reflective on the random nature of what had happened. I found the interview moving and wrote a song based on what I had heard. I called it *Jackie Copeland.*

Jackie Copeland he was my good friend
When we went to fight on France's field
And I lived on to this good age
But Jackie, just sixteen was killed
And I have lived a good life now
That might have just as well been his
Many times I've thought on Jackie's fate
And wonder where the justice is.

The Battle of the Somme is an event of particular significance for unionists in Northern Ireland owing to the participation in the battle of the 36th Ulster Division, and the heavy losses they sustained in July 1916. Many Catholic Irish also lost their lives in the First World War, but that reality was obscured in retrospect by the 1916 Easter Rising and the War of Independence which led to the creation of the Irish Free State in 1921. The song I wrote imagines the dilemma faced by soldiers who returned to Ulster following the Armistice in 1918.

Well, I returned to civil war
And Ireland was divided
By a conflict to this very day
Remaining undecided
And I wondered what would Jackie think,
And would strain to hear his voice,
Hoping counsel of a wiser mind
Would help me make my choice.

In writing this song I was no doubt influenced by the Scottish-Australian singer, Eric Bogle, and his two great songs of the First World War, *The Green Fields of France* and *The Band Played Waltzing Matilda.* I don't imagine my mother was aware of either, but I knew she would be sympathetic to the themes of the song I had written and interested in the fact that I had used Mrs Ferris's family name of Copeland for the sixteen-year-old boy who had been killed, memory of whom is the touchstone of the song.

When I had finished, my mother turned to my father and asked the meaning of the word "acrimonies" which I had used in the penultimate verse of the song. It was a word I would not have expected her to struggle with and I thought her difficulty not a good sign in the progression of her illness.

Now Europe is at peace
With our foe become our friend
Yet we still distrust our neighbours,
Can't let old acrimonies end
But I have seen the folly
And the fault on every side
As blood still runs on Ulster streets
For the sake of foolish pride.

Clan Foley

Evidence of musicality on the Foley side of the family was provided when Ma's brother Uncle Bill and Aunty Mary made the trip from Toronto. Bill was happy to sing for us. My mother's younger sisters, Myrtle, Olive and Rose were also present at that gathering of the Foleys, having travelled from their homes in Bury St. Edmunds, Leicester and, in Rose's case, Queensland Australia. As Rose departed, she spoke to me with a characteristic directness. "I don't think I'll see your mother again." She was correct in this surmise.

The final period of my mother's life was punctuated by occasional crises which would land her in hospital, but each time she would rally and return home to be cared for by my father until her death in September 1989.

Peter, Michael, Da, Ma, Deirdre with my niece Katie, Stephen, my nephew Joe with dinosaur, Elaine. Photo taken 17th September 1989, Inishowen, Dumfries.

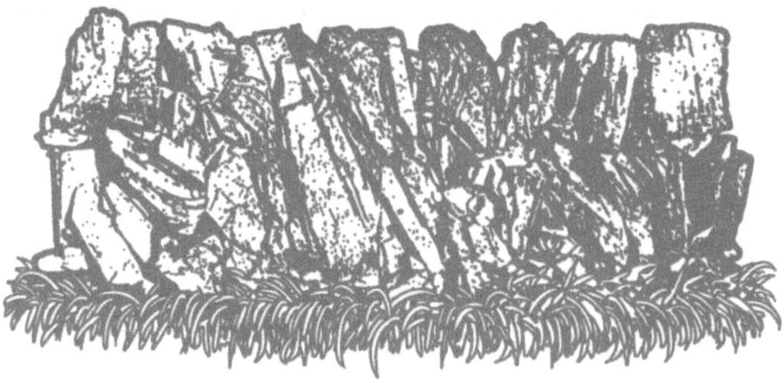

8: Accidental Teacher

Hare Crosses the Border

Somewhere south of Slieve Gullion
In a long line of broken curves and fluid turns,
Hare crosses the Border.
Perhaps hesitating for a moment,
But not as fox hesitates or badger hesitates,
Hare lopes forward instinctively
Into his inescapable future
All senses scoping the hazards of his universe,
Crossing and crossing again
The imperceptible line that separates human from human.

2012

Elmbank

At the time my mother died I was still working in Elmbank with pupils excluded from the region's schools. I had some reservations about the regime, but I liked being part of the team and admired the resilience of my colleagues in the face of what I knew to be challenging work. I could have happily remained there, but of course I was on the lookout for other options which might be suited to my abilities and make a better contribution to the mortgage which Elaine and I had taken on.

The fact that I had a teacher training qualification was a subject occasionally discussed with my colleagues and an interesting possibility emerged from this; though I couldn't be a subject teacher in a secondary school in Scotland, it seemed that my GTC registration as a Scottish primary school teacher would serve as a Learning Support qualification at secondary level. I didn't initially make any serious effort to explore this option but then, in October 1990, I gathered that a crisis had arisen in the Learning Centre in Sanquhar Academy, just thirty miles north of Dumfries. One of the staff had gone off on maternity leave, and all efforts to find a temporary replacement had failed. I was given encouragement to apply.

Though Sanquhar is a Royal Burgh of some antiquity, the community of which it is part had been going through difficulties owing to the closure of the coal mines which had, for many years, been an important employer in the area. The desperation of Sanquhar Academy for someone to fill the Learning Centre post provided me with an opportunity. I went up there on a Friday and was interviewed by the Head Teacher. He was affable and welcoming. He showed me around and seemed interested in the answers I gave to his questions. Could I start on Monday? I said "Yes," and set off back to Dumfries.

I made an early start on the Monday to be sure to arrive in good time to meet with Flora, who was in charge of the Learning Centre. It was principally for pupils who, it was felt, could make better progress outside the framework of a conventional timetable. There could be many reasons for this, but a good number of those I worked with had difficulties with reading, or with speech or had some other conspicuous impairment to their ability to learn. Flora was in charge and was quick to give me encouragement for the way in which I was working. I spent a very agreeable three months there and it is possible that period might have been extended had it not been for the fact that I was offered a similar post in Dumfries Academy starting in the New Year.

I accepted this offer, the most obvious advantage over Sanquhar Academy being that I could cycle to work in about ten minutes, a definite improvement on the thirty-mile trek to Sanquhar. The emphasis of my work was different from that in the Learning Centre in Sanquhar. I was deployed to other teachers' classes, providing support to pupils who were struggling. Usually there were three or four identified, but I could offer help to anyone in the class if that was needed. I liked working across the full range of subjects and observing the diverse strategies by which teachers managed their classes. However, I felt, if anything, a little under-employed. At the risk of being disloyal to my Learning Support colleagues, I would say the preparation required for what I had to do was not demanding. I just had to turn up in the class. I envied those colleagues who stood up and delivered the lessons. It was a more challenging role and yet I had a hankering for the performance involved. When a job came up in Dumfries and Galloway College, working with students with Learning Difficulties, but planning and delivering classes, I was interested and attracted by the fact that I would be working in Further Education. I applied, was interviewed and offered the post. My start was in March 1992 and the college was to be my employer until my retirement in June 2020, my final term there overlapping with the first lockdown of the Covid-19 pandemic.

First We Take Manhattan

When I reflect on the more than 25 years I spent working at Dumfries and Galloway College, I am reminded of the Leonard Cohen song, *First We Take Manhattan*, in which he speaks of the "sentence" of boredom exacted for becoming part of a system and then attempting to change it from within. My reluctance to become a teacher in the first place was based on a view of education which seemed less applicable in a Further Education context where students, at least in theory, had chosen to be present; but in any case, to call my subsequent experience "boredom" would not be fair. True, there were long and often pointless meetings; there was stifling and burgeoning bureaucracy designed to hold lecturers such as myself to account and constantly shifting technology, which was either, out of date or a challenge to work with because, occasionally, it was brand new. And yet, what comes to mind most readily in my recollection is the good humour and resourcefulness that I experienced daily. Whilst the Shangri-La of retirement opens fresh possibilities — such as writing a memoir — I miss my colleagues and I miss the students. Not every colleague was a friend to me or every student easy to work with. In the span of that teaching career, I had a few challenging encounters on both of those fronts. But overwhelmingly I consider myself blessed to have had the career I did. And for goodness' sake, I wasn't paid half badly for it and the holidays were generous, though they never quite matched the glorious expanse of summer holidays when I was still at school.

Da

Following the death of my mother, my father had rapidly concluded that he should sell up in Castle Douglas and move to Dumfries. He bought a former council house just around the corner from where Elaine and I were living at the time and with his usual efficiency and lack of sentimentality was soon installed as our near neighbour. About this time Michael finished his piano tuning apprenticeship in Thornaby in northeast England and returned to live for a period with Da, though he was soon to find his way into other accommodation. In a couple of instances these billets seemed less than ideal but eventually he accepted the offer of a Housing Association flat in the town and at that point his life started to change for the better.

For my father, living in Dumfries was an arrangement that worked well. Peter and Deirdre and their two children, Joe and Katie also lived close by, and Michael was in walking distance. We saw a good deal of one another and yet my father did not rely on us and was quick to establish an independent existence. He tried out different churches, eventually settling on Maxwelltown West Presbyterian Church, a break with the Church of Ireland and the Episcopalian tradition which had defined his religious practice hitherto. Maxwelltown West was close to where he was living; he could walk there on a Sunday, and he liked the Minister officiating. He continued to be a member of the Dumfries Choral Society, which he had joined on arrival in Castle Douglas. We had been concerned, at the outset, as the Dumfries Choral had auditions, and by the time he applied to join, he was in his late seventies and his baritone voice not as strong as it had once been. He was accepted and attendance at the weekly practices was one of his great pleasures. He became something of a spectacle in the neighbourhood, still riding his bicycle which, by that stage, he had further customised with a new handlebar arrangement, essentially an upturned version of drop bars, but in his case optimised for an erect sitting position from which he could survey all that he passed. Despite the obvious appeal of gears to a mathematician he had previously resisted such newfangledness, but finally caved in and accepted the logic of a five-speed hub. When concerts for the Choral Society were scheduled, he would hang a hand-written notice of the event from the crossbar of his bike and advertise it wherever he went.

When he had been a teacher and we were pupils at Newry High School, it was behaviour of this kind which could make him a difficult father to own up to, but by the time of his arrival in Dumfries, the three of us had come to terms with such eccentricity, perhaps even begun to recognise similar impulses in our own character. They say you don't ever get a second chance to give a first impression, but my father didn't appear to suffer any detriment from his idiosyncrasies and made good friends with his neighbours and with members of the Choral Society and the church.

I made a point of going in to see him at least once each week and we would sit and talk. His attendance at church, I could see, was for social reasons; he liked being part of a community. However, belief in God was another matter; he didn't really have time for the certainties that defined much religious belief and said what really interested him was the mystery. As he grew older his mind, if anything, became more open. For me, those weekly meetings were not a duty; I looked forward to our conversations and felt I was getting to know him better than I had done at any previous stage of my life.

We had snow on Christmas Day 1995. The family gathered at Peter and Deirdre's home for our Christmas Dinner. By about three o'clock we were in recovery from our main meal. The day was perfect; cold, a clear blue sky, no wind. Peter proposed we go tobogganing. We crossed the road to the golf course and found a lovely slope on which to enjoy our sport. Da came along, I thought, as a spectator. He was then aged eighty-four, but still walking and cycling. When he got the chance in summer, he would find a bend in the Nith and go for a swim, or a bathe, as he liked to call it. I only ever remember teenagers doing this so close to the town. Bathing was, I think for him, one of life's essential pleasures; I assumed, however, that he was beyond tobogganing, but I was mistaken. The experience of watching our fun was just too much for him and he became impatient with his role as spectator. He made it clear that he wished to take a turn. Tobogganing is not a high-risk sport but still, I wondered, was this a good idea? He shot off down the hill, hit a bump not far from the bottom and came off. After a few moments he clambered to his feet, clearly undamaged and delighted, though a single turn was sufficient to satisfy his spirit on that occasion.

Early one morning in January 1997 I got a phone call from him asking me to come round. He was experiencing a severe pain in his lower back. The worst of this seemed to pass quickly but he knew that the matter was serious. A visit to the doctor and a scan confirmed that he had a growth in one of his kidneys and it was agreed that it should be removed. He had to wait until the end of June for the operation. Whatever interim treatments were provided he seemed well during the waiting period and optimistic that the outcome of his operation would be good. Initially it seemed to have gone well, but on return home it became increasingly apparent that there was something very wrong with his health; He was experiencing an unpleasant taste all the time and feeling nauseous.

He was getting some help in the house but continued to be very independent, though it was then that he reported to me he was finding it difficult to get out of his bath, a weekly ritual. As I was just round the corner I would attend and wait while he took his leisure and then would assist him in clambering out. I was at that time making some effort to build on the piano lessons I had resigned from as a teenager and attempting to learn some simple arrangements of classical pieces. I thought that this would please him and whilst I was waiting remember attempting Debussy's Claire de Lune which I could more or less get through without stumbling. He expressed some appreciation of this accomplishment. It was in reality the highpoint of my piano playing and not long after I decided that being even a moderately competent pianist was going to demand more time than I was prepared to give up to the task.

My father's decline continued over the summer and into the autumn and it would not be entirely wrong to say that, after a short illness, he passed away early in the month of November: not entirely wrong, but wrong, nevertheless.

When I was still in my twenties, Da took me aside to converse about the matter of his own mortality. He was at the time perfectly healthy and in good spirits but let me know that if he were ever to become terminally ill, he would consider ending his own life, the determining factor being its quality. He made it clear that it was a subject he was very ready to talk about and, occasionally over the years he would discreetly remind us of his settled view.

Peter went to his house on the evening of the fifth of November 1997 and having knocked and received no response, used a key to gain entry, but was immediately confronted by a notice in my father's hand, advising caution. Peter guessed what this meant and came to get me so we could go in together. We hurried back to his front door, well aware of what to expect. He lay on his bed, one might say peacefully, there being no evidence of either physical or emotional trauma, but he was clearly deceased. On his open desk lay a number of documents; his will, a letter intended to be read following his death and some other notes including a list of questions to his doctor, concerning the symptoms he was experiencing. This was very upsetting, and yet nothing more than what we had anticipated. The letter he left was, in part, a reflection on the many things which he felt were positive in his life; he spoke lovingly of my mother and of his close family. He mentioned periods of difficulty, most particularly the tragic death of his younger brother Dell, when they were both in their twenties. In conclusion, he spoke of how, as a young man, he had enjoyed going to dances, but had always preferred to leave a little early when the event was still in full swing; he did not like hanging on until the bitter end.

In circumstances where there is a sudden death at home, a police and medical investigation is legally mandated. As part of this enquiry all of the documents to which I have referred were taken away by the police. The formalities were managed sensitively and, when the due process was complete, the documents were returned to us and we were discreetly made aware that those officers who had handled the case were very respectful for what my father had done.

As I mentioned earlier, it was the evening of the fifth of November when Peter and I discovered my father had taken his life. As we entered the house that night there was a bonfire blazing in a nearby park and fireworks bursting in the skies close by. I don't imagine that this was an intended theatrical framing for the event, but it certainly has made the anniversary an easy one to remember.

Three Variations on the Theme of Marriage

For twenty years, Elaine and I had been living together and saw no reason to change this status. I was happy, when speaking of our relationship, to refer to her as "my partner," and she was similarly content with this. In 2004 we began to take a closer look at the financial implications of our situation. At that time there was no such thing as a Civil Partnership which might offer the equivalent legal status and financial security which were available to a married couple. We decided that the time had come to do something about this.

We did not wish our marriage to involve any of the traditional trappings and were confident we could accomplish the necessary without telling anyone beyond those required to officiate and record the details. We both enjoyed the clandestine and unorthodox character of our plans. The ceremony was set for the registry office in Gretna which is situated just over thirty miles east of Dumfries. The detail that I liked best was that the necessary witnesses could be found on the street outside the office.

When our big day came, we dressed soberly, attended in good time, secured our witnesses, said all that was required by the celebrant, and the deed was done. Following the event, we made our way to Carlisle and treated ourselves to a meal out. It was a romantic occasion, for several more years, very much our secret.

Peter and Deirdre had been thinking along similar lines and some years later invited Elaine and I to be witness to their marriage which took place in the registry office in Dumfries, again, a happy event.

In 2005 Michael announced that he was getting married. Following his return from Thornaby to Dumfries he worked informally as a piano tuner whilst also developing friendships in a community of people, some of whom had, like himself, experienced mental health challenges. There is no question that he derived immense support from being part of this informal social network. Increasingly he became more assured, and then, after some years of this more settled life, he met Ruth. She had previously been married and had a grown family. They became inseparable and eventually decided to formalise their relationship. As Michael said to me at the time, "In for a penny, in for a pound."

My mother and father would of course have been delighted by this turn of events, but there were others in our extended family who knew Michael well and who made the journey on the 15th of April, to join us for the celebration; my mother's younger sisters, Olive and Myrtle, my cousin Cathryn and her husband Anthony. Robin, Michael's old school friend, who had been the drummer in a band in which Michael had played guitar when they were both pupils at Newry High School, came up from London. And then of course there was Ruth's family and the many locally-based friends of both Michael and Ruth. Though the marriage took place in a hotel, a Presbyterian minister, who Ruth knew well, officiated. Following the ceremony a buffet meal was laid out for the guests. Musicians from Michael and Ruth's circle of acquaintances provided entertainment. It was a wonderful day for us all.

The First Minister Comes to Town

In late September 2007 Ian Paisley was booked as the opening speaker for Wigtown Book Festival, an event which Elaine and I had attended and enjoyed in previous years. In May 2007 Reverend Paisley had become First Minister of Northern Ireland and, against all the odds, seemed to be working amicably with Deputy First Minister, Martin McGuinness. I had very mixed feelings about this, regarding Reverend Paisley as an obdurate opponent of progress over the preceding forty years. He had been very seriously ill in the early years of the new millennium, and perhaps this, and age, had mellowed him, though the fact that the top job seemed suddenly to fall into his lap may also have moved him towards a more generous view of the Good Friday Agreement. On the surface of it, despite his reputation as a ruthless IRA commandant, Martin McGuinness's reincarnation as a man of peace seemed more credible. Even as Deputy First Minister he continued to live in the house in the Bogside where he had grown up. When I had heard him interviewed, he spoke warmly of cross-community friendships he had made in his home city. He was someone I thought who, in another and better world, might have joined the Social Democratic and Labour Party — and yet, I could not forget the stories which Mervyn's young friend Kevin had told me and which seemed to implicate McGuinness, former Brigade Commander of the Derry Provisional IRA, in some very dark dealings.

Whatever misgivings I had about Reverend Paisley, I decided to attend. Elaine was not enthusiastic but understood my desire to witness the event and came with me. The subject of Reverend Paisley's talk was the Wigtown Martyrs, a story well known in Galloway, of two women, Margaret Maclauchlan and Margaret Wilson who were Scottish Covenanters and who, in 1685, were executed for their religious beliefs. "Executed" does not really capture the barbarity of what happened to them. They were tied to stakes in the mudflats below Wigtown not far from where we were sitting listening to Reverend Paisley and left there to drown in the rising tide.

The First Minister gave his talk, low key despite the drama of the events which were his subject, perhaps because in this case, it was Episcopalians and not Roman Catholics, who were his "villains". Nevertheless, he was in good form, affable, self-assured as ever. Once he had spoken the event was opened to questions from the audience, all of which, so far as I can remember, ignored the subject of the talk and focused instead on the elephant in the marquee. I was anxious to ask a question myself which might in some way cut through his defences and hold him to account. I can't recall what that question was. There were many possibilities. Why had he not shown greater willingness to work with moderate nationalists in support of the Sunningdale Agreement of 1974? Why had he supported the strike which had collapsed the agreement — a strike in which my brother Michael had been a reluctantly caught up when he worked in the Armagh Down Creamery. I would like to have asked Dr Paisley how he could justify the paramilitary threat implicit in that occasion in February 1981 when he had led journalists to a place in the Antrim hills where, in military formation and paramilitary attire, were assembled 500 men, each brandishing a firearms certificate?

Whatever question I did manage to articulate, the big man hardly noticed it; as is the way of many politicians, he answered a question he wanted to answer rather than the one that I had asked him. And yet there he stood, in some way changed, enabling a new dispensation, talking mildly of the Sinn Feiners. Michael Longley's poem *Ceasefire* comes to mind, written in response to the 1994 Provisional IRA ceasefire, its closing lines the words of the Trojan King Priam:

> *I get down on my knees and do what must be done*
> *And kiss Achilles' hand, the killer of my son.*

Following the event, Elaine and I stood outside in the square at the centre of Wigtown where the marquee had been pitched. We watched as Reverend

Paisley emerged into the streetlights, his security entourage in close attendance. They did not tarry to savour the atmosphere of the Book Festival but instead climbed into a waiting people carrier, a sleek grey vehicle with darkened windows which swept out of the town, enroute for Stranraer and the ferry crossing to Belfast.

One of These Days

In January 2008, news reached me that Michael had collapsed at his home in Kelloholm, and had been taken to the Dumfries Royal Infirmary, where he was unconscious and on a life support machine.

He had not appeared unwell when I had last seen him. However, sometime in the previous year he confided in me that his doctor had told him, repeatedly, he must give up smoking. "I know it's serious," Michael had said. Ruth also smoked. Together they attempted to give up, but did not succeed.

What I didn't realise was that Michael's problem was a progressive loss of lung capacity. His main symptom was shortness of breath when he exerted himself physically. He wasn't in any obvious pain or discomfort, but he did have advanced emphysema.

He was never to recover consciousness. When I went to see him in the Infirmary, he was still on a life support machine. Despite the critical nature of his condition, he looked well, healthy even; but the reality was otherwise. After about a week Ruth accepted that there was nothing that could be done for him and his life support systems were withdrawn.

From where I write I can look up to see a picture I took of Michael and Ruth in the doorway of their house in Kelloholm. They are standing close to one another, looking directly at the camera. Michael's right arm draws Ruth gently towards him, his hand resting lightly on her shoulder. They look relaxed and are smiling. I think of that time, forty years ago, in the dining room at Warrenpoint when Mrs Ferris was there and Ma asked Michael to play something, and he sang *One of These Days*.

Plugging the Gaps

With every new college session came a new teaching timetable and this would frequently bring surprises, some welcome, others less so. The fact that I had a Social Sciences background was doubtless the reason I started to be given classes in Psychology. It had been only a small fraction of my degree so it was fortunate I found the subject interesting. The level I was asked to teach at, in the first instance, was not a huge challenge though the classes I took were coming in from schools in the region and were not always filled with enthusiastic learners. From my point of view, as long as I wanted a job, there really wasn't much choice in the matter. This was business for the college and if a fully qualified lecturer wasn't readily available, then some less perfectly fitted soul was likely to get the job. I imagine the thought process of the timetabler: "Umm — Stephen — he could do that!"

After a few years of teaching Psychology at entry level I found myself teaching Higher classes. Highers are somewhat similar to A-Levels, though the course is generally completed in a single year. In 2013, as a consequence of this more advanced teaching experience, I became part of a team which was developing a new Higher National Certificate in Social Sciences. There were to be a couple of Sociology units. That was my degree, but one of my colleagues was already well-established as a Sociology lecturer and was the obvious person to deliver these. One of the other options was Politics; but who would teach it? So much of what happened in college involved responsibilities, sometimes unwelcome responsibilities, being pushed in your direction. This time, however, I did not shuffle uncomfortably and look for excuses and instead put my head above the parapet saying: "I think I could do that." I don't recall much discussion of the matter. In fact, once I'd stepped through the door it snapped shut behind me and there was no going back. I was given time to develop the units ready for the first intake of students the following year.

Teaching Politics is not to be confused with having knowledge of current events. Historical and constitutional aspects of the United Kingdom and Scottish political systems were at the heart of the units that I was to deliver. Nevertheless, current affairs can provide an interesting reference point for discussion and in that respect you could say I got lucky: there was an independence referendum in Scotland in 2014, the first year the course was to run, a General Election in 2015 and then, in 2016, a UK-wide referendum which set the United Kingdom on its very troubled journey out of the European Union. Adding spice to the mix was the perplexing entry of Donald Trump onto the United States electoral stage. The world of politics had suddenly gone a bit mad and this made an interesting backdrop to my initiation as a teacher of the subject.

I naturally had views on all of this turmoil but, as a Politics lecturer, it was not my job to argue in favour of one side or another, or one individual or another, but rather to encourage the students to consider all points of view. I enjoyed that challenge and was pleased when in 2014 one of my students said, in a disgruntled tone, with regard to the coming Scottish Independence Referendum: "I don't suppose you'll be telling us which way you're going to vote!"

One area where I feel I may have slipped up occasionally in this responsibility of impartiality was when I would find myself in a rather too impassioned critique of the First Past the Post voting system for the House of Commons, but even then, I was careful to slip in a few arguments in favour of the status quo. I would also acknowledge that I found it difficult to be impartial where Donald Trump was concerned but then I was not teaching US politics so could afford to be a little more unguarded in my commentary.

I liked the students who came on the course, but mostly they questioned the relevance of the Politics units and were more easily persuaded that Sociology and Psychology were the real heart of their studies, with Politics a filler to be suffered rather than enjoyed. But despite this resistance it was a pleasure to me to teach those classes and I found some students who were keen and persuaded a few others that politics was something worth paying attention to and got along fine with those who continued to resist the charms of the subject.

Despite this being a new subject to me, I worked hard at keeping ahead of my students. On one occasion, however, a girl put her hand up in my class; she pointed out, by way of correction of what I had just said, that the Law Lords were no longer the highest appeal court in the UK and that this was now the job of the UK Supreme Court. I looked sceptical. "No, no — that's the US Supreme Court you're thinking of." A minute or two later she put her hand up again. This time she had the evidence to back up her correction, displayed on a government website right there on her smartphone. What could I say? "Thank you. Well done! That puts me in my place." I felt some shame in admitting that I had not properly registered this change in the UK

Constitution which had taken place not long after Steve Jobs launched the iPhone, the instrument of my downfall. It was a fair cop.

In the HNC I was working with a great team of lecturers. I was the least experienced at that level but felt valued and supported by my colleagues. I was pleased to take responsibility in relation to any problems which arose from our use of information and computing technology where I already had a formal cross-college role in developing the use of computing and the Internet in the delivery of lessons. Indeed, I found it hard to resist exploring the emerging opportunities for managing students' work online though I could see others, including my students, were not so keen and were themselves weary of constant change and the need to become familiar with new systems. Despite their obvious obsession with their hand-held devices, they were not enthusiastic about being asked to problem-solve the difficulties at their end of an online transaction in formal education and resistant to the idea that there would be any real advantages in what was on offer. I, on the other hand, was pretty certain this was a road we were all going to have to travel, whether we liked it or not.

The workload involved in teaching on the HNC was well beyond anything I had previously encountered in my college career. It wasn't just the demands of being well prepared for classes: I had to mark essays, and though I enjoyed providing feedback, the task was time consuming, in addition to which, it was dispiriting to sometimes receive work that fell significantly short of the required standard. One then had the bleak responsibility of telling a student they would have to repeat their essay on a different topic; more work for them and more for me further down the line.

When I first started at college, I regularly stayed late to prepare my classes for the following day, but then I had very little work to mark. In a Learning Support context all feedback was immediate and provided verbally during the course of classes. I was contracted for thirty-five hours each week and might easily have imagined that I did a great deal more than this, but when I worked it out, I was rarely working for the college much above forty hours a week. By contrast, when I was teaching Higher Psychology and then the HNC, I could see that I was becoming a bit of a college lackey. They were getting a good deal, not just from me, but from all of my colleagues on the HNC team. As I was getting towards the date when I might retire, I started to reduce my hours, first going down to four days a week, then three. For the last couple of years, I taught only the Politics unit, and went into college just one day a week. Once I had taught my class, I would spend time at my workstation collecting my thoughts, preparing for the following week, occasionally going down some rabbit hole on the internet, whilst not forgetting to enjoy leisurely coffee and lunch breaks in the company of my colleagues and friends. It was, for me, an agreeable contract and though I could see that all around me college lecturing and support staff were being squeezed, I was happy to linger on the payroll, less concerned with finding a way out than were many others. But nevertheless, I decided that session 2019-20 would be my last.

It all started well. I was comfortable with the units I had to teach and enjoying my weekly outing to the college. Then in December 2019 we began to hear reports of a strange new respiratory illness in the Chinese city of Wuhan. On 20th January 2020 the World Health Organization declared the outbreak "a public health emergency of international concern." When people started dying from the virus in the UK I began to pay serious attention. To begin with it was mostly in the south of England. Dumfries and Galloway felt safe. Early in March I had spotted that there was a folk club running in Dalbeattie, not far west of where I live. I thought I might attend and perhaps step up as a floor singer. As the day approached the spread of the coronavirus became increasingly concerning and I decided that this was not the right moment to relaunch my "career" on the folk circuit. I stayed at home. The first confirmed death from Covid 19 in Scotland was on the 13th of March.

On the 16th of that month the Prime Minister and clown laureate, Boris Johnson, announced that the time had come "for everyone to stop non-essential contact and travel." Shortly after that the college closed down all of its face-to-face classes, and we were in lockdown.

Whatever Boris Johnson's appeal to people tired of the compromises and blatant evasions of politics and politicians, I found it difficult to forgive him the cavalier way in which he had dealt with Brexit. For all its flaws, forty years in the European Union had done more for prosperity and harmony in the island of Ireland, north and south of the border, than three hundred years in the United Kingdom. The manner of our exit from the EU showed absolutely no concern for the fragilities of the Good Friday Agreement and the fact that a majority in Northern Ireland, as in Scotland, had voted Remain. And now the same Boris Johnson was presiding over a pandemic. This did not inspire confidence.

By good fortune all of my teaching was complete by that stage of the session and so far as the units I was delivering were concerned I had only to mark essays and deal with the fallout from this. There remained, however, the delicate task of how we were going to award grades to our students, on the basis of which they might apply for a place on a university course or in other ways progress.

Normally we had what amounted to a final examination for this purpose, but that was no longer possible. We would have to award grades on the basis of essays submitted across the year. All of these issues were discussed in online meetings and we worked out a formula. There was some minor complaint from one student who protested that he had been keeping his powder dry for the exam and had been coasting when writing his essays. His argument did not carry much weight though, it is fair to say, that is exactly how some people approach their studies. There was in fact little push back against the grades that we allocated.

I was pleased to have had some experience of the online meetings which were to become such a feature of the workplace in the months that followed. I thought that they worked well. I was equally pleased, however, that I was not having to teach classes online. That challenge was waiting for the lecturers who would be returning in August to begin the next college session, and I would not be in their number.

Sadly, there would be no meals out to mark the end of term, no staffroom gatherings or speeches to bid me farewell. I was sent cards and gifts through the post. I circulated my own farewell message on the college email. When my final online meeting concluded, I waved goodbye to my colleagues across the ether of the Internet. Clicking the button to log out, I turned my head to gaze through the south-facing window of my home-office and savour the fine weather which had settled over the United Kingdom and which one could almost believe had been turned on by the arrival of the pandemic. As far as I could see stretched a perfect expanse of blue sky, untroubled by clouds or jet trails.

I got up from my seat at the computer and found my way downstairs to join Elaine who was sitting watching Politics Live, a socially distanced panel of politicians, journalists, academics, experts and contrarians, picking over the latest Government statements on the health crisis, the utterances of the Health Secretary and the Chief Medical Officer. As Elaine caught sight of me, she picked up the remote control and put the programme on pause: with a quizzical look, she threw me a question: "You been in a meeting?" It was my turn to look quizzical. She knew I'd been in a meeting! But in a flash, she provided the required qualification: "Looking like that?"

A View from Across the Water

I have now been in Dumfries for more than forty years. I am fortunate to live in lovely countryside not far from the town. Elaine and I have enough space to keep four Shetland sheep and five hens. Our household is shared with our dog Lucas and our two cats, Macklin and Lenny. I have family and friends close by. Yet, though I haven't visited for some years, I still nurture a strong affection for the country of my birth, both north and south of the border. I take a continuing interest in its people, its landscape, its towns and cities, its culture, its politics, its history, its sporting successes and failures.

A favourite haunt of mine in Dumfries and Galloway is Portpatrick, where in a previous era there was once a ferry to and from Donaghadee. Portpatrick is a lively place in the tourist season. During the months of July and August, yachts from across the water are often to be seen in the little harbour and Ulster voices mingle with those of the locals and other tourists in the harbour-front bars and hotels.

From the campsite along the cliff tops by the ruin of Dunskey Castle, where Elaine and I have often stayed, it is possible, most days, to see across to the Ards peninsula, and further north, to the Antrim coast. On a clear day, looking south, you can see the Mournes and, if I strain my imagination a little, I can glimpse the plain at the foot of the eastern flank of the mountains, which stretches out beyond the remnants of the Second World War airfield at Greencastle, to the outer strand at Cranfield. From there, I can trace the walk beyond the Coast Guard station and, descending to the rocky shore at the southern margin of the beach, on around the headland — past the rock pools, where Philip, Nicholas and I searched for crabs and shellfish, and then on to the lighthouse strand, the dreamland of my teenage years.

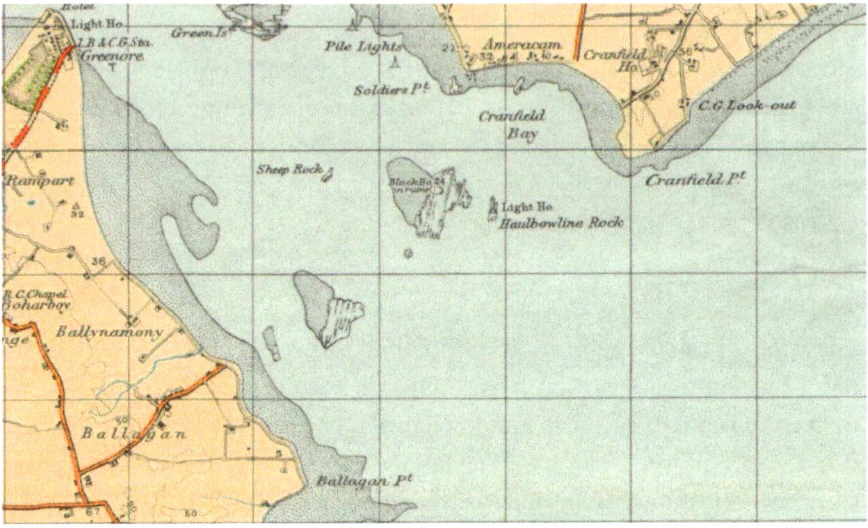

Cranfield Point. Extract from Ordnance Survey one inch, sheet 11, Northern Ireland, published in 1955. Full map image available from Wikimedia.org.

It is my hope that, if they have not already done so, the young people growing up now where I grew up, will shake off the ill-fitting clothes of unionism and republicanism and will forge and celebrate new ways of identifying themselves which criss-cross and obliterate the old, worn-out divisions. Whether this plays out in the form of a united Ireland or some other formulation that is yet to be imagined, is a matter of small importance.

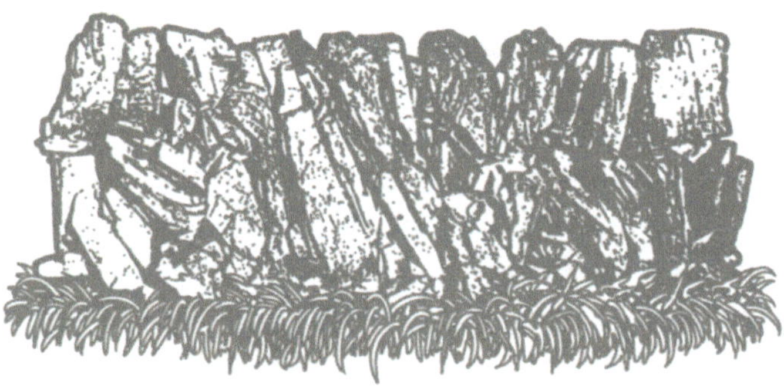

Acknowledgements

This memoir has gone through several incarnations and I sent early drafts to a number of people who gave useful feedback which has encouraged me, despite some surprises and upsets along the way, to press on and extend the project.

For important help, encouragement and suggestions at the outset I owe a special debt to Marie-France Browne, Christopher Williamson, Victor Wright, Alan Fell and Jeannie Truell. Likewise, Ann Yuill for encouragement and challenge to Section 1 through to Section 4, at a moment when confidence was faltering. Martin Price continued to express interest in my progress based on his reading of the section covering my first summer in Reading. Colin Craig gave essential and detailed help with the Ballycastle section.

As the project developed, I continued to get extremely useful help from Alan Fell. Angie Briggs came on board to look at my recollections of working at Dumfries and Galloway College, and whilst much of this detail has been cut, she also expressed interest in reading the earlier sections and made many corrections. Janis Crawshaw took an important interest at this stage, sharing her thoughts with me in places as unlikely as outside the Post Office next to the bins by the traffic lights in Galloway Street. Angus Macmillan, a co-editor of *Southlight*, Dumfries and Galloway's literary magazine, was kind enough to read an early full-length version and to make insightful comments about where he felt the principal strengths of the manuscript were to be found.

Thanks also to my brother, Peter, who has pointed out important errors of detail and also contributed anecdotes whilst allowing me to believe that I might be doing something worthwhile.

Many thanks to my Canadian cousin, Alison Foley, for all her work on the history of the Foley family, to which I frequently referred. Though I have never met him, thanks also to my cousin Geoffrey Foley for his family history which included a lovely recollection of Overton by our Aunty Myrtle and from which I have pinched a fine photograph of the wedding of our grandparents.

It was delight to find reference to my grandmother, Kathleen Pemberton, in Pat Quigley's biography of Stasko Markiewicz. The book provided very useful background detail which has given me a better understanding of my grandmother's connection with the Markiewicz family.

Thanks to Brian King for drawing Brendan Kennelly's poem *To You* to my attention. I have extracted the second half of the poem to use as my epigraph and this was to give me the title for this memoir. Brian was a teacher for a few years at Newry High School in the late 1960s and early 1970s and, with his wife Alice, was a good friend to the Shellard family. For some reason, the poem stuck with me, though I don't think it was part of any lesson and I never made any attempt to learn it by heart.

I owe particular thanks to my wife, Elaine Kennedy, always my best critic who, whilst unafraid of pointing out errors of spelling, grammar, style and substance continues to encourage me that the effort involved in completing the project will be worthwhile.

I would credit Elaine and Alan for persuading me that I had, in my original manuscript, written two books, one of which might be of interest to a general reader, the other, probably not. This is the first of those books. I hope, in the course of time, to complete the second, a reflection on my experiences working with young people, (which does form a small part of this first book). If I do progress with that it will be a book of essays, and I thank Angus for encouraging me to use this format for my work.

Whilst Elaine, Alan and Angie have made many corrections, my subsequent reworking of the manuscript has no doubt introduced further errors for which I happily accept responsibility.

Quotation from Songs and Poems

Earlier versions of this memoir included more extensive quotation, both from songs and poems. When I started to enquire into the matter of permission to use such quotation I was in for a shock. In most cases I had assumed that to quote a few lines would be considered acceptable and permission granted free of charge. After all, I was not trying to pass the work off as my own and, in every case, was drawing attention to lines which might encourage the reader to look beyond my quotation and explore the work of the featured writer in more detail. However, in those cases where I received a response to my request for permission, I was bluntly told that there would be a charge which in turn would be related to factors such as my selling price, projected sales figures, duration of publication and other such matters. Poetry, I would have to say, comes relatively cheap — £75 for the use of half a poem as an epigraph, for example. The minimum charge for quoting the work of Leonard Cohen on the other hand, was £600. Cohen's catalogue has been sold to Sony who have sub-contracted management of the rights of his lyrics to the sheet music publisher, Hal Leonard, so I am not holding Leonard Cohen responsible for this daylight robbery.

The British Government's guidance says: "Fair dealing is a legal term used to establish whether a use of copyright material is lawful or whether it infringes copyright. There is no statutory definition of fair dealing — it will always be a matter of fact, degree and impression in each case." This suggests that I might put my case in court and hope for a judgement in my favour in relation to my use of assorted quotations, but really, is it likely that I would succeed against the Sony corporation? Or their proxies? Even if I could afford to have a go, which I cannot.

In the end, with regret, I took most of the quotation out of the text. Titles of work do not fall into copyright and when an author has been dead for more than seventy years, their work is no longer in copyright, so that has freed me up to use quotation in a number of cases. It remains for me to thank various people, to whom I have paid or am happy to pay their asking price, for permission to use work.

Thank you to Bloodaxe Books for permission to use lines from Brendan Kennelly's poem *To You*, as my opening epigraph.

I continue to seek permission to use lines from Michael Longley's wonderful poem *Ceasefire* and also for permission to use lines from Colum Sands' songs *The Last House in Our Street* and *Newry Market*. I have also written to the estate of Hamish Henderson for permission to quote from his *Elegies for the Dead in Cyrenaica* but to date have received no reply. Finally, I quote a line from a Judy Sill song, *The Kiss,* and again am happy to consider terms for the use of the five words involved, though I may be obliged to withdraw the quotation if these are not favourable.

Maps

I have used a number of map images, all of which are in the public domain. I wish to acknowledge the work of Wikimedia in making these images available and clarifying their public domain status. Three of the images are old Ordnance Survey maps. In 1984, Elaine and I were lucky enough to see, in Newry Town Hall, a production of Brian Friel's celebrated play, *Translations*, concerning the Ordnance Survey of Ireland which began in 1824 and which, as the play points out, struggled to render the original Irish place names into written English. Still, those maps are a work of art.

Book Design

I thank my nephew, Joe Shellard, (pictured on page 201, holding a dinosaur.) for providing the cover design and also end of chapter icon and Carruchan Press logo. My wife Elaine also has a very sharp eye for such matters as widows and orphans in the text and the aesthetic of book design in general.

Playlist – Remembered Fragments

Due to the frustrations I encountered in obtaining permission to use song lyrics, I have created a play list on Spotify which includes all of the songs mentioned in *Remembered Fragments*, and a few others which I think were playing in the background of the events I describe, for example, Helen Shapiro's *Walking Back to Happiness*, the first song that I can remember which qualifies as modern pop. It was released in the United Kingdom in September 1961 when I was eight years old. I remember listening to it on our wireless, probably played between *The Laughing Policeman*, as sung by Charles Penrose, and the theme music to *Rawhide*, as sung by Frankie Laine:

> *Keep them dogies movin', rawhide*
> *Don't try to understand 'em*
> *Just rope and throw and brand 'em,*
> *Soon we'll be living high and wide*

Details of the play list may be found at:
carruchan.wordpress.com/2024/04/27/remembered-fragments-playlist/

Reading

Many books have influenced the ideas expressed in this memoir but the following I think deserve a mention.

- *Killing Rage*, by Eamon Collins, published by Granta, London, 1997
- *Once Upon a Hill: Love in Troubled Times*, by Glen Patterson, published by Bloomsbury Paperbacks, 2009
- *Before the Bandits,* by Shane White, published by Lagan Press, 2011
- *Northern Protestants: On Shifting Ground,* by Susan McKay, published by Blackstaff Press, 2021
- *We Play Here*, by Dawn Watson, published by Granta Poetry, 2023

About the Author

Stephen Shellard was born in July 1953 in Newry, Co. Down, where he attended Newry High School. He left Newry for Reading University in October 1972 graduating in Sociology in 1975 and then spending a year as editor of the Students' Union magazine before training as a teacher in Liverpool. Following this, he returned to Reading and worked first as a social services ambulance driver and then, for two years, as a Detached Youth Worker, seconded to a youth counselling service. He resigned this position and, continuing to live in the Reading area, worked for short periods as a delivery driver and for Pickford's Removals, before being invited to Ballycastle in Co. Antrim to work for a year as a volunteer at the Ramoan Centre, the first direct alternative to custody for serious and persistent young offenders in Northern Ireland, managed by Save the Children in co-operation with the Probation Service. During a career intermission, he went grape picking in France and spent several months in West Berlin, living in a squatted house and working as a hotel dishwasher, before returning to the United Kingdom and settling in Southwest Scotland. There he found employment supporting people with learning difficulties to live independently and spent time as a self-employed gardener before taking a job in a unit for excluded school pupils. Following this he taught secondary school pupils with additional support needs before becoming a lecturer at Dumfries and Galloway College. He worked in Further Education for more than twenty-five years, until his retirement in 2020. At the outset he taught students with Learning Difficulties but, eventually, also Psychology and Politics classes.

Over the years he has written and performed songs as a floor singer at folk clubs and open mic events. From his early years he acquired a writing habit, resulting in, amongst other things, publication of letters in the *Irish Times* (circa 1970), *the Reading Chronicle*, the *Newry Reporter*, the *Belfast Telegraph*, the *Belfast News Letter*, the *Dumfries and Galloway Standard* and the *Dumfries Courier*. He has written two plays, one of which, in 1981, was staged in a pub in Reading to modest acclaim. The other, written in 1982, whilst living in Ballycastle, Co. Antrim — a possible companion piece to the *Billy* trilogy of television plays which launched Kenneth Branagh's acting career — the author is very happy to keep in a drawer. In 1993 he had a submission included in the Opsahl Report on Northern Ireland. Whilst working as a lecturer in Further Education, he wrote several articles on the developing implications of new technologies in the classroom for the Scottish Further Education Unit journal, *Broadcast.* More recently, he has written a blog which has a small and occasionally appreciative audience. Work on his blog has been on hold for some time whilst he has been writing his memoir, *Remembered Fragments.*

Printed in Dunstable, United Kingdom

73132990R00137